Basic English Grammar Workbook

for
dummies®
A Wiley Brand

Basic English Grammar Workbook

by Geraldine Woods

for
dummies®

A Wiley Brand

Basic English Grammar Workbook For Dummies®

Published by: **John Wiley & Sons, Inc.,** 111 River Street, Hoboken, NJ 07030-5774, www.wiley.com

For general information on our other products and services, please contact our Customer Care Department within the U.S. at 877-762-2974, outside the U.S. at 317-572-3993, or fax 317-572-4002. For technical support, please visit https://hub.wiley.com/community/support/dummies.

Wiley publishes in a variety of print and electronic formats and by print-on-demand. Some material included with standard print versions of this book may not be included in e-books or in print-on-demand. If this book refers to media that is not included in the version you purchased, you may download this material at http://booksupport.wiley.com. For more information about Wiley products, visit www.wiley.com.

Library of Congress Control Number: 2025933230

ISBN 978-1-394-33099-7 (pbk); ISBN 978-1-394-33102-4 (ebk); ISBN 978-1-394-33101-7 (ebk)

SKY10100830_032425

Contents at a Glance

Contents at a Glance

Table of Contents

Introduction

John leaves a note for his dad:

> I had to write a report for school. I sat at your desk because your chair is more comfortable than mine. I typed the report on your computer. Everything was fine for the first ten minutes. Then it broke! I'm sorry.

What does John's dad think?

> Where's my toolbox? I can fix that chair.

or

> That desk is an antique. Only an expert can repair it.

or

> I hate when my computer breaks.

Here's what I think: John needs to sharpen his grammar skills. Surprised? Many people believe that grammar is a set of meaningless rules. In fact, grammar is the structure of language. It comes from traditions, from the way people speak and write. If you obey commonly accepted grammar rules, more people will understand your message. By the way, I don't know what broke — the chair, the desk, or the computer. I do know that the pronoun *it* is unclear. That's the grammar rule that John broke. *Basic English Grammar Workbook For Dummies* can help John. It can help you, too, whether you have spoken English all your life or you're learning the language now.

About This Book

In *Basic English Grammar Workbook For Dummies*, I focus on the information you need to improve your grasp of Standard English. That's the version of the language that educated people use when they're in formal situations. I explain the rules of Standard English, but I also tell you when you can bend or break them in casual situations.

For the most part, I stay away from technical vocabulary. You can speak and write perfectly well without labeling everything in a sentence! I provide grammar terms only when you need them to understand a rule. Don't worry: I define every grammar term I use and give examples.

Each topic begins with a short explanation of the rules. Then, a set of questions prompts you to apply the rules. The final section of each chapter is "Calling All Overachievers." Its questions cover all the rules in the chapter. Once you've answered the questions, you can check your work. The answer key at the end of the chapter tells you what's correct and explains why it's correct. For even more practice, take an online quiz. (See "Beyond the Book" later in this introduction for details on how to access online material.)

Basic English Grammar Workbook For Dummies is divided into five parts:

>> **Part 1** explains how to tailor your writing style to fit your audience and purpose. This part also introduces you to the building blocks of language — the parts of speech — and explains what you need to know in order to use them correctly.

>> **Part 2** explores three important elements of a sentence: verbs, subjects, and complements. In this part, you also practice recognizing and writing complete sentences.

>> **Part 3** covers capitalization and punctuation (periods, commas, question marks, and so forth).

>> **Part 4** connects grammar to modern life. You apply your grammar knowledge to texts, emails, online posts, presentation slides, and bulleted lists. One chapter takes grammar to work and to school, with questions about reports, memos, letters, and other such tasks.

>> **Part 5** covers common mistakes so you can avoid making them. Questions direct your attention to words that sound alike but have different meanings, nonstandard expressions, confusing comparisons and descriptions, spelling, and more.

A NOTE ABOUT PRONOUNS

A *pronoun* is a word that stands in for a noun or another pronoun. Because of pronouns, you can write "George said that he forgot his phone" instead of "George said that George forgot George's phone." The pronouns *he* and *his* make the sentence flow more smoothly.

A pronoun should match the word it refers to. A singular pronoun (referring to one) pairs with a singular noun or another singular pronoun. A plural pronoun (referring to more than one) pairs with a plural noun or another plural pronoun. Gender matters, too. Some pronouns are masculine (*he, him, his*), some are feminine (*she, her, hers*), and others are neuter (*it* and *they* when referring to objects, ideas, or places). The rules for these pronouns have stayed the same. So have the rules for pronouns referring to a group of people (*they, them, their, theirs*).

The rules have changed, though, when a pronoun refers to a person whose gender is unknown or not accurately described as "male" or "female." For these situations, many grammarians (including me) select *they, them, their,* and *theirs*. Each of these pronouns may be either singular or plural, depending on the word it refers to. Take a look at some examples:

- **The children ate their lunches.** (The plural pronoun *their* pairs with the plural noun *children.*)

- **If anyone forgot their lunch, the teacher will give them something to eat.** (The singular pronouns *their* and *them* refer to the singular pronoun *anyone*.)

- **Alix arrived late because they were stuck in traffic.** (The singular pronoun *they* pairs with the singular noun *Alix*, the pronoun Alix prefers.)

The first two examples may look familiar to you. From the 14th century onward, *they*, *them*, and *their* have been used to refer to one person or a group, just as the pronoun *you* does. In the 18th century, though, a few grammarians decided that the pronouns *they*, *them*, *their*, and *theirs* were correct only for references to a group. According to these grammarians, the forms *he*, *him*, and *his* and *she*, *her*, and *hers* were the only appropriate references to one person. If the gender was unknown, *he*, *him*, and *his* were said to be the proper choice. You can imagine how popular this decision was with supporters of women's equality! In the late 20th century, many writers used pairs — *he or she*, *him or her*, and *his or her* — for singular references. That practice often resulted in awkward sentences like "Everyone must bring his or her gym suit with him or her." Paired pronouns also ignore people whose identity isn't described by a male or female label, such as the situation in the third example about Alix. The singular *they/them/their/theirs* solves these problems.

It may take a while to get used to *they* as a singular word. If you're expecting one dinner guest and hear "they're on the way," you may rush to cook more food before you remember that *they* is your guest's preferred pronoun. You may also find yourself writing for an authority figure who insists you use *they*, *them*, *their*, and *theirs* as plurals only. In that situation, you can reword the sentence to avoid using pronouns. You can find more examples and information about pronouns in Chapter 2.

Conventions Used in This Book

As you work your way through this book, I want your mind focused on grammar. I don't want you to spend time wondering why some words are in **bold**, some are in *italics*, and some are underlined. Here's the key:

>> **Bold** calls your attention to the main idea of each item on a list.

>> **Underlining** identifies the portion of a sentence I'm discussing.

>> *Italics* signal a new term or a word I'm discussing. For example, I might tell you to examine *signal*, the second word in this bullet point.

Foolish Assumptions

I have never met you, but I have spent quite a bit of time with you — the reader, I imagine. When I write, you sit on the corner of my desk, asking questions and keeping me on track. This is how I see you:

>> You know the English language, but you're open to learning more.

>> You want to sharpen your grammar skills.

>> You have a busy life.

The last idea on the list is the most important. I don't want this book to sit on the shelf or in the cloud. I want you to use it! You're more likely to do so if the explanations are clear, simple, and short. If you want more detailed explanations and additional examples, pick up a copy of the companion book, *Basic English Grammar For Dummies*, 2nd Edition.

Beyond the Book

As they say in late-night television commercials, "Wait! There's more!" Look online at www.dummies.com to find a cheat sheet for *Basic English Grammar Workbook For Dummies*, where you can zero in quickly on crucial information. Competitive? You can also test yourself with online quizzes oriented to a single chapter or to a heftier amount of information. To get this Cheat Sheet, simply go to www.dummies.com and search for "Basic English Grammar Workbook For Dummies Cheat Sheet" in the Search box.

You also get access to online practice tests. To gain access to the online practice, all you have to do is register. Just follow these simple steps:

1. Go to www.dummies.com/go/getaccess.

2. Create a new account or log in to an existing account.

   If you create a new account, you'll receive an email confirmation. Click through to finish creating a new account.

   Note: If you do not receive a confirmation email after creating your account, please check your spam folder before contacting us through our Technical Support website at http://support.wiley.com or by phone at 877-762-2974.

3. After you've logged into your new or existing account, select "Dummies" under the "Select the brand for your product" header.

4. Select your title from the drop-down list. Choose "[need product name here]."

5. Answer a validation question about the product, and then click "Redeem."

You must choose the correct title and edition from the drop-down list. Select the option that says **"Basic English Grammar Workbook For Dummies."**

Now you're ready to go! You can come back to the practice material as often as you want — simply log on with the username and password you created during your initial login.

Your registration is good for one year from the day you redeem your product.

Icons Used in This Book

Icons are little drawings that alert you to key points, pitfalls, and question sets. Here's what they mean:

I live in New York City, and I often see tourists wandering around. They need someone who lives here to help them find their way. The Tip icon is like a helpful New Yorker, giving you inside information.

When you're walking through a minefield, it's nice to have a map. The Warning icon tells you where the traps are so you can avoid them.

This icon notifies you that it's time to get to work. It appears at the beginning of each set of exercises.

Where to Go from Here

To the refrigerator for a snack. Nope, I'm just joking! If you know which grammar issues confuse you, turn to those chapters first. If you aren't sure what you need, browse through the Table of Contents. Select a chapter that interests you. Sample a couple of questions from the "Calling All Overachievers" section or from the chapter's online quiz because they cover everything in the chapter. Next, check your answers. If all your answers are correct, give yourself a gold star and skip that chapter. If anything puzzles you, read the explanations and examples. Then, work through the rest of the questions in the chapter. Repeat the process with another chapter, and keep going. You're on the road to grammar mastery!

1

Mastering the Basics

Chapter 1

Tailoring Language to Suit Your Audience and Purpose

Suppose you invented a video game. The way you tell a teacher or boss about the game differs from the way you explain it to friends. If you're like most people, you probably switch levels of formality easily, dozens of times a day. But sometimes, you may find yourself wondering how to express yourself. If you hit the wrong note, your message may not receive the reaction you want. Very few investors would say yes to someone who writes, "Yo, want in on this?" Nor will you find it easy to get a date if you ask, "Would you consider dining with me at an informal Italian restaurant that offers relatively good pizza?" In this chapter, you identify levels of formality and examine situations in which each is appropriate.

Climbing the Ladder of Language Formality

Proper English is important. The only problem with that statement is the definition of *proper*. Language has many levels of formality, all of which are "proper" in some situations and completely wrong in others. To make things simple, I think of English as divided into three large categories: what I call "friendspeak" (the most casual), "conversational" (one step up), and "formal," "Standard" English. Take a look at these examples:

c u in 10 (friendspeak)

There in ten minutes. (conversational English)

I will arrive in ten minutes. (Standard English)

All three statements say the same thing in very different ways. Here's the deal:

» **Friendspeak** breaks some rules of Standard English on purpose to show that people are comfortable with each other. Friendspeak shortens or drops words and often includes slang and references that only close friends understand. (That's why I call it *friend*speak.) No one has to teach you this level of English. You learn it from your pals, or you create it yourself and teach it to your buddies.

» **Conversational English** sounds relaxed, but not too relaxed. It's the language equivalent of jeans and a T-shirt. Conversational English is filled with contractions (*I'm* instead of *I am, would've* instead of *would have,* and so forth). Abbreviations appear in conversational English, but only those that are widely understood (*etc., a.m., p.m.,* and the like). You may also see acronyms, which come from the first letter of each word of a name (*NATO* for the *North Atlantic Treaty Organization* or *AIDS* for *Acquired Immune Deficiency Syndrome,* for example). Conversational English may drop some words and break a few rules. The sample sentence for conversational English at the beginning of this section, for instance, has no subject or verb, a giant no-no in formal writing but perfectly acceptable at this level of language.

» **Standard English** is the most formal. It follows every rule (including some you never heard of) and avoids slang and abbreviations.

Think about your audience when you're selecting friendspeak, conversational English, or Standard English. What impression are you trying to give? Let your goals guide you. Also, consider the situation. At work, you may rely on conversational English when you run into your boss at the coffee machine, but not when you're submitting a quarterly report. At school, choosing conversational English is okay for a teacher–student chat in the cafeteria but not for homework. More on situation and language appears in the next section, "Matching Message to Situation."

Can you identify levels of formality? Before you try the questions, check out this example:

YOUR TURN

Q. Place these expressions in order of formality, from the most formal to the least. Note: Two expressions may tie. For example, your answer may be A or B and C — in which case, expression A is the most formal, and expressions B and C are on the same, more casual level.

A. sus block

B. That is a dangerous neighborhood.

C. Where gangs rule.

A. B, C , A. Expression B is the most formal because it follows all the rules of Standard English. Every word is in the dictionary, and the sentence is complete. (See Chapter 8 for more practice with complete sentences.) Expression C, on the other hand, is an incomplete sentence and is therefore less formal. Also, in Expression C, the verb *rule* has an unusual meaning. Your readers or listeners probably understand that gangs aren't official authorities but instead have a lot of unofficial power. The statement is less formal than in Standard English. Expression A employs slang (*sus* means "suspicious, maybe dangerous"), so it fits into the friendspeak category.

1

A. regarding your proposal

B. in reference to your proposal

C. about that idea

2

A. earlier, bro

B. heretofore

C. until now

3

A. Please don't abbreviate.

B. abbreevs not ok

C. I prefer that you write the entire word.

4

A. Awkward!!!!

B. Your behavior disturbs me.

C. Calm down, guys!

5

A. Are you into electronic dance music?

B. edm 2nite?

C. Tonight that club features electronic dance music. Would you care to go?

6

A. M left J's FOMO

B. Mike left John's house when he got a text from Fran about her party.

C. M = gone FOMO F's party

7

   A. #newbaby #thnxmom #notkillingmewhenIcriedallnight

   B. Super tired. Baby cried all night. Feeling grateful to my mom.

   C. Now that I'm caring for my new baby, I am grateful to my mother for tolerating me when I was an infant.

8

   A. In retrospect, jumping into the pool blindfolded was foolish.

   B. broken ankle but YOLO

   C. No water in the pool. Who knew? Broken ankle!

9

   A. 2G2BT

   B. 4real?

   C. u sure?

10

   A. ATM card not working.

   B. My bank card was rejected.

   C. ATM?!?!?

Matching Message to Situation

When you're listening or reading, you probably notice the difference between formal and informal language. Recognizing levels of language, however, isn't enough. You also must select a level of formality to express yourself. Before you choose, consider these factors:

>> **Your audience.** If your message is going to a person with more power or higher status than you (an employee writing to a boss or a student to a teacher, for example), you should probably be more formal. If you're speaking or writing to someone with less power or lower status than you, conversational English is fine. In a higher-to-lower situation, however, the person with more authority may choose formal English in order to serve as a role model or to establish a professional atmosphere. When you're dealing with equals, conversational English is a good bet. Only your closest friends rate — and understand — friendspeak.

>> **The situation.** At the company picnic or in the cafeteria, most people speak less formally. In the same way, at get-togethers with family and friends, formal language may sound too stiff. In an official meeting with a client or teacher, however, Standard English — the most formal choice — is best.

»» The format. When you're speaking, you have more leeway than when you're writing. Why? Unless you're reading prepared remarks, you probably can't produce perfect sentences. Not many people can! The writing in texts, tweets, and instant messages tends to be in conversational English or, with your buddies, in friendspeak. Exceptions occur, though. A text to a client should be more formal than one to a friend, and journalists or officials often tweet in formal English. Email can go either way. Because it's fast, the dropped or shortened forms of conversational English are generally acceptable, but if you think the reader expects you to honor tradition (the written equivalent of a curtsy or a hat-tip), go for Standard English. Always employ Standard English for business letters and reports and school assignments.

TIP

Listen to those around you or read others' work that appears in the same context you're navigating. Unless you want to stand out, aim for the same level of formality you hear or see.

YOUR TURN

Think about the audience, situation, and format. In the following example, decide whether the writing or speech is appropriate or inappropriate.

Q. Text from a department head to the CEO requesting a salary increase:

greenlight $20K or I walk

A. Inappropriate. Think about the power ladder here. The CEO is on the top rung, and the department head somewhere farther down. Even though texts tend to be informal, this one is about money. When you ask for money, do so in Standard English. The department head should have written something like, "If you cannot raise my salary by $20,000, I will seek employment elsewhere."

11 Email from student to professor about the assigned reading of Shakespeare's *Hamlet*:

Best. Play. Ever.

12 Chat between friends:

There's this prince, he's named Hamlet. He's freaking out about his mother's marriage to his uncle only a couple of months after Hamlet's father died.

13 Portion of an essay about the play, written as a homework assignment:

The Queen's new husband is not a sympathetic character. Dude's a murderer!

14 Cover letter from a job applicant to a potential employer:

Attached please find my resume, pursuant to your advertisement of July 15th.

15 Texts between classmates, discussing their grades:

A+!!!

sick

ttyl

ok bfn

16 Portion of a letter to the editor of the town paper from a citizen:

The lack of a stoplight on that corner has led to several car crashes. The city council is right to think about the expense of installing one, but what about the cost of human life and suffering?

17 Comment on a social media post about a tax to finance improved traffic flow:

You morons should stop stealing our money. We coulda bought five stoplights made outta gold for the amount of money you spent on office furniture. To conclude, shut up!

18 Email to the mother of a potential tutoring client:

I have an advanced degree in mathematics and many years of experience teaching algebra. My rates are on par with those of other tutors in the area. Also, I get along well with kids!

19 Tweet from the president to the members of the local garden association:

Meeting tonight at 8 p.m. #springplanting

20 Speech by the class president to fellow students at graduation:

We made it! We're out of this place! We're gonna be great, especially Roger. He's got rizz!

Answers to "Tailoring Language to Suit Your Audience and Purpose" Questions

In this section, you will find all the answers you're looking for. Well, maybe not the answers to "What is the meaning of life?" or "Why is the sky blue?" but definitely the right answers to the questions in this chapter.

1. **A and B, C.** Both A and B are formal English expressions. Each employs businesslike vocabulary (*regarding your proposal,* and *in reference to*). Expression C takes the formality level down a little, substituting *idea* for *proposal* and *about* for *regarding* and *in reference to.*

2. **B, C, A.** Expression B sounds fancy, and it is. You find *heretofore* in legal documents and in many other types of formal English writing. (It means "before this time," by the way.) Expression C is something you probably hear and say all the time. It's conversational. Expression A might be conversational without *bro* (a slang term for friend), but adding that little word puts this one in the friendspeak category.

3. **C, A, B.** Expression C hits the top of the formal meter, and B is at the bottom. (You probably already guessed that *abreevs* isn't a real word. Also, B breaks its own rule by including *ok* instead of *okay.*) In between expressions C and B is A, which is grammatically correct without being stuffy.

4. **B, C, A.** Expression B is a complete sentence, and so is C. But *guys* isn't formal, so C slips into conversational English. Expression A pops up in friendspeak, whenever someone does something impolite or embarrassing. The four exclamation points (which is three too many in Standard English) also marks this one as friendspeak.

5. **C, A, B.** Expression C features two complete sentences, and every word is in the dictionary. Expression A is also a complete sentence, but asking if someone is *into* this type of music (or anything else) brings slang to the sentence. Slang is never formal. Expression B has an abbreviation (*edm* = electronic dance music) and a "word" (2*nite,* or "tonight") that is okay only when you're texting friends. (For more about texting, see Chapter 13.)

6. **B, A, and C.** Both expressions A and C are written in friendspeak. They use abbreviations and an acronym: *M* and *J's* stand for names — probably *Mike* and *John's* — and *FOMO,* which is "fear of missing out." This usage shows up only in the least formal situations, usually texts between friends. Expression B is a full sentence with all the words written correctly and completely.

7. **C, B, A.** Expression C explains the speaker's situation in clear, Standard English. Expression B has half-sentences (probably because the speaker needs sleep!), so it's less formal in the category of conversational English. Expression A, using only hashtags (the # sign) is the least formal.

8. **A, C, B.** Expression A is a complete sentence and employs some advanced vocabulary. (*Retrospect* means "a review of the past.") It's the most formal. Expression C has incomplete sentences (*No water in the pool* and *broken ankle*). The one complete sentence is a humorous, short comment (*Who knew?*). For these reasons, C represents conversational English. Expression B is the least formal, for friends only. *YOLO* is an acronym for "you only live once."

9. **A and B and C.** Did I catch you here? All three of these texts are informal, what I think of as friendspeak. Expression A expresses doubt with an abbreviation for "too good to be true." Expression B asks if something is "for real." Expression C also asks for confirmation, saying, "Are you sure?"

10 **B, A, C.** Expression B is a complete, correct sentence, so it's the most formal. Expression A drops a couple of words, as you would in conversation. Expression C makes sense only if you know that the person who texted this stops for cash often and freaks out when the card doesn't work. This is clearly the least formal.

11 **Inappropriate.** Professors and teachers aren't your friends. They're in charge of your education. English teachers, in particular — even the ones who show up in class wearing jeans and sneakers — value language. True, the message may appeal because English teachers tend to think that everything they assign is great. However, the message may fail (and the student also) if the teacher expects Standard English.

12 **Appropriate.** This chat is a good example of conversational English that's perfectly fine. The friends are conversing — your first clue. They break a few rules, such as illegally stringing together two complete sentences: *There's this prince, he's named Hamlet.*

13 **Inappropriate.** Homework assignments have no room in them for *Dude*, unless you're writing fiction and a character says that word. The first sentence establishes a formal tone; the second sentence should match, not lower, the level of formality.

14 **Inappropriate.** Job applicants should be formal, but they should also avoid old-fashioned expressions like "pursuant to." "In response to" is more suitable wording. "Attached please find" should be "Attached is."

15 **Appropriate.** This one's entirely fine for friends texting each other. Translated for those who need actual words, this exchange reads as follows: Friend 1: I got an A+.

Friend 2: That's great. (*Sick* is slang for "excellent, wonderful.")

Friend 1: I will talk to you later. (The first letter of each word creates this expression.)

Friend 2: All right (or okay). Bye for now.

16 **Appropriate.** This paragraph is quite formal, and its purpose is to persuade readers that a stoplight is needed. To convince someone, you want to sound informed and thoughtful. Standard English fills that slot!

17 **Inappropriate.** Social media has a reputation as an "anything goes" sort of medium, but before you post, think about your purpose. Who would pay attention to this writer? To persuade someone not to tax — or to persuade someone of anything — you need a real argument, not just a set of insults like *morons, stealing,* and *shut up.* Proper grammar isn't essential, but if your goal is to be taken seriously, mistakes such as *coulda* (instead of *could have)* and *outta* (instead of *out of)* don't help.

18 **Appropriate.** Job applicants usually want to sound competent, and those seeking teaching roles should be even more formal than others. Why? Because language in academic situations is generally formal. You may have wondered about the last sentence, which includes the informal term *kids.* Here, the writer breaks into conversational English, but with a reason: to show that the writer can relate to and be comfortable with the child to be tutored.

19 **Appropriate.** Dropping words is fine in tweets, as is *#springplanting,* a tag that directs people who are interested in attending the meeting to other tweets about spring planting.

20 **Inappropriate.** Unless you're in a school that is proud of breaking the rules (and those places do exist), a graduation speech should be something that appeals to the entire audience. The graduates may know that *rizz* means to be attractive, but some in the audience will be puzzled.

Chapter **2**

Noticing Nouns and Perfecting Pronouns

W ave a magic wand. Make all people, places, things, ideas, and emotions disappear. What's left? Not much. That's how important nouns are. This part of speech names all the things your magic wand wiped out. Pronouns are an important part of speech, too. They refer to or replace nouns. Pronouns can also refer to other pronouns. Without pronouns, you'd have to write "Geraldine is writing Geraldine's book, with help from a friend of Geraldine's" instead of "She is writing her book, with help from a friend of hers." In this chapter, you identify nouns and pronouns and practice using them correctly.

Getting to Know Nouns

Everything needs a name. Sometimes, it's specific: *Geraldine Woods, Chicago, Walmart.* Sometimes it's general: *woman, city, store.* Both types of names are nouns. Nouns also name feelings (*love, anger*) and ideas (*loyalty, democracy*).

Did you notice that specific names are capitalized and general terms aren't? For more on capitalization, turn to Chapter 12.

TIP

Identifying nouns

I admit it: You can speak and write perfectly well without knowing which of your words are nouns. That extra knowledge is interesting, I believe. If you disagree, skip this section. If not, try your hand at identifying nouns.

Identify the nouns in each sentence.

YOUR TURN

Q. Grandpa bought a house in the most expensive area of Brooklyn.

A. **Grandpa, house, area, Brooklyn.** The names of people (*Grandpa*), places (*area, Brooklyn*), and things (*house*) are nouns.

1. My grandfather is a retired attorney who practiced law for more than forty years.

2. Grandma teaches chemistry and physics to juniors and seniors at Cole College.

3. Her students call her "Granny Science."

4. Chemistry is a tough course, but good teaching makes the subject easier.

5. Three times a week, my grandfather volunteers at the community center.

6. Many people come to the center for free legal advice.

7. The clients express gratitude.

8. Sometimes, Grandma calls her husband "Grandaddy Law."

9. The grandchildren like that nickname.

10. On Thanksgiving, the law books and lab equipment that usually sit on their kitchen table will be stacked on the floor.

Forming plurals

When small children ask Santa for a *present* (a singular noun), chances are they really hope for *presents* (a plural noun). Here's some guidance on how to form a regular plural noun: Add the letter *s* to the end of the word unless the noun ends with *sh, ch, ss,* or *x.* (*bank → banks, arrow → arrows, shoe → shoes*)

>> If the singular noun ends with *sh, ch, ss,* or *x,* add *es* to the end of the word. (*wish → wishes, watch → watches, loss → losses, tax → taxes*)

>> When a noun ends with *o,* you usually add the letter *s* if the letter before the *o* is *a, e, i, o,* or *u.* (*radio → radios, tornado → tornados*) You generally add *es* if the letter before the *o* is not *a, e, i, o,* or *u.* (*tomato → tomatoes, hero → heroes*) However, some words ending with the letter *o* don't follow these rules. (*halo → halos, zero → zeros*)

>> When a noun ends with *y*, add s if the letter before the *y* is *a, e, o*, or *u*. (*bay → bays, key → keys, boy → boys, guy → guys*)

>> When a noun ends with *y*, and the second-to-last letter isn't *a, e, o*, or *u*, change the *y* to *i* and add *es*. (*story → stories, party → parties, baby → babies*)

>> When a noun ends with *f* or *fe*, you generally change the *f* to *v* and add *es*. (*life → lives, half → halves*). However, many words don't follow this rule (*roof → roofs*)

>> Some irregular plurals don't add *s*. (*child → children, man → men, goose → geese, deer → deer*)

If you're unsure how to form the plural, check the dictionary.

TIP

Write the plural form of each noun.

Q. bowl _____

YOUR TURN

A. **bowls.** The singular noun does not end with *sh, ch, ss*, or *x*. Therefore, you add only the letter *s* to form the plural.

11 dash _____

12 donkey _____

13 potato _____

14 hex _____

15 fuss _____

16 sauce _____

17 calf _____

18 church _____

19 floor _____

20 moose _____

21 runway _____

22 copy _____

23 suitcase _____

24 espresso _____

25 switch _____

26 tattoo _____

27 kitten _____

28 jury _____

29 woman _____

30 foot _____

Attaching "this," "that," "these," and "those" to nouns

Which grammar rule: <u>This</u> rule or <u>that</u> one? Which annoying questions: <u>These</u> questions or <u>those</u>? The underlined words point to nouns. They're descriptions, and they're helpful when, for example, you're pointing to the dessert you want. The rule for using these words is simple: *this* and *that* attach to singular nouns (a word naming one person, place, or thing), and *these* and *those* attach to plural nouns (a word naming more than one person, place, or thing). So, you live with *this cat* or *that cat*, but if you really love animals, you probably live with *these cats* or *those cats*.

Mark each phrase as correct or incorrect.

YOUR TURN **Q.** this dictionaries

A. **Incorrect.** *Dictionaries* is a plural word, so you cannot attach *this* or *that* to it.

31 that flower _____

32 those doorknob _____

33 these cloud _____

34 this statue _____

35 these answers _____

Pinning Down Pronouns

Pronouns take the place of nouns. (See the preceding section, "Getting to Know Nouns," for more information.) Besides pinch-hitting for nouns, pronouns can replace other pronouns. Pronouns must match the word they replace in three ways:

>> **Number:** This is the term English teachers use for singular (one) or plural (more than one). In the world of grammar, singular pronouns must pair with singular nouns, and plural pronouns with plural nouns. When nouns and pronouns pair up correctly, English teachers say they're in agreement.

>> **Gender:** Some pronouns represent females, some represent males, and some are gender-neutral. A few pronouns — *it*, for example — refer to things.

>> **Case:** Pronouns may change form depending on their role in the sentence. For instance, the pronouns *I* and *me* always refer to the speaker, but *I* works as a subject and *me* as an object. (For more on subjects and objects, see Chapter 7.) *My*, another pronoun referring to the speaker, is possessive because it shows ownership.

TIP

Language mirrors people's experiences and understanding of the world. Because people never stop changing, language doesn't either. Recently, the pronoun *they* has attracted attention and sometimes arguments. Turn to "A Note about Pronouns" in the Introduction for more information.

Before you work on number, case, and gender, you should learn to recognize the most common pronouns:

>> *I, me, my, myself,* and *mine* are pronouns representing the person who is speaking or writing. The plural pronouns *we, us, our, ourselves,* and *ours* represent the group that is speaking or writing.

>> *You, your, yours, yourself,* and *yourselves* are pronouns representing the audience — whoever is listening to or reading the sentence. *You, your,* and *yours* may be either singular or plural. *Yourself* is singular, and *yourselves* is plural.

>> Many pronouns represent whoever or whatever is being talked about. The most common singular pronouns in this category are *he, him, his, himself, she, her, hers, herself, it, its,* and *itself*. The pronouns *they, them, their,* and *theirs* may be either singular or plural. Themselves refers to a group or to one person without specifying gender. (Some people choose *themself* as a nongendered, singular pronoun.) Another common plural pronoun is *both*.

>> Some pronouns represent a group: *everyone, everybody, everything, someone, somebody, something, anyone, anybody, anything, no one, nobody,* and *nothing*. The *every-* pronouns take the place of the names of all the people or things in the group. The *any-* and *some-* pronouns represent one person or thing in the group without specifying which one. The *no-* pronouns rule out every member of the group.

WARNING

In Standard English, the *self* pronouns have only two jobs. They can emphasize (*I myself* will take charge of the cooking), and they can show action that doubles back. (*The cat washed himself.*) Don't use a *self* pronoun in any other way:

>> NONSTANDARD: Diego and myself will introduce the guests.

>> STANDARD: Diego and I will introduce the guests.

YOUR TURN

Identify the pronouns. If the word the pronoun represents appears in the sentence, identify it.

Q. Maria asked herself whether she should look for a new job.

A. **herself, she → Maria.** Both pronouns refer to the noun *Maria*.

36 Her supervisor was the meanest man on the planet, and she didn't like him.

37 Actually, Maria didn't like anyone!

38 Once he told her to complete a project only ten minutes after he gave it to her.

39 The project had seventeen parts, yet Maria had experience with only two of them.

40 She knew nothing about marketing, for example.

41 The supervisor himself was an expert in marketing.

42 "You should take care of the job yourself," he told her when she asked for help.

43 "The first two parts are mine," declared Maria, "but the other fifteen are for somebody else."

44 Everyone thinks Maria will be fired.

45 Maria herself told us that she was quitting.

46 "My aunts will help me out while I look for work," Maria said.

47 They retired when they bought a winning lottery ticket.

48 "Don't worry about us," they told Maria. "We have enough money to support ourselves and you."

Coming to an agreement with pronouns

To make a good match, as every online dating service knows, you have to pair like with like. That's true for grammar, too. Singular pairs with singular and plural with plural. No mixing allowed! Here's how to sort singular and plural pronouns:

>> **Singular:** *I, me, my, mine, myself, yourself, he, him, his, him, himself, she, her, hers, herself, it, its, itself, themself, everyone, everybody, everything, someone, somebody, something, anyone, anybody, anything, no one, nobody, nothing*

>> **Plural:** *we, us, yourselves, both*

>> **Singular and plural:** *you, your, yours, they, them, their, theirs, themselves*

TIP

I listed *themself* as an acceptable singular pronoun, but not everyone agrees with me. *Themself* was used from the 16th to the 19th centuries to refer to one person without specifying gender. *Themselves* was the pronoun used to refer to a group, again without specifying gender. Then, some grammarians rejected *themself*. In recent years, *themself* has gained popularity. What should you do? You can use *themselves* for both singular and plural, nongendered situations, or you can use *themself* as a singular pronoun and *themselves* as a plural pronoun. (Or, if you're unsure, you can rewrite the sentence so that you don't need a pronoun at all!)

You can sort pronouns by gender, too:

Feminine (for females): *she, her, hers, herself*

Masculine (for males): *he, him, his, himself*

Gender-neutral: *I, me, my, myself, we, us, our, ourselves, you, your, yours, it, its, itself, they, them, their, theirs, themself, themselves, everyone, everybody, everything, someone, some-body, something, anyone, anybody, anything, no one, nobody, nothing, both*

YOUR TURN

In the blank, write a pronoun that may replace each underlined noun or phrase. Here's a list of characters and how they identify themselves:

Helen, female

Georgie, gender neutral (neither male nor female)

Tomas, male

Q. <u>All the people</u> stayed overnight. _____

A. **everyone, everybody.** Both pronouns include the entire group without naming them. Did you choose *they?* Count yourself correct because that pronoun may also refer to a group.

49 My name is Georgie, and <u>Georgie</u> just won the lottery.

50 "Georgie, that's fantastic! Tomas and I can give <u>Georgie</u> investment advice," screamed Helen, the money manager of a large company.

51 "For sure," <u>Tomas</u> said, nodding <u>Tomas's</u> head.

52 <u>Not one person</u> in the room was calm.

53 "You can invest in government bonds because <u>government bonds</u> are safe," <u>Helen</u> remarked.

54 "So much money! You can put <u>the money</u> under your mattress," Tomas joked, laughing at <u>Tomas's</u> own joke.

55 "The money will be too bumpy to sleep on," Helen whispered to <u>Helen</u>.

56 <u>Tomas and Georgie</u> heard what Helen said.

57 "Give <u>Tomas and Helen</u> some money, and <u>the bed</u> will be smoother," said Helen.

58 "Georgie said, "<u>Georgie</u> can deal with bumps in the bed!"

Solving pronoun case

When you select a pronoun, do you ever wonder whether to say *I, me,* or *my?* Perhaps you must decide between *he* and *him* or *their* and *them.* Don't call a detective to help you with pronoun case — the quality of a pronoun that shows its role in a sentence. Instead, learn how to sort out these pronouns.

>> **Subject pronouns represent the person performing the action or existing in the state of being expressed by the sentence.** In Chapter 7, you practice identifying subjects. In this preview, the subject pronouns are underlined:

> <u>He</u> is cooking.

> <u>I</u> am hungry.

> <u>We</u> will eat soon, and <u>they</u> will clean up.

>> **Object pronouns are on the receiving end of the action.** In other words, the action is directed at an object pronoun. Object pronouns answer the questions *whom?* or *what?* after a verb or a preposition. (For more about the object of a verb, see Chapter 7. For more about the object of a preposition, turn to Chapter 5.) In these sentences, the object pronouns are underlined:

> Give <u>him</u> a cookbook!

> The food delivery is for <u>me</u>.

> Yesterday's meal made <u>us</u> ill.

>> **Possessive pronouns show ownership.** In these sentences, the possessive pronouns are underlined:

> <u>His</u> cooking skills are terrible.

> Ellen and Abdul graduated from cooking school, and <u>their</u> meals are delicious.

> They wrote a cookbook. <u>Its</u> recipes are easy to follow.

WARNING

Possessive pronouns are never written with apostrophes. For example, the correct word is *theirs*, not *their's*.

Here are the most common pronouns sorted into cases:

>> **Subject pronouns** *I, you, he, she, it, we, they, who, whoever*

>> **Object pronouns** *me, you, him, her, it, us, them, whom, whomever*

>> **Possessive pronouns** *my, mine, our, ours, your, yours, his, her, hers, its, their, theirs, whose*

Some pronouns, such as *you* and *it*, appear on both the subject and the object lists. Other pronouns that work as both subjects and objects are *either, most, other, everyone, everybody, everything, someone, somebody, something, anyone, anybody, anything, no one, nobody, nothing, both.*

WARNING

Don't unnecessarily buddy up a pronoun and the noun it replaces. "My brother he goes swimming" is fine in many languages, but in English, it's wrong because the pronoun (*he*) is meant to replace the noun (*brother*). "My brother goes swimming" or "He goes swimming" are both correct.

YOUR TURN

Check your sorting skills. In each sentence, you find one blank. At the end of the sentence is information about the pronoun you should insert. Try not to peek at the lists as you answer these questions. Search your memory first!

Q. Frieda told _____ about the film premiere. (referring to the speakers, object pronoun)

A. us.

(59) _____ was seated in the same row as the star. (referring to a woman, subject pronoun)

(60) The director sat behind the five co-stars, but he didn't speak to _____. (referring to a group, object pronoun)

(61) _____ eyes were focused only on the screen. (referring to a man, possessive)

(62) The director should have cut some scenes from the film because _____ was more than three hours long. (referring to a thing, subject pronoun)

(63) Even the co-stars yawned, hiding behind _____ programs. (referring to a group, possessive pronoun)

(64) The director is sure that the film will win many awards and has even built a special shelf to display _____. (referring to things, object pronoun)

(65) _____ is empty now and is likely to stay that way! (referring to a thing, subject pronoun)

(66) I went with Alix, and _____ reaction to the film was negative. (referring to the speaker and another person, possessive)

(67) Alix has been _____ friend since kindergarten. (referring to the speaker, possessive)

(68) At the end, _____ in the audience clapped. (referring to all the people in a group, subject pronoun)

(69) We were so glad _____ was over! (referring to a thing, subject pronoun)

(70) _____ all hope the director doesn't read the reviews. (referring to a group that includes the speaker, subject pronoun)

Calling All Overachievers: Extra Noun and Pronoun Questions

Still interested in perfecting your knowledge of nouns and pronouns? Excellent! Here's a page from a manual explaining how to set up your new television. (Don't look for this product. It isn't real.) Check the underlined words and decide whether they are correct or incorrect. If you find an error, correct it by changing the underlined word.

Congratulations on (1) your new Floogle TV! Follow (2) this ten simple steps to set up your TV. Don't worry! Soon (3) you will be watching (4) your favorite (5) comedies.

Step One	Open the two small (6) <u>boxs</u>.
Step Two	Carefully pull out (7) <u>those</u> cord (shown in the diagram) and place (8) <u>it</u> on a table.
Step Three	Plug the power cord into (9) <u>it's</u> slot on the back of the TV.
Step Four	If you see (10) <u>sparkes</u> or get a shock, call 1-800-555-5555 and ask to speak with Mr. Smith.
Step Five	(11) <u>Mr. Smith, he</u> is our lawyer and will explain why you should not sue.
Step Six	Connect the TV to (12) <u>you</u> wifi network.
Step Seven	Put (13) <u>batterys</u> in the remote. This is so easy that even (14) <u>childs</u> can do it.
Step Eight	If the remote doesn't work, don't call (15) <u>our</u> helpline.
Step Nine	Pay the cable company to fix (16) <u>everything</u> you did wrong.
Step Ten	Do you like (17) <u>movies</u> and sports? (18) <u>Them</u> channels cost extra.

Note: If you return the TV to (19) <u>us</u>, you will receive a full refund, minus the 90 percent we charge for (20) <u>deliveries</u>.

Answers to Noun and Pronoun Questions

1. **grandfather, attorney, law, years.** Two nouns name people (*grandfather, attorney*). Two name things (*law, years*).

2. **Grandma, chemistry, physics, juniors, seniors, Cole College.** In this sentence, you find three nouns naming people (*Grandma, juniors, seniors*), one naming a place (*Cole College*) and two naming things (*chemistry, physics*).

3. **students, Granny Science.** Did you count *Granny Science* as two nouns? Both words form one name.

4. **Chemistry, course, teaching, subject.** All four of these nouns name things. Did I catch you with *teaching*? In some sentences, that word may be part of a verb (*is teaching, were teaching,* and so forth). In this sentence, however, it's a quality — a thing. Therefore, it's a noun.

5. **times, week, grandfather, center.** Here, you have two nouns for things (*times, week*), one for a place (*center*) and one for a person (*grandfather*). Note: If you wrote *community center*, count yourself correct. *Center* is the important word, but you can take *community center* as one name.

6. **people, center, advice.** The first noun (*people*) names a person (actually, persons!), the second (*center*) a place, and the third (*advice*) a thing.

7. **clients, gratitude.** The first noun names people, and the second names a feeling.

8. **Grandma, husband, "Grandaddy Law."** All three nouns name people.

9. **grandchildren, nickname.** The first noun names people, the second a thing.

10. **Thanksgiving, books, equipment, table, floor.** Holidays are considered things, so their names are nouns. Did you include some descriptions with your other choices — *kitchen table* instead of just *table*, for example? Descriptions aren't nouns. (Chapter 4 tells you what you need to know about descriptions.)

11. **dashes.** When a noun ends with *sh, ch, ss,* or *x*, add *es* to form the plural.

12. **donkeys.** When a noun ends with *y* and the letter before *y* is *a, e, i,* or *o*, add *s* to form the plural.

13. **potatoes.** When a noun ends with *o* and the letter before *o* is not *a, e, i, o,* or *u*, you generally add *es* to form the plural.

14. **hexes.** When a noun ends with *sh, ch, ss,* or *x*, add *es* to form the plural.

15. **fusses.** When a noun ends with *sh, ch, ss,* or *x*, add *es* to form the plural.

16. **sauces.** When a noun doesn't end with *sh, ch, ss,* or *x*, add *s* to form the plural.

17. **calves.** Words ending with *f* or *fe* generally form plurals by changing the *f* to *v* and adding *s* or *es*.

18. **churches.** When a noun ends with *sh, ch, ss,* or *x*, add *es* to form the plural.

19. **floors.** When a noun doesn't end with *sh, ch, ss,* or *x*, add *s* to form the plural.

(20) **moose.** This irregular noun is the same in both singular and plural forms.

(21) **runways.** When a noun ends with *y* and the letter before *y* is *a, e, i,* or *o,* add *s* to form the plural.

(22) **copies.** When a noun ends with *y* and the letter before *y* is not *a, e, i,* or *o,* change the *y* to *i* and add *es* to form the plural.

(23) **suitcases.** When a noun doesn't end with *sh, ch, ss,* or *x,* add *s* to form the plural.

(24) **espressos.** When a noun ends with *o* and the letter before *o* is not *a, e, i, o,* or *u,* you generally add only *s* to form the plural.

(25) **switches.** When a noun ends with *sh, ch, ss,* or *x,* add *es* to form the plural.

(26) **tattoos.** When a noun ends with *o* and the letter before *o* is *a, e, i, o,* or *u,* you generally add only *s* to form the plural.

(27) **kittens.** When a noun doesn't end with *sh, ch, ss,* or *x,* add *s* to form the plural.

(28) **juries.** When a noun ends with *y* and the letter before *y* is not *a, e, i,* or *o,* change the *y* to *i* and add *es* to form the plural.

(29) **women.** This is an irregular plural.

(30) **feet.** This is an irregular plural.

(31) **Correct.** *Flower* is a singular noun, so you can correctly attach *this* or *that* to it.

(32) **Incorrect.** *Doorknobs* is a plural noun, so you cannot attach *this* or *that* to it.

(33) **Incorrect.** *Cloud* is a singular noun, so you cannot attach *these* or *those* to it.

(34) **Correct.** *Statue* is a singular noun, so you can correctly attach *this* or *that* to it.

(35) **Correct.** *Answers* is a plural noun, so you can correctly attach *these* or *those* to it.

(36) **Her, she → Maria, him → supervisor, man.** *She* and *her* refer to *Maria.* The pronoun *him* refers to *supervisor* and *man,* two nouns that name the same person.

(37) **anyone.** The pronoun *anyone* singles out but doesn't name one person from a group.

(38) **he, her, he, it → project, her.** *He* refers to *supervisor* (twice). *Her* refers to *Maria* (whose name is not in the sentence), and *it* refers to *project.*

(39) **them → parts.** The pronoun *them* refers to *parts.*

(40) **nothing.** The pronoun *nothing* rules out all the things Maria could know about marketing.

(41) **himself → supervisor.** This pronoun refers to and emphasizes *supervisor.*

(42) **You, yourself, he, her, she.** Both *You* and *yourself* refer to the person listening to the supervisor. *He* refers to the supervisor, who doesn't appear in the sentence. *Her* and *she* refer to *Maria,* even though her name isn't in the sentence.

(43) **mine → Maria, somebody.** The first pronoun refers to the speaker, *Maria,* and the second to the an unnamed person from a group.

(44) **Everyone.** This pronoun represents all the people in the group without naming them.

(45) **herself → Maria, us, she → Maria.** The pronoun *herself* adds emphasis to *Maria*, the word it refers to. *Us* represents the audience hearing the message, but they aren't named in the sentence. The pronoun *she* represents *Maria*.

(46) **My, me, I, she.** All three pronouns refer to the speaker, whose name doesn't appear in the sentence. *She* refers to *Maria*, which doesn't appear in the sentence.

(47) **They, they.** Both pronouns refer to the aunts, but they don't appear in the sentence.

(48) **us, they → aunts, ourselves, you.** The first pronoun (*us*) refers to the speakers, whose names don't appear in the sentence. The second (*they*) refers to *aunts*. *Ouselves* refers to the speakers, and *you* to the person hearing the words. Those names aren't in the sentence.

(49) **I.** The sentence begins with "My name is," so you know that Georgie is speaking. The underlined portion should be replaced with *I*, the pronoun referring to the speaker or writer.

(50) **you.** Because the sentence is addressed to Georgie, the underlined word should be *you*, the pronoun that represents the audience for Helen's words.

(51) **his.** This pronoun replaces *Tomas's*.

(52) **No one, Nobody.** The sentence rules all every person in the room, so you need a pronoun that excludes people. Both *no one* and *nobody* fit. If you wrote either one of them, count yourself correct. (If you wrote both, give yourself a star!)

(53) **they, she.** The plural pronoun *they* can represent people, but here *they* represents things. Because Helen is female, the pronoun *she* fits.

(54) **it, his.** The noun is singular, so the pronoun *it* is the best choice to replace *money*. The pronoun *his* replaces *Tomas's*.

(55) **herself.** When an action doubles back (*Helen → Helen*), you need a *self* pronoun.

(56) **They.** Two people are represented by the pronoun *they*.

(57) **us, it.** Helen is speaking about herself, but also about Tomas. The plural pronoun *us* refers to both. *It* is the pronoun that represents one thing (*bed*, in this sentence).

(58) **I.** This pronoun represents the speaker, Georgie.

(59) **she.**

(60) **them.**

(61) **His.**

(62) **it.**

(63) **their.**

(64) **them.**

(65) **It.**

(66) **our.**

(67) **my.**

(68) **everyone.**

(69) **it.**

(70) **We.**

Here are the answers to the overachiever questions:

(1) **Correct.** The pronoun *your* properly refers to the reader. You need a possessive pronoun here to show ownership of the TV.

(2) **Incorrect, these.** Because *steps* is plural, you can't attach the singular word *this* to it. *These* is the plural form of *this*.

(3) **Correct.** *You* is the proper pronoun to address the reader.

(4) **Correct.** The possessive pronoun *your* shows that the favorite shows belong to the reader.

(5) **Correct.** In its singular form, *comedy* ends with a *y*. The letter before the *y* is not *a, e, o,* or *u*, so you must change the *y* to *i* and add *es* to make the plural form.

(6) **Incorrect, boxes.** The singular noun *box* ends with *x*, so you add *es* to make the plural form.

(7) **Incorrect, that.** *Cord* is a singular noun, so it doesn't match *those*, a plural. *That* is the singular form of *those*.

(8) **Correct.** *It* is a singular pronoun, a good match for the singular word (*cord*).

(9) **Incorrect, its.** No possessive pronoun has an apostrophe.

(10) **Incorrect, sparks.** Form the plural of *spark* by adding *s*.

(11) **Incorrect, Mr. Smith is OR he is.** Don't double up a pronoun with the word it represents, unless you're adding emphasis with a *self* pronoun.

(12) **Incorrect, your.** You need the possessive pronoun *your* to show that the network belongs to the reader.

(13) **Incorrect, batteries.** *Battery* (a singular noun) ends with *y*, and the letter before the *y* is not *a, e, o,* or *u*. In this situation, change the *y* to *i* and add *es* to form the plural.

(14) **Incorrect, children.** *Children* is an irregular plural.

(15) **Correct.** *Our* is a plural possessive, referring to the speaker or writer.

(16) **Correct.** The pronoun *everything* is used properly in this sentence.

(17) **Correct.** To form the plural of the noun *movie*, add *s*.

(18) **Incorrect, Those.** *Them* is an object pronoun, so it can't describe the noun *channels*.

(19) **Correct.** The object pronoun *us* properly follows the preposition, *to*.

(20) **Correct.** *Delivery* (a singular noun) ends with *y*, and the letter before the *y* is not *a, e, o,* or *u*. In this situation, change the *y* to *i* and add *es* to form the plural.

Chapter **3**

Getting Acquainted with Verbs

Before you do anything to a sentence — write, analyze, or edit — you have to locate its heart, also known as the *verb*. Words that express action or state of being are verbs; they pump meaning into a sentence, just as a real heart pumps blood into veins and arteries. In this chapter, you practice identifying verbs and their helpers, sorting out the ways verbs express time, and selecting irregular forms.

Treasure Hunt: Finding the Verb

To find the verb, think about the meaning of the sentence. Ask two questions: *What's happening? What is, was, or will be?* The answer is a verb. You may find more than one verb in a sentence:

This morning, I showered and washed my hair.

In this sentence, *showered* and *washed* are both verbs.

Each verb family starts with a base word — an *infintive*. Infinitives are often written with *to* in front: *to be, to juggle, to plop.* In Standard English, every sentence must have a verb. Often, it's just the base word or the base word with extra letters. In the example above, the base words *shower* and *wash* appear with *ed* attached because the action occurred in the past.

More on verbs and time appears in the next section, "Using Past, Present, and Future Tense at the Right Time."

TIP

Sometimes, the verb in a sentence is formed with two or more words: *will go, has arrived, can sleep*. The words forming a verb may be next to each other, or they may be separated, especially in questions and negative statements. You have to locate all the parts of a verb in order to understand how the sentence works. (More on other types of multi-word verbs appears in "Recognizing and Using Helping Verbs" later in this chapter.)

YOUR TURN

Q. Find the verb or verbs in each sentence.

Gloria is a tennis fan, so she rushed to buy tickets for the championship match.

A. **is, rushed**. This sentence makes two statements, one about Gloria and one about her actions. To locate the verbs, ask the verb questions: *What's happening?* The answer is *rushed*, which is a verb. *What is, was, or will be?* The answer is the verb *is*.

TIP

Did you choose *to buy*? That's an infinitive. Oddly, infinitives don't function as verbs in a sentence. If you reread the statement about Gloria, you see that the sentence doesn't say that she bought tickets. She *rushed*. Maybe she was successful, and maybe she wasn't. Either way, *to buy* is an infinitive, not a verb.

1. The fire engine raced down the street.

2. Around the curve, just ahead of the railroad tracks, stood seven donkeys.

3. One of the donkeys, frightened by the noise of the siren, ran away.

4. Another looked worried but did not move.

5. Was she brave or was she foolish?

6. Most likely, the animal did not notice the noise or did not care.

7. The donkey was eating George's lawn!

8. George's house was not on fire, but several others on his street were burning.

9. George left the donkey alone and went inside for an extra-long lunch.

10. Because of the donkey, George did not mow his lawn.

Using Past, Present, and Future Tense at the Right Times

Even without a watch or a smartphone, verbs tell time. This quality is known as *tense*. In this section, I hit you with time questions. Not "Why are you late again?" but "Which verb do I need to show what's completed, not yet begun, or going on right now?"

Verbs fall into one of three categories: *past*, *present*, and *future*. In this chapter, you practice the *simple tenses*. In Chapter 6, you work on *progressive tenses* (the *ing* form of a verb), which emphasize a process or an action that spans a time period. Chapter 6 also deals with the *perfect tenses*, which establish a timeline. Here's a taste of each simple tense:

>> *Past tense* **tells what happened at a specific, previous time.** Past tense may also describe a pattern of behavior in the past. In the sentence, *Diane tattooed a skull on her arm, tattooed* is a past-tense verb. In the sentence, *Diane always covered her tattoo before job interviews, covered* is a past-tense verb. Regular past-tense verbs end with *ed,* which is tacked onto the base word of the infinitive. (*I walked, you cooked, Yasser and his friends rested,* and so on.)

>> *Present tense* **tells you what's going on now at the present moment, or more generally speaking, what action is happening over and over again.** In the sentence *Grace rides her bike, rides* is a present-tense verb. All regular present-tense verb forms, except for one, are the base word of the infinitive. (*I carry, you buy, we trust,* and so on.) The exception is the verb form you use to talk about one person or thing. To make this form, add *s* to the base word of the infinitive. (*Maria talks, the dog barks, the vase breaks,* and so on.)

>> **Future tense looks ahead.** The verb in *Grace will give Diane a ride around the block* is *will give,* which is a future-tense verb. Regular future-tense verbs add *will* (or occasionally, *shall*) to the base word of the infintive.

YOUR TURN

Q. Fill in the blank with the correct form of the base word in parentheses. Be sure to choose the correct tense.

Yesterday, reacting to a tiny taste of arsenic, Mike _____ his evil twin brother of murder. (*accuse*)

A. accused. The clue here is *yesterday*, which tells you that you're in the past.

11   Fashion is important to Abe, so he always _____ the latest and most popular style. (*select*)

12   Last year's tight, slim lines _____ Abe, who likes more comfortable clothing. (*challenge*)

13   When he goes shopping next week, Abe _____ (find) something that _____ (make) him look and feel good. He always does!

14 Abe hopes that the next fashion fad _____ his favorite color, blue. (*highlight*)

15 Tomorrow Diane _____ an article for the fashion press stating that purple and orange are trending. (*write*)

16 She once _____ a purple pantsuit and wore it with an orange blouse. (*purchase*)

17 Every time she _____ the pantsuit, she receives many compliments. (*wear*)

18 An hour ago, Grace _____ about show-offs who "spend too much time and money on clothing." (*complain*)

19 However, as soon as Grace saves enough cash, she _____ in an expensive wardrobe for herself. (*invest*)

20 At next year's Fashion Gala, Abe _____ Diane the "Best Dressed" trophy. (*award*)

21 Two minutes after receiving the trophy, Diane _____ it on a shelf next to her "Best Fashion Writer" medal. (*place*)

22 Every day when I_____ the medal, I wonder who voted for Diane. (*see*)

23 Abe _____it to me in detail yesterday. (*explain*)

24 "She earned the medal for her writing style," he _____, not for her fashion sense. (*state*)

25 Grace, who_____ Diane tomorrow, says that Diane got the award because she bribed voters. (*visit*)

Getting a Handle on Common Irregular Forms

Life would be easier — well, at least grammar would be easier! — if all verbs followed the rules. They don't. Past-tense verbs, especially, stray from the regular path and wander all over the place. So do some important verbs, *be, do,* and *have.* In this section, you survey the rule-breakers.

Digging into the past

Regular past-tense verbs tack *ed* onto the base verb. Irregulars don't. Because English has so many irregular verbs, I can list only a few here. The dictionary can help you out with any verb that doesn't appear here.

Base Verb	Past Tense	Base Verb	Past Tense
become	became	begin	began
bite	bit	break	broke
bring	brought	catch	caught
choose	chose	come	came
drink	drank	eat	ate
fall	fell	feel	felt
fly	flew	freeze	froze
get	got	go	went
know	knew	lead	led
lend	lent	lose	lost
ride	rode	ring	rang
rise	rose	run	ran
say	said	see	saw
shake	shook	sing	sang
sit	sat	slide	slid
speak	spoke	take	took
throw	threw	wear	wore
win	won	write	wrote

Fill in the blanks with the correct irregular past tense form, working from the base verb in parentheses.

YOUR TURN

Q. With one leg 3 inches shorter than the other, Natalie seldom _____ into first base, even during important softball games. (*slide*)

A. **slid**. No *ed* for this past tense! *Slid* is the irregular past form of *slide*.

26 The last time she played, Natalie _____ her leg. (*break*)

27 Our team _____ with fear when she _____ over. (*shake, fall*)

28 Antonio, who believes that safety is more important than winning, _____ an email to the whole team. (*send*)

29 He _____ that everyone should keep their eyes on the ground and avoid potholes. (*write*)

30 He _____ to the team about safety before the game. (*speak*)

31 He _____ a bell whenever he saw someone playing recklessly. (*ring*)

32 Natalie _____ to speak with league officials about what she called "Antonio's overreaction." (*go*)

33 The league _____ to investigate Antonio's coaching style. (*begin*)

34 Soon after, Antonio _____ the team and _____ a new hobby. (*leave, find*)

35 Natalie _____ a job coaching chess because she _____, it was more relaxing than softball. (*take, say*)

be, do, and *have*

Three irregular verbs — *be, do,* and *have* — appear more frequently than a movie star with a new film to promote. Like movie stars, they also tend to cause trouble. Both change according to time and according to the person with whom they're paired. (Amazing that the movie-star comparison works on so many levels!) Table 3-1 shows the proper present-tense and past-tense verb forms to pair with *I, we,* and *you* (both singular and plural). The table also gives you the matching verb form for *they* (both singular and plural, as well as any plural noun). The last line of the table shows the verb form you need for *it, he,* and *she,* as well as any singular noun. Are you wondering why I didn't include the future tense? The future forms of these verbs are regular. All you do is add *will* to the base word: *will be, will do, will have.* That's it!

Table 3-1   Verb Forms for the Irregular Verbs *To Be* and *To Have*

Pronouns and Nouns	Present Tense Verb Forms for "Be"	Past Tense Verb Forms for "Be"	Present Tense Verb Forms for "Do"	Past Tense Verb Forms for "Do"	Present Tense Verb Forms for "Have"	Past Tense Verb Forms for "Have"
I	am	was	do	did	have	had
you, we, they, any plural noun	are	were	do	did	have	had
he, she, it, any singular noun	is	was	do	did	has	had

Note: The form of *be* used with helping verbs is *been.*

YOUR TURN

Fill in the blanks with the correct form of the verb in parentheses at the end of the sentence.

Q. The woman in charge of the county fair _____ very tan today because yesterday she stayed in the sun for hours. (be, present tense)

A. **is.** *Woman* is a singular noun, which makes a good match with *is.*

36 My apple muffins _____ very tasty and should win a blue ribbon this year. (*be*, present tense)

37 At last year's county fair, my corn muffins _____ very well, too. The judges asked for the recipe! (*do*, past tense)

38. This year, I am bringing a large salad to the picnic because I believe you can never _____ enough green vegetables. (*have*, present tense)

39. Mikeyla told me not to bring salad. She said, "I _____ sure the amount of green vegetables I already _____ will feed everyone." (*be*, present tense; *have*, present tense)

40. Last year, Karl _____ a different idea. (*have*, past tense)

41. "Dmitri and I _____ firmly anti-vegetable," he commented. (*be*, present tense)

42. Two hours from now, Dmitri _____ three slabs of meat on his plate. (*have*, future tense)

43. Mei _____ everything she can to win the cooking competition. (*do*, present tense)

44. Yesterday, Mei _____ second thoughts about her entry; she now thinks that she should have prepared a dessert instead of a main dish. (*have*, past tense)

45. The soon-to-be-announced winners in each category _____ extremely pleased with the prizes this year. (*be*, present tense)

46. "Give me a taste because I _____ a judge," I said. (*be*, present tense)

47. "No kidding!" exclaimed Dmitri. "I thought you _____ a participant." (*be*, past tense)

48. Mikeyla doesn't like desserts, but I _____. (*do*, present tense)

49. Mikeyla _____ a heavy hand with hot sauce. (*have*, present tense)

50. "You _____ to taste her dish anyway," she told me. (*have*, future tense)

Recognizing and Using Helping Verbs

Sometimes, a one-word verb is all your sentence needs. To ask a question or to make a negative statement, though, you nearly always have to add a *helping verb*. Often, the helper is a form of the verbs *be, do,* or *have*. Other helping verbs — *can, should, might,* and *must,* for example — add shades of meaning. In this section, you practice getting the help the verb in your sentence needs.

Questioning with verbs

In many languages, you say the equivalent of "Liked the cake?" to find out whether someone enjoyed what you baked. To create a question in English, you generally combine a form of *be*, *do*, or *have* with the base form of the verb:

> Did you like the cake?

Notice that the combo form (*did like*) is different from the past tense form used in statements (*liked*).

Other question-creators, underlined in these examples, change the tense:

> <u>Will</u> you <u>eat</u> that cake?

> <u>Do</u> you *eat* cake?

The first example reaches into the future; the second stays in the present, asking about an ongoing action.

When *be* or *have* acts as the base verb for a question, you don't always need to attach a helper:

> <u>Are</u> they good bakers?

> *Have* they any cake left?

TIP

You probably noticed that in a question with a two-word verb, the two words are separated by another word. That's the *subject* (who or what does the action or exists in the state of being expressed by the verb). For more about subjects, turn to Chapter 7.

YOUR TURN

Rewrite each statement so that it becomes a question. Add words or rearrange the sentence as needed.

Q. **You found a wallet on the ground.**

_____

A. **Did you find a wallet on the ground?** The helping verb *did* comes before *you* in this question. The past-tense form, *found*, changes to *find*, the base word.

51 You took the wallet to the police station.

_____

52 The cops always accept lost items.

_____

53 The wallet was stolen.

_____

54 The detectives seemed interested.

_____

55 They noticed the seven credit cards, each with a different name.

_____

56 The photo on the license matches a mug shot.

_____

57 The police will act swiftly.

_____

58 You want the reward for recovering stolen property.

_____

Choosing the correct verb for negative expressions

Three little letters — *not* — turn a positive comment ("I like your boots") to a negative one ("I do not like your boots"). Apart from the fashion critique, what do you notice about the negative statement? The verb changes from *like* to *do like*. You need the extra word because "I not like" isn't correct in Standard English. In addition to forms of the verb *do*, the helping verbs *have*, *has*, or *had* may help turn a positive sentence into a negative one. Sentences with a *be* verb can turn negative without any helping verb at all. In this section, you can try your hand at *not* creating the wrong negative verb.

YOUR TURN

Q. Rewrite each sentence as a negative expression.

Mark's acting received an Academy Award.

_____

A. **Mark's acting did not receive an Academy Award.** Two things change when the positive verb (*received*) becomes negative (*did not receive*). *Received*, a past-tense form, is replaced by the base word of the infinitive (*receive*). The helping verb *did* pairs with it. As you probably noticed, *not* is tucked between the two parts of this verb, its usual spot.

59 My phone buzzes like a bee.

_____

60 Sheila is in love with bees.

_____

61 She wanted to be a beekeeper.

_____

62 Looking at bee hives gives her hives.

_____

63 The bee flying near our picnic table left Sheila alone all afternoon.

_____

64 Sheila will ask me to change my ringtone.

_____

Adding shades of meaning with helping verbs

In addition to _has_, _have_, _had_, and the _be_ verbs (_am_, _is_, _are_, _was_, _were_, and so on), you can attach a few other helpers to a base verb, and, in doing so, change the meaning of the sentence slightly. Consider hiring the following helpers:

>> **_Should_ and _must_ add a sense of duty.** Notice the sense of obligation in these two sentences: "Otto should put the ice cream away before he eats the whole pint." "Otto must reduce the number of calories he eats, according to his doctor."

>> **_Can_ and _could_ imply ability.** _Could_ is the past tense of _can_. Choose the tense that matches the tense of the base verb or the time period expressed in the sentence, as in these examples, "If Mei can help, she will." or "Cedric could run faster than anyone else on the track team."

>> **_May_ and _might_ add possibility to the sentence.** Strictly speaking, _might_ is for past events, and _may_ for present, but these days, people interchange the two forms: "I may go to the picnic if the weather is good." "I told Sven that he might want to bring sunscreen."

>> **_Would_ usually expresses a condition or willingness.** This helper explains under what circumstances something may happen. ("I would have brought the cat had I known about the mouse problem.") _Would_ may also express willingness. ("He would catch many mice.") _Would_ sometimes communicates repeated past actions. ("Every Saturday, he _would_ go to the pet store for more cat food.") The present tense of _would_, the helping verb _will_, may also indicate a condition in the present or future. ("I will go if I can get a free ticket.")

Add a helper to the base verb. The information in parentheses after the fill-in-the-blank sentence explains what meaning the sentence should have.

YOUR TURN

Q. Lisa said that she _____ consider running for Parks Commissioner, but she hasn't made up her mind yet. (possibility)

A. **might or may.** The _might_ or _may_ shows that Lisa hasn't made up her mind yet.

65 The mayor, shy as ever, said that she _____ go to the tree planting ceremony only if the media agreed to stay outside the forest. (*condition*)

66 Kirk, an influencer, _____ not agree to any conditions because his followers expect eyewitness coverage. (*ability*)

67 Whenever he met with the mayor, Kirk _____ always urge her to invite the media to special events, without success. (*repeated action*)

68 The mayor _____ make an effort to be more open to the press. (*duty*)

69 Lisa, who writes the popular "Trees-a-Crowd" blog, explained that she _____ rely on her imagination to supply details. (*possibility*)

70 Lisa knows that Kirk's report _____ go viral, and she doesn't want to miss an important story. (*ability*)

71 All good reporters _____ know that if a tree falls or is planted in the forest, the sound is heard by a wide audience only if a reporter is there. (*duty*)

72 Sound engineers, on the other hand, _____ skip all outdoor events if they _____ do so. (*condition, ability*)

CALLING ALL OVERACHIEVERS: EXTRA PRACTICE WITH VERBS

Check the underlined words in this email from a teacher to parents. If everything is okay, write "Correct." If you find a mistake, write "Incorrect" and revise.

I (1) are sure you (2) will enjoy the second grade's musical performance, which (3) took place next Wednesday. The children (4) has great pride in their work. They are so good, they (5) could be professional singers! Of course, a few (6) did not paid attention during the first few practices. (7) Were I discouraged then? No! I (8) bringed donuts and bribed them. All have now learned their parts and (9) will perform perfectly when you are present. Note: You (10) should wear earplugs.

Answers to Questions about Verbs

Have you conquered verbs? Check your answers to find out.

1. **raced.** Ask *what's happening?* The answer is *raced. Raced* is the verb.

2. **stood.** Even though *stood* sounds like inaction, it's still expressing what happens, so it's a verb.

3. **ran.** What's happening? The frightened animal *ran,* that's what's happening! *Ran* is a verb. Did you focus on *frightened?* That word can be a verb in a sentence such as "The monster frightened the child." In question 3, though, *frightened* is a description.

4. **looked, did move.** The verb *looked* tells you about the donkey's state of being. *Did move* tells you what's happening, so it's an action verb. If you wrote *move* and omitted *did,* give yourself partial credit. Both words combine to create one question. Are you wondering why *not* isn't listed here? *Not* is not a verb. It's an adverb. (For more on adverbs, turn to Chapter 4.)

5. **was, was.** Each of these verbs tells you about the donkey's state of being.

6. **did notice, did care.** Negative statements often rely on forms of the verb *do.* Here you find *did notice* and *did care,* both of which tell you what's happening.

7. **was eating.** The answer to *what's happening?* is *was eating,* which is the verb.

8. **was, were burning.** In the first part of this sentence, *was* expresses state of being. The second part of the sentence tells you what was happening, using the verb *were burning.*

9. **left, went.** Both verbs tell you what's happening.

10. **did mow.** Did you include *not?* Nope. *Not* is an adverb, not a verb. Chapter 4 tells you more about adverbs. *Did mow,* on the other hand, tells you what's happening, so it's a verb.

11. **selects.** Notice the time clues? The first part of the sentence contains the present-tense verb *is,* and the second part includes the word *always.* You're in the present with a recurring action.

12. **challenged.** Another time clue: *last year's* places you in the past.

13. **will find, will make OR makes.** The time clue here is next week — the future —so *will find* is perfect for this slot. The second verb can be in the future (*will make*), but if you chose the present tense (*makes*), you're not wrong. Present tense can express something that always happens.

14. **will highlight.** The key here is *next,* which puts the sentence in the future.

15. **will write.** The time clue *tomorrow* puts this sentence in the future.

16. **purchased.** Diane's bad-taste choice happened *once,* which means it took place in the past.

17. **wears.** For something that happens over and over again, use the present tense.

18. **complained.** The clue to the past is *an hour ago.*

(19) **will invest.** The time words here, *as soon as*, tell you that the action hasn't happened yet.

(20) **will award.** The expression *next year* puts you in the future.

(21) **will place.** The expression *two minutes after* seems to set the sentence in the past, but because Diane hasn't received it yet, the action of placing the award on the shelf is in future tense.

(22) **see.** The time clue here is *every day*, which tells you that this action occurs over and over. Therefore, the verb should be in present tense.

(23) **explained.** The *yesterday* is a dead giveaway; go for past tense.

(24) **stated.** The story of the award is in past tense, and this sentence is no exception. Even without the story context, you see the first verb (*earned*) is in past tense, which works nicely with the past-tense verb *stated*.

(25) **will visit.** The time clue is *tomorrow*, which places the verb in the future.

(26) **broke.**

(27) **shook, fell.**

(28) **sent.**

(29) **wrote.**

(30) **spoke.**

(31) **rang.**

(32) **went.**

(33) **began.**

(34) **left, found.**

(35) **took, said.**

(36) **are.** This verb form matches the plural noun *muffins*.

(37) **did.** The past-tense form of *do* is *did*.

(38) **have.** This form matches the pronoun *you*.

(39) **am, have.** Both verbs correctly pair with the pronoun *I*.

(40) **had.** The past-tense form of *have* is *had*.

(41) **are.** You need a plural verb form to pair with *Dmitri and I*.

(42) **will have.** To create a future-tense verb, place *will* before the base word of the infinitive. (Some people attach *shall* if the verb pairs with the pronoun *I*.)

(43) **does.** *Diane* is a singular noun, so it pairs with *does*.

(44) **had.** The past-tense form of *have* is *had.*

(45) **are.** You need *are* to pair with the plural noun *winners.*

(46) **am.** *Am* pairs with *I* in the present tense.

(47) **were.** *Were* pairs with *you* in the past tense.

(48) **do.** *Do* pairs with *I* in the present tense.

(49) **has.** *Mikeyla* is a singular noun, which pairs with *has.*

(50) **will have.** *You* pairs with *will have* in the future tense.

(51) **Did you take the wallet to the police station?** Typical question format: the two parts of the verb, *did* and *take,* are separated by the subject, *you.*

(52) **Do the cops always accept lost items?** This one's in present tense because the original statement contains the present-tense verb, *accept.*

(53) **Was the wallet stolen?** Because the verb in this sentence is a form of *be,* you don't need a helping verb to form a question.

(54) **Did the detectives seem interested?** The base verb, *seem,* needs the helping verb *did* to create a question.

(55) **Did they notice the seven credit cards, each with a different name?** The helper *did* works with the base verb, *notice,* to form this question.

(56) **Does the photo on the license match a mug shot?** The helping verb *does* joins the base verb, *match,* to ask a question.

(57) **Will the police act swiftly?** The helper, *will,* always pairs with the base verb in the future tense, whether you're asking a question or making a statement. In a question, though, the subject (who or what is involved in the action the verb expresses) sits between *will* and the base verb.

(58) **Do you want the reward for recovering stolen property?** To form this question, you add *do* to the base verb, *want.*

(59) **My phone does not buzz like a bee.** The positive verb *buzzes* turns into *does buzz* in the negative, with *not* between the two parts of the verb.

(60) **Sheila is not in love with bees.** With your sharp eyes, you probably noticed that no form of the verb *do* appears in this sentence. The verb *be* is special because it doesn't require a helping verb to ask a question or make a negative statement. A simple *not* does the job here.

(61) **She did not want to be a beekeeper.** The past-tense verb form *wanted* turns to *did want.* *Not* completes the negative transformation.

(62) **Looking at bee hives does not give her hives.** Here, the present-tense form *gives* changes to *does give,* with *not* in between.

(63) **The bee flying near our picnic table did not leave Sheila alone all afternoon.** The past-tense verb form *left* changes to *did leave,* which becomes negative with the addition of *not.* Were you confused by *flying?* Although *flying* expresses action, it isn't the verb in this section. (For more information about this sort of "fake verb," turn to Chapter 18.)

(64) **Sheila will not ask me to change my ringtone.** The positive, future-tense verb form *will ask* needs no other helping verb. The word *not* does the job when it's tucked between *will* and *ask*.

(65) **would.** The going is dependent upon the press arrangement. Thus, *would* is the best choice.

(66) **could.** The agreement wasn't possible, so *could* wins the prize.

(67) **would.** This helping verb expresses repeated actions in the past.

(68) **should or must.** Once you imply duty, *should* or *must* is the helper you want. *Should* makes a suggestion, and *must* creates a requirement.

(69) **may or might.** Lisa, if she's in the mood, will cover the tree-cutting without seeing it. This possibility is expressed by the helpers *may* and *might*.

(70) **can.** You need to express ability in the present tense, which *can* can do.

(71) **should or must.** To express duty, *should* or *must* works perfectly. *Should* is a suggestion, *must* a requirement.

(72) **would, could.** *Would* expresses a condition, and *could* adds ability to the sentence.

Answers to "Overachievers Questions"

(1) **Incorrect. am.** The pronoun *I* pairs with *am*, not with *are*.

(2) **Correct.** Because the performance is "next Wednesday," the future tense is what you need here.

(3) **Incorrect. will take.** You need future tense, not past, because the performance has not yet taken place.

(4) **Incorrect. have.** *Children* is a plural noun, so you need *have*, not *has*.

(5) **Correct.** *Could* implies ability or possibility, both of which fit the meaning of this sentence.

(6) **Incorrect. did not pay.** In a negative expression, the usual past-tense form of the verb isn't appropriate. You need a helping verb and the base form, which is *pay*.

(7) **Incorrect. Was.** *I* pairs with *was*, not with *were*.

(8) **Incorrect. brought.** The verb *bring* has an irregular past-tense form, *brought*.

(9) **Correct.** The future-tense form, *will perform*, is appropriate.

(10) **Correct.** The helping verb *should* joins the base verb *wear* to express necessity.

Chapter 4

Writing Good or Well: Adjectives and Adverbs

D o you write *good* or *well* — and what's the difference? Is your snack *a apple* or *an apple* or *the apple*? Is your cold *worse* or *more bad*? If you're stewing over these questions, you've come to the right chapter. Here, you can practice choosing between two types of descriptions — adjectives and adverbs — and decide whether *a, an,* or *the* is best for any situation. You also work on making comparisons with adjectives and adverbs.

Identifying Adjectives and Adverbs

Adjectives describe nouns — words that name a person, thing, place, or idea. They also describe pronouns, which are words that stand in for nouns (*other, someone, they,* and similar words). Adjectives usually come before the word they describe, but not always. In the following sentence, the adjectives are italicized:

The *rubber* duck with his *lovely orange* bill sailed over the *soapy bath* water. (*Rubber* describes *duck; lovely* and *orange* describe *bill; soapy* and *bath* describe *water.*)

An *adverb*, on the other hand, describes a verb, usually telling how, where, when, or why an action took place. Adverbs may also change the intensity of another descriptive word or add information about another description. In the following sentence, the adverbs are italicized:

> The alligator snapped *furiously* as the duck *very violently* flapped his wings. *(Furiously describes snapped, violently describes flapped, and very describes violently.)*

Whether you're speaking or writing, you should take care to use adjectives and adverbs correctly. But first, you have to recognize them. To identify an adjective, locate the nouns and pronouns. Ask *which one? what kind? how many?* about each one. If you get an answer, you've found an adjective. To locate an adverb, first check every verb. Ask *how? when? where? why?* If you get an answer, you've identified an adverb. Also, look at the adjectives and adverbs. Does any word strengthen (*very*, for example) or weaken (*less*, perhaps) the description? That's an adverb at work.

WARNING

Sometimes, when you ask the adjective or adverb questions, the answer is a group of words. Don't panic. Longer descriptions can function as adjectives and adverbs, too. In this exercise, concentrate on one- or two-word adjectives and adverbs.

YOUR TURN

Q. Underline and label every adjective or adverb in each sentence.

Followed by three little dogs, Debbie slowly crossed the dark street.

A. **three (ADJ), little (ADJ), slowly (ADV), dark (ADJ).** What kind of *dogs? Little dogs. Little* is an adjective describing the noun *dogs.* How many dogs? *three dogs. Three* is an adjective describing *dogs.* How did *Debbie cross? Slowly. Slowly* is an adverb describing the verb *crossed.* What kind of *street? The dark street. Dark* is an adjective describing the noun *street.* In case you're wondering, *the* is also a type of adjective — an *article.* You can find out more about articles later in this chapter. For now, ignore *a, an,* and *the.*

1 Slipping onto the comfortable, old sofa, Mei quickly grabbed the black plastic remote. _____

2 "I arrived early because I desperately want to watch the new motorcycle show," she said to Lamar. _____

3 Lamar, who was intently watching the latest news, turned away silently. _____

4 Everyone present knew that Mei would get her way. She always did! _____

5 Lamar resisted fiercely, but he was curious about the show, which featured a different motorcycle weekly. _____

6 If he held out a little longer, he knew that Mei would offer him a snack — something delicious! _____

7 Mei's backpack always held a few goodies, and Lamar was extremely fond of chocolate brownies. _____

8   He could almost taste the sweet hazelnut flavor that Mei sometimes added to the packaged brownie mix. _____

9   Lamar sighed loudly and waved a long, thin hand. _____

10   "You can watch anything good," he remarked in a low, defeated voice, "but first give me two brownies." _____

The Right Place at the Right Time: Placing Adjectives and Adverbs

You don't need to stick labels on adjectives and adverbs, but you do need to send the right word to the right place. A few wonderful words (*fast*, *short*, *last*, and *likely*, for example) function as both adjectives and adverbs, but for the most part, adjectives and adverbs are not interchangeable. In this section, you choose between adjectives and adverbs and insert them into sentences.

TIP   Most adverbs end in *ly*, but some adverbs vary, and adjectives can end with any letter in the alphabet, except maybe *q*. If you're not sure which form is an adjective and which is an adverb, check the dictionary. Most definitions include both forms, with handy labels telling you what's what.

YOUR TURN   Which word is correct? The parentheses contain both an adjective and an adverb. Circle your selection.

Q.   While (soft, softly) music played, Alix (gentle, gently) placed the new table near the fireplace.

A.   **soft, gently.** What kind of music? *Soft* music. *Soft* is an adjective describing *music.* How did Alix *place* the table? The word you want from the second parentheses must describe an action (the verb *placed*), so the adverb *gently* wins the prize.

11   "I love my (new, newly) furniture!" exclaimed Alix (loud, loudly).

12   "You made some (great, greatly) choices," replied Marc as he dropped his (damp, damply) gloves on top of Alix's wooden table.

13   "How dare you treat my table (careless, carelessly)!" said Alix (angry, angrily).

14   "You don't have to talk (nasty, nastily) to me!" replied Marc (firm, firmly).

15   Alix (swift, swiftly) grabbed the gloves and threw them in the wastebasket.

16   "Why are you (extreme, extremely) nervous about this plain (wooden, woodenly) table?" Marc (final, finally) said.

17   Alix eyed the table (fearful, fearfully), worrying that the water stain was (permanent, permanently).

18. Just then, a (poor, poorly) dressed man appeared in the doorway.

19. "I am (real, really) sorry to interrupt," he said, "but I have (extensive, extensively) experience in (fine, finely) carpentry."

20. As Alix and Marc stared (silent, silently), the newcomer added, "I can (sure, surely) help you with this water stain."

21. To Alix and Marc, the man seemed (odd, oddly).

22. The man opened his backpack and took out a cloth that was (near, nearly) five feet in length.

23. He (immediate, immediately) rubbed the water off the table and then spread polish (even, evenly) over the surface.

24. "Look!" he ordered in a (cheerful, cheerfully) voice. "It's as good as new."

25. Having finished the job, the (happy/ happily) worker smiled.

26. "Don't put any more wet clothing on it," he said (gentle, gently).

27. "Never," replied Marc as he plopped himself on the (clean, cleanly) sofa. "I promise."

28. Alix sighed (sad, sadly).

29. "You have not made a (serious, seriously) promise," Alix added.

30. It had rained all day, and Marc's pants were (definite, definitely) wet.

How's It Going? Choosing Between Good/Well and Bad/Badly

For some reason, adjective and adverb pairs that pass judgment (*good* and *well*, *bad* and *badly*) cause a lot of trouble. Here's a quick guide: *Good* and *bad* are adjectives, so they have to describe nouns — people, places, things, or ideas. ("I gave a *good* report to the boss." The adjective *good* describes the noun *report*. "The *bad* dog ate my slippers this morning." The adjective *bad* describes the noun *dog*.) *Well* and *badly* are adverbs used to describe action. ("In my opinion, the report was particularly *well* written." The adverb *well* describes the verb *written*. "The dog slept *badly* after his meal." The adverb *badly* describes the verb *slept*.) *Well* and *badly* also describe other descriptions. In the expression, *a well-written essay*, for example, *well* describes *written*. When they're connected by a hyphen — the short line between *well* and *written* — the two words form a single description of the noun *essay*. (For more information about hyphens, see Chapter 9.)

Well can be an adjective in one particular circumstance: health. When someone asks how you are, the answer (I hope) is "I am well" or "I feel well." You can also — and I hope you do — feel *good*, especially when you're talking about your mental state, though this usage is informal. Apart from health questions, however, *well* is a permanent member of the adverb team.

When a description follows a verb, danger lurks. You have to decide whether the description gives information about the verb or about the person/thing who is doing the action or is in the state of being. If the description describes the verb, go for an adverb. If it describes the person/ thing (the subject, in grammatical terms), go for the adjective.

Circle the correct word in each set of parentheses.

Q. The trainer works (good/well) with all types of dogs, especially those that don't outweigh him.

A. well. How does the trainer work? The word you need must be an adverb because you're giving information about an action (*works*), not a noun.

31 My dog Caramel barks when he's run (good, well) during his daily race with the letter carrier.

32 The letter carrier likes Caramel and feels (bad, badly) about beating him when they race.

33 Caramel tends to bite the poor guy whenever the race doesn't turn out (good, well).

34 I named him after a type of candy I think is (good, well).

35 The letter carrier's opinion is that high-calorie snacks are (bad, badly).

36 He also hates candy because, he says, it tastes (bad, badly).

37 Caramel once ripped off a corner of the dog food bag and chewed a (good, well) meal.

38 Caramel ate (good, well)!

39 Caramel, who didn't feel (good, well) after eating too much, barked quite a bit that day.

40 Tired of the noise, I screamed, "(Bad, Badly) dog!"

Mastering the Art of Articles

Three little words — *a, an,* and *the* — pop up in just about every English sentence. Sometimes, they show up where they shouldn't. Technically, these three words are adjectives, but they belong to the subcategory of articles. As always, forget about the terminology. Just know how to use them:

>> *The* refers to something specific. When you say that you want *the book,* you're implying one particular text, even if you haven't named it. *The* attaches nicely to both singular and plural words.

>> *A* and *an* are more general in meaning and work only with singular words. If you want *a book*, you're willing to read anything. *A* precedes words beginning with consonants (every letter except *a, e, i, o*, and *u*) and words that begin with a long *u* sound, similar to what you hear when you say "you." *An* comes before words beginning with vowels *(an ant, an encyclopedia, an uncle)* except for the long *u* sound *(a university)*. *An* also precedes words that sound as if they begin with a vowel *(hour*, for example) because the first letter is silent.

TIP

If you want a general term but you're talking about a plural, try *some* or *any* instead of *a* or *an*, because these last two articles can't attach to plurals.

Write the correct article in each blank in the sentences that follow.

YOUR TURN

Q. When Lulu asked to see _____ wedding pictures, she didn't expect Annie to put on _____ twelve-hour slide show.

A. **the, a.** In the first half of the sentence, Lulu is asking for something specific. Also, *wedding pictures* is a plural expression, so *a* and *an* are out of the question. In the second half of the sentence, something more general is appropriate. Because *twelve* begins with the consonant *t, a* is the proper choice.

41   Although Lulu was mostly bored out of her mind, she did like _____ picture of Annie's Uncle Fred snoring in the back of the church.

42   _____ nearby guest, one of several attempting to plug up their ears, can be seen poking Uncle Fred's ribs.

43   At Annie's wedding, Uncle Fred wore _____ antique tie pin that he bought in _____ department store next door to his apartment building.

44   _____ clerk who sold _____ tie to Uncle Fred secretly inserted _____ microphone.

45   Uncle Fred's snores were posted on _____ social media site, along with his photo.

46   _____ post went viral.

47   Many people commented that Fred's snore was _____ amazing sound.

For Better or Worse: Forming Comparisons

If we human beings weren't so tempted to compare our situations with those of others, life (and grammar) would be a lot easier. In this section, I tell you everything you need to know about creating comparisons, whether they show up as one word — *higher, farthest*, for example — or two words — *more beautiful, least sensible,* and so forth. (For information on longer comparisons, see Chapter 19.)

Visiting the ER (and the EST): One- or two-word comparisons

Single-word adjectives and adverbs are the base upon which two types of comparisons may be made: the *comparative* and the *superlative.* Comparatives (*dumber, smarter, neater, more interesting, less available,* and the like) deal with only two elements. Superlatives (*dumbest, smartest, neatest, most interesting, least available,* and so forth) identify the extreme in a group of three or more. Here are the guidelines for regular comparisons:

» **Tack *er* onto the end of a one-syllable descriptive word to create a positive comparative form.** When I say *positive,* I mean that the first term of the comparison comes out on top, as in "parakeets are noisier than canaries," a statement that gives more volume to *parakeets.* Occasionally a two-syllable word forms a comparative this way also (*lovelier,* for example).

» **To make the comparative forms of a word with more than one syllable, you generally use *more* or *less,* not *er.*** This guideline doesn't hold true for every word in the dictionary, but it's valid for most. Therefore, you say that "canaries are more popular than parakeets," not "canaries are popularer." Just to be clear: *popularer* isn't a word!

» **Glue *est* to one-syllable words to make a positive superlative.** A positive superlative gives the advantage to the element cited in the comparison. For example, *canaries* have the edge in "canaries are the finest singers in the bird world." Also, a few two-syllable words use *est* to create a superlative (such as *loneliest*).

» **Add *most* or *least* to longer words to create a superlative.** The definition of *longer* isn't set in stone, but a word containing two or more syllables, such as *beautiful,* generally qualifies as long. The superlative forms are *most beautiful* or *least beautiful.*

» **Negative comparative and superlative forms always have two words.** If you want to state that something is *less* or *least,* you have to use those words and not a tacked-on syllable. Therefore, "the canary's song is *less clear* when he has a head cold," and "my parakeets are *least annoying* when they're sleeping."

» **Check the dictionary if you're not sure of the correct form.** The entry for the plain adjective or adverb normally includes the comparative and superlative forms if they're single words. If you don't see a listing for another form of the word, take the *less/more, least/most* option.

A few comparatives and superlatives are irregular. I discuss these in the next section, "Going from bad to worse (and good to better): Irregular comparisons."

WARNING

Never add *er* or *est* AND *less/more* or *least/most.* These forms together are not correct.

Ready for some comparison shopping? Insert the comparative or superlative form as needed into the blanks for each question. The base word is in parentheses at the end of the sentence. There I also tell you whether to make the comparison positive or negative.

YOUR TURN

Q. Elena is the _____ of all the computer techs in that company. (*intelligent* — positive)

A. **most intelligent**. The sentence compares Elena to other agents in the office. Comparing more than two elements requires the superlative form. Because *intelligent* is a long word, *most* creates a positive comparison. (*Least intelligent* is the negative version.)

48 Elena is hoping to work remotely from France, where the cost of living is _____ than in her hometown, but the nightlife is _____. (*high* — positive, *lively* — positive)

49 Elena's manager claims that she is the _____ and _____ of all his employees. (*efficient* — positive, *valuable* — positive)

50 We work with Elena, and we know that she is _____ and _____ than the manager thinks. (*slow* — positive, *accurate* — negative)

51 Plus, Elena has the _____ work area. (*sloppy* — positive)

52 Everyone else's desk is _____ and _____ than Elena's. (*neat* — positive, *professional* — positive)

53 Elena has been angry with me ever since I said that the coffeemaker she bought for the office makes coffee that is _____ and _____ than the machine it replaced. (*weak* — positive, *tasty* — negative)

54 Oscar added that the new coffeemaker breaks _____ than the old one. (*frequently* — positive)

55 If Elena works remotely, the office will be _____ but _____ than it is now. (*calm* — positive, *boring* — positive)

56 Big news! The manager just announced that Elena's request wasn't approved, and she is in the _____ mood imaginable, even _____ than she was when her desk caught fire. (*irritated* — positive, *annoyed* — positive)

57 Natalie, who considers herself the _____ person in the company, wanted Elena's corner desk, so she is even _____ than Elena. (*essential* — positive, *upset* — positive)

58 "I am the _____ of the three coders on my team," she commented, "and I deserve that desk!" (*productive* — positive)

59 She added, "I am absent _____ than everyone else." (*often* — negative)

60 Today, Elena and Natalie are _____ than usual. I think they're uploading their resumes and looking for new jobs. (*quiet* — positive)

Going from bad to worse (and good to better): Irregular comparisons

The preceding section explains the rules for regular comparisons, and luckily, most comparisons are regular! A couple of basic descriptions, however, break all the rules. Table 4-1 shows you the irregular comparative and superlative forms of *good, well, bad, ill, much,* and *many.*

Table 4-1   Forms of Irregular Comparisons

Description	Comparative	Superlative
Good or well	Better	Best
Bad or ill	Worse	Worst
Much or many	More	Most

YOUR TURN

Choose the correct comparative or superlative form of the word in parentheses and write your answer in the blank.

Q. Ed's scrapbook, which contains souvenirs from his trip, is the _____ example of a boring book that I have ever seen. (*good*)

A. **best.** Once you mention the top or bottom experience of a lifetime, you're in the superlative column. Because *goodest* isn't a word, *best* is the one you want.

61 Ed explains his souvenirs in _____ detail than anyone would ever want to hear. (*much*)

62 Bored listeners believe that the _____ item in his scrapbook is a set of menus, which Ed can discuss for hours. (*bad*)

63 On the bright side, everyone knows that Ed's appreciation of good food is _____ than any restaurant critic's. (*good*)

64 When he has the flu, Ed actually feels _____ if his chicken soup isn't perfectly prepared. (*bad*)

65 Although he is only nineteen years old, Ed has the _____ menus of anyone in his family. (*many*)

66 Our family's kitchen is well equipped, but everyone relies on Ed to make it run even_____. (*well*)

67 Ed's special cupboard contains thirteen brands of olive oil; Ed thinks Time-Ola Oil is the _____ choice. (*good*)

68 Mom disagrees; she thinks O'Tree's oil is _____ than Time-Ola. (*good*)

Calling All Overachievers: Extra Practice with Adjectives and Adverbs

YOUR TURN Read this page from a dress catalog. Twenty-five words or phrases are underlined and numbered. Some are correct, and some aren't. Look for adjectives trying to do an adverb's job and vice versa, articles that should be changed, and comparisons that need some work. When you find an error, correct it. If the underlined expression is fine, leave it alone.

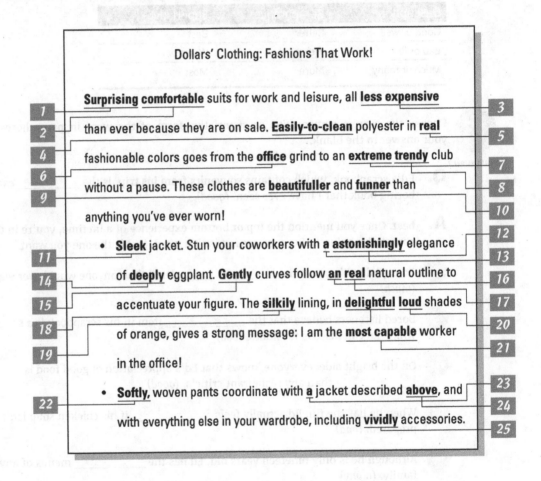

Dollars' Clothing: Fashions That Work!

1 **Surprising** **comfortable** suits for work and leisure, all **less expensive** **3** **2** than ever because they are on sale. **Easily-to-clean** polyester in **real** **5** **4** fashionable colors goes from the **office** grind to an **extreme trendy** club **7** **6** without a pause. These clothes are **beautifuller** and **funner** than **8** **9** anything you've ever worn! **10**

- **11** **Sleek** jacket. Stun your coworkers with **a astonishingly** elegance **12** **13** **14** of **deeply** eggplant. **Gently** curves follow **an real** natural outline to **16** **15** accentuate your figure. The **silkily** lining, in **delightful loud** shades **17** **18** of orange, gives a strong message: I am the **most capable** worker **20** **19** **21** in the office!

- **Softly,** woven pants coordinate with **a** jacket described **above**, and **23** **22** **24** with everything else in your wardrobe, including **vividly** accessories. **25**

Answers to Adjective and Adverb Questions

I hope the challenging exercises in this short chapter on descriptive words didn't give you too much trouble. Find out how you did by comparing your work to the following answers.

1. **comfortable (ADJ), old (ADJ), quickly (ADV), black (ADJ), plastic (ADJ).** The adjectives *comfortable* and *old* tell you what kind of sofa. The adverb *quickly* tells you how Mei *grabbed*. The adjectives *black* and *plastic* tell you what kind of *remote*.

2. **early (ADV), desperately (ADV), new (ADJ), motorcycle (ADJ).** The adverb *early* tells you when Mei *arrived*. The adverb *desperately* answers the question *want how?* The adjectives *new* and *motorcycle* answer the question *what kind of show?*

3. **intently (ADV), latest (ADJ), away (ADV) silently (ADV).** The adverb *intently* answers the question *watching how? Latest*, an adjective, tells you what kind of *news. Away* and *silently*, both adverbs, answer *turned how?*

4. **present (ADJ) always (ADV).** *Present* is an adjective describing the pronoun *everyone*. This adjective breaks the pattern because it appears after the word it describes, not before. It also doesn't fit perfectly into the adjective questions (how many? which one? what kind?), but it serves the same purpose. It limits the meaning of *everyone*. You aren't talking about everyone in the universe, just *everyone present. Always* answers the question *did when?* and is therefore an adverb. You may be wondering about *her. Her* is a possessive pronoun, not an adjective.

5. **fiercely (ADV), curious (ADJ) different (ADJ), weekly (ADV).** *Fiercely*, an adverb, answers the question *resisted how? Curious* is an adjective appearing after a linking verb (*was*). *Curious* describes the pronoun *he. Different* is an adjective answering the question *which motorcycle? Weekly*, an adverb, answers the question *features when?*

6. **little (ADV), longer (ADV), delicious (ADJ).** The adverb *little* changes the intensity of another adverb, *longer*. Together they answer the question *held out when?* The adjective *delicious* describes the pronoun *something*.

7. **few (ADJ), extremely (ADV), fond (ADJ), chocolate (ADJ).** How many *goodies?* A *few goodies. Few* is an adjective. (*A* is an article, which is technically an adjective.) The adverb *extremely* intensifies the meaning of the adjective *fond. Fond*, which appears after a linking verb, describes *Lamar. Extremely* answers the question *how fond?* The adjective *chocolate* answers *what kind of brownies?*

8. **almost (ADV) sweet (ADJ), hazelnut (ADJ) sometimes (ADV), packaged (ADJ), brownie (ADJ).** The adverb *almost* answers the question *taste how?* What kind of *flavor? Sweet, hazelnut.* Both are adjectives. *Added* when? *Sometimes* — an adverb. What kind of *mix? Packaged, brownie mix.* Both *packaged* and *brownie* are adjectives.

9. **loudly (ADV), long (ADJ), thin (ADJ).** *Loudly*, an adverb, answers *sighed how?* The adjectives *long* and *thin* tell you what kind of hand.

10. **good (ADJ), low (ADJ), defeated (ADJ), first (ADV), two (ADJ).** *Good* is an adjective describing the pronoun *anything. Low* and *defeated* are adjectives answering *what kind of voice? First* is an adverb answering *give when? Two* is an adjective answering *how many brownies?*

11. **new (ADJ), loudly (ADV).** Because *furniture* is a noun, you need an adjective to describe it. The adjective *new* tells you *what kind of furniture.* The adverb *loudly* describes *exclaimed*, a verb.

12. **great (ADJ), damp (ADJ).** The adjective *great* explains what kind of choices Alix made. *Choices* is a noun. *Gloves* is a noun, so the adjective *damp* should describe it.

(13) **carelessly (ADV), angrily (ADV).** You need adverbs in this sentence to describe two actions: the verbs *treat* and *said*.

(14) **nastily (ADV), firmly (ADV).** To describe actions, you need adverbs. In this sentence, the adverb *nastily* describes the verb *talk*. (Actually, *do talk*. See Chapter 3 for more information on helping verbs.) The adverb *firmly* describes the verb *replied*.

(15) **swiftly (ADV).** The adverb *swiftly* is what you need here to describe the verb *grabbed*.

(16) **extremely (ADV), wooden (ADJ), finally (ADV).** Adverbs can make another description more or less intense. In this sentence, *extremely*, an adverb, answers the question *how nervous?* A *table* is a thing, so it's a noun, and it must be described by the adjective *wooden*. The adverb *finally* answers the question, *said when?*

(17) **fearfully (ADV), permanent (ADJ).** To describe the verb *eyed*, you need the adverb *fearfully*. A stain is a thing and, therefore, a noun, which must be described by the adjective *permanent*. In sentences containing any form of the verb *be*, an adjective describing the subject may appear after the verb. (For more information on subjects, turn to Chapter 7.)

(18) **poorly (ADV).** Did I catch you on this one? Adverbs sometimes describe adjectives. The adjective *dressed* describes *man*, and the adverb *poorly* tells you how he was dressed.

(19) **really (ADV), extensive (ADJ), fine (ADJ).** The verb in this sentence is *am*, a form of the verb *be*. *Be* verbs act like giant equal signs, connecting what comes before and after the verb. (See Chapter 3 for more information.) The sentence connects *I* with *sorry*. *I*, a pronoun, represents the speaker. Pronouns are described by adjectives, so *sorry* is an adjective describing *I*. Now ask *how sorry?"* The answer is *really sorry*. The adverb *really* intensifies the adjective *sorry*. Next, you have two adjectives: *extensive* describes the noun *experience*, and *fine* describes the noun *carpentry*.

(20) **silently (ADV), surely (ADV).** *Stared* and *can help* are actions, so they're verbs. The adverb *silently* tells you how the friends stared. The adverb *surely* describes the verb *can help*.

(21) **odd (ADJ).** The verb *seemed* links what comes before and after it. In this sentence, *seemed* links the noun *man* to its description, the adjective, *odd*.

(22) **nearly (ADV).** One description describing another? That's an adverb's job! Here, *five* tells you how many *feet*. The adverb *nearly* describes *five*, showing that the cloth is slightly shorter than *five feet*.

(23) **immediately (ADV), evenly (ADV).** Two verbs — *rubbed* and *spread* — are described by adverbs, *immediately* and *evenly*.

(24) **cheerful (ADJ).** A *voice* is a thing, even though you can't see or touch it. Therefore, it's a noun described by the adjective *cheerful*.

(25) **happy (ADJ).** The adjective *happy* describes the noun *worker*, answering the question *what kind of worker?*

(26) **gently (ADV).** The adverb *gently* describes the action verb *said*.

(27) **clean (ADJ).** The noun *sofa* must be described by an adjective, in this case *clean*.

(28) **sadly (ADV).** How did Alix sigh? The adverb *sadly* answers that question. Descriptions of actions must be adverbs.

(29) **serious (ADJ).** A *promise* is a thing, so it's a noun and must be described by the adjective *serious*.

30. **definitely (ADV).** The word *wet* is an adjective, and therefore, you need an adverb to describe it. *Definitely* answers the question *how wet?*

31. **well.** The adverb *well* tells you how Caramel has run.

32. **bad.** This sentence illustrates a common mistake. The description doesn't tell you anything about the letter carrier's ability to feel (touching sensation). Instead, it tells you about a state of mind. Because the word is a description of a person, not of an action, you need an adjective, *bad*. To feel *badly* implies that you're wearing mittens and can't feel anything through the thick cloth.

33. **well.** The adverb *well* describes the action to *turn out* (to result).

34. **good.** The adjective *good* describes the noun *candy*. It appears after *is*, a form of the verb *be*. Adjectives in that spot generally describe the subject of the sentence. (Turn to Chapter 7 for more about subjects.)

35. **bad.** The description *bad* applies to the *snacks*, not to the verb *are*. Hence, an adjective is what you want.

36. **bad.** This one is tricky. The verb *tastes* sounds like an action, and in many sentences, it is. Here, though, *tastes* gives you information about *candy*, a noun, not about the act of tasting.

37. **good.** The adjective (*good*) is attached to a noun (*meal*).

38. **well.** You're talking about the action (*ate*), so you need an adverb (*badly*).

39. **well.** The best response here is *well*, an adjective that works for health-status statements. *Good* will do in a pinch, but *good* is better for psychological or mood statements.

40. **Bad.** The adjective *bad* applies to the noun *dog*.

41. **the.** The sentence implies that one particular picture caught Lulu's fancy, so *the* works nicely here. If you chose *a*, no problem. The sentence would be a bit less specific but still acceptable. The only true clunker is *an*, which must precede words beginning with vowels (except for a short *u*, or uh sound) — a group that doesn't include *picture*.

42. **A.** Because the sentence tells you that several guests are nearby, *the* doesn't fit here. The more general *a* is best.

43. **an or the, the.** In the first blank, you may place either *an* (which must precede a word beginning with a vowel) or *the*. In the second blank, *the* is best because it's unlikely that Fred is surrounded by several department stores. *The* points out one particular store.

44. **The, the, a.** Lots of blanks in this one! The first two seem more particular (one clerk, one tie pin), so *the* fits well. The second blank needs the more general word *a*, because the clerk selected one from a group of many, not a particular microphone.

45. **a.** The site isn't named, so the general word *a* is proper here.

46. **The.** The sentence is about one particular post, so you want *the*, not the more general word *a*.

47. **an.** The word *amazing* begins with a vowel sound, so you need *an*, not *a*.

48. **higher, livelier.** The comparative form is the way to go because two places, Paris and Elena's hometown, are compared. One-syllable words such as *high* form comparatives with the addition of *er*. Most two-syllable words rely on *more* or *less*, but *lively* is an exception.

(49) **most efficient, most valuable.** In choosing the top or bottom rank from a group of three or more, go for superlative. *Efficient* and *valuable*, both long words, need *most* for a positive comparison.

(50) **slower, less accurate.** Comparing two elements — in this case, what coworkers think of Elena's performance and what the manager thinks — calls for the comparative form. The one-syllable word takes *er*, and the longer word relies on *less*.

(51) **sloppiest.** The superlative form is needed here because the work area is at the extreme in terms of sloppiness. The one-syllable word becomes superlative with the addition of *est*. (The *y* changes to *i* when *est* is added. For more spelling tips, see Chapter 20.)

(52) **neater, more professional.** After you read the word *everyone*, you may have thought that superlative (the form that deals with comparisons of three or more) was needed. However, this sentence actually compares two elements (Elena's desk and the group of other desks). *Neat* has one syllable, so *er* is all you need to add. Because *professional* is a long word, you must use *more* for the comparative form.

(53) **weaker, less tasty.** In comparing two coffeemakers, go for the comparative form. Both are short words, but a negative comparison always requires two words; here, *less tasty* does the job.

(54) **more frequently.** Two coffeemakers are being compared, and *frequently* is a long word. Therefore, you need the comparative form, *more frequently*.

(55) **calmer, more boring.** When you compare two things (how calm and boring the day is now and how long and boring it will be if Elena works remotely), go for the comparative, with *er* for the short word and *more* for the two-syllable word.

(56) **most irritated, more annoyed.** The extreme in a group calls for the superlative, and Elena's mood is at the extreme end of what is imaginable. Therefore, *most irritable* is correct. In the second portion of the sentence, two things are being compared: Elena's mood when her desk caught fire and Elena's mood now. *More* creates a two-word comparative form.

(57) **most essential, more upset.** Natalie is singled out as the extreme in a large group. Hence, the superlative is the one that fits the first blank. Three-syllable words need *most* to form the superlative *most essential*. In the second blank, two moods are compared, so you need *more upset*, the comparative form of a long word.

(58) **most productive.** When you choose the extreme from a group of three or more, you need the superlative form. Because *productive* is a long word, add *most*.

(59) **less often.** The comparison is between the speaker and every other employee, one at a time. Therefore, comparative is appropriate. A negative comparison needs the word *less*.

(60) **quieter.** Two behaviors, one now and one "usual," are being compared. The short word becomes comparative when you add *er*.

(61) **more.** Two elements are being compared here: the amount of detail Ed uses and the amount of detail people want. When comparing two elements, the comparative form rules.

(62) **worst.** The superlative form singles out the extreme (in this case, the *most boring*) item in the scrapbook.

(63) **better.** The sentence pits Ed's skills against the skills of one group (*restaurant critics*). Even though the group has many members, the comparison is between two elements — Ed and the group — so the comparative form is what you want.

(64) **worse.** Two states of being are in comparison in this sentence, Ed's health before and after he eats soup. In comparing two things, go for comparative form.

65 **most.** The superlative form singles out the extreme, in this case, Ed's menu collection.

66 **better.** The comparative deals with two states — how the kitchen runs with and without Ed's presence.

67 **best.** To single out the top or bottom rank from a group of more than two, go for the superlative form.

68 **better.** The sentence compares two types of olive oil, so you need the comparative form.

Answers to "Overachievers Questions"

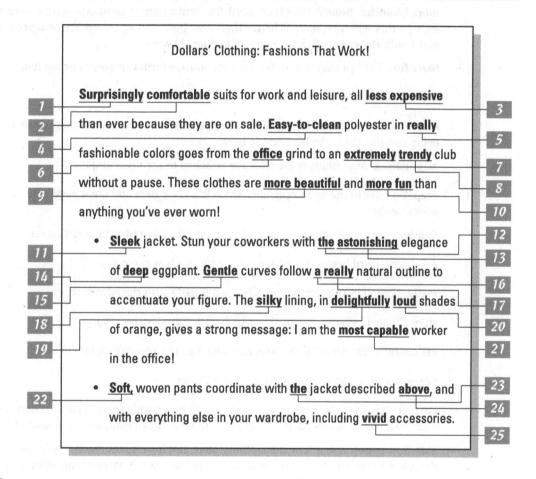

Dollars' Clothing: Fashions That Work!

1 **Surprisingly comfortable** suits for work and leisure, all **less expensive** **3**

2 than ever because they are on sale. **Easy-to-clean** polyester in **really** **5**

4 fashionable colors goes from the **office** grind to an **extremely trendy** club **7**

6 without a pause. These clothes are **more beautiful** and **more fun** than **8**

9 anything you've ever worn! **10**

    • **Sleek** jacket. Stun your coworkers with **the astonishing** elegance **12** **13**

11 of **deep** eggplant. **Gentle** curves follow **a really** natural outline to

14 accentuate your figure. The **silky** lining, in **delightfully loud** shades **16**

15 of orange, gives a strong message: I am the **most capable** worker **17**

18 in the office! **20**

19 **21**

    • **Soft,** woven pants coordinate with **the** jacket described **above,** and **23** **24**

22 with everything else in your wardrobe, including **vivid** accessories. **25**

1 **Surprisingly.** The adverb *surprisingly* is what you need attached to the description *comfortable*, an adjective.

2 **Correct.** The adjective *comfortable* answers, "what kind of *suits*?" *Suits* is a noun.

3 **Correct.** *Less expensive* is a negative comparison, which is always formed with two words. *Less* is better than *least*, the superlative form because you're comparing two things — how expensive these suits were before with how expensive they are now.

(4) **Easy-to-clean.** *Easily* is an adverb, but the three-word description is attached to a noun, *polyester*. *Easy* is an adjective and is the word you want here. Are you wondering why this phrase is hyphenated? Check Chapter 9 for more information.

(5) **really.** The adjective *fashionable* is intensified by the adverb *really*. *Real*, an adjective, is out of place here. By the way, if it were an adjective describing colors, *real* would be separated from the next adjective by a comma. For more information on commas, turn to Chapter 10.

(6) **Correct.** *Office* can be a noun, but here, it functions as an adjective, describing the noun *grind*.

(7) **extremely.** How *trendy*? *Extremely trendy*. Intensifiers are adverbs.

(8) **Correct.** The adjective *trendy* describes the noun *club*.

(9) **more beautiful.** *Beautiful* is a long word. To form a correct comparison, use *more*, *most*, *less*, or *least*. In this sentence, *more* is better than *most* because two things are being compared: this outfit with the group of clothes you've previously worn.

(10) **more fun.** *Fun* is a short word, but its comparative form is *more fun* or *less fun*.

(11) **Correct.** *Sleek*, an adjective, describes the noun *jacket*.

(12) **the.** Elegance is defined in a specific way in this sentence: It's *deep eggplant*. Because you're being specific, *the* is the best article here.

(13) **astonishing.** *Astonishing* is an adjective attached to the noun *elegance*.

(14) **deep.** To refer to the noun *eggplant*, which is a color here and not a vegetable, use the adjective *deep*.

(15) **Gentle.** *Gentle* is an adjective, just what you need to describe the noun *curves*.

(16) **a.** Before a word beginning with a consonant, such as *r*, place *a*.

(17) **really.** *Natural* is an adjective, which you intensify with the adverb *really*.

(18) **silky.** *Lining* is a noun, so you describe it with the adjective *silky*.

(19) **delightfully.** To intensify the adjective *loud*, use the adverb *delightfully*.

(20) **Correct.** This adjective describes the noun *shades*.

(21) **Correct.** Many people work in an office, so the superlative form of comparison is what you want here. Because *capable* is a long word, the two-word comparison is needed.

(22) **Soft.** You're describing how the clothing feels, not how it was made. The adjective *soft* describes the noun *pants*. (The comma is a clue that you have two adjectives; turn to Chapter 10 for more information.)

(23) **the.** The text makes it clear that you're talking about the "sleek jacket" that has already been identified. To refer to that specific jacket, use *the*.

(24) **Correct.** The adverb *above* works perfectly here to explain where the jacket is described.

(25) **vivid.** You need an adjective, *vivid*, to describe the noun *accessories*.

Chapter **5**

Packing Plenty of Power: Prepositions, Conjunctions, and Interjections

Are you interested in relationships? I'm not referring to stars' dating partners. Instead, I'm talking about two parts of speech: prepositions and conjunctions. Both express the relationship between two or more elements of a sentence. In this chapter, you practice identifying prepositions and conjunctions so you can use them effectively in your speech and writing. This chapter also helps you perfect your knowledge of interjections. Fantastic! *Fantastic*, written that way, is an interjection.

Pinning Down Prepositions

Prepositions are relationship words connecting two ideas. If I mention *the grammar book by Geraldine Woods*, I'm connecting the source of my income (*book*) to myself (*Geraldine Woods*) with the preposition *by*. The book can sit *on the shelf*, relating an action (*sit*) to a place (*shelf*).

If I'm lucky, the book can also *sell like hotcakes,* connecting the action *(sell)* to a legendary, best-selling item *(hotcakes)* with the preposition *like.* As you've probably noticed, the preposition appears with at least one other word — my name, in the first example, and *shelf* and *hotcakes* in the other examples. Each of those words is the *object of the preposition.* You can have one object or more than one object (in the phrase *near cafes and restaurants,* the preposition *near* has two objects, *cafes* and *restaurants*). A few descriptions may show up between the preposition and its object (*in cheap cafes and expensive restaurants,* for example), but they're not objects.

To locate a prepositional phrase, find the preposition and ask *whom?* or *what?* after it. The most important word in the answer is the object.

You need to locate prepositional phrases mostly so you can ignore them. Surprised? Prepositional phrases may confuse you when you're hunting subject-verb pairs, which must match. (For more on pairing off subjects and verbs, turn to Chapter 7.)

Time to hunt prepositional phrases and underline them. Write the object of the preposition in the blank.

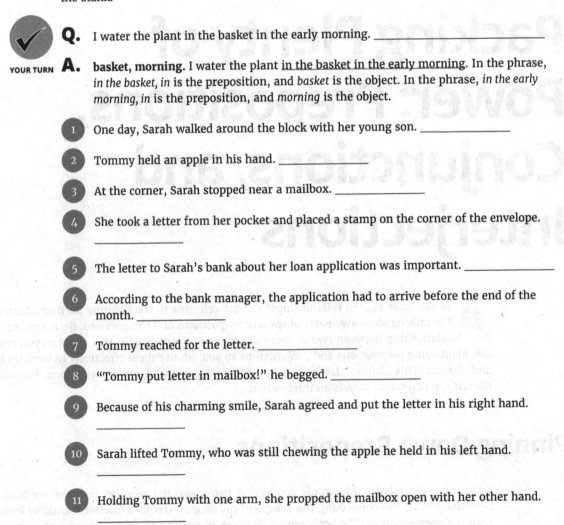

Q. I water the plant in the basket in the early morning. _____

YOUR TURN **A.** **basket, morning.** I water the plant <u>in the basket in the early morning</u>. In the phrase, *in the basket, in* is the preposition, and *basket* is the object. In the phrase, *in the early morning, in* is the preposition, and *morning* is the object.

1. One day, Sarah walked around the block with her young son. _____

2. Tommy held an apple in his hand. _____

3. At the corner, Sarah stopped near a mailbox. _____

4. She took a letter from her pocket and placed a stamp on the corner of the envelope. _____

5. The letter to Sarah's bank about her loan application was important. _____

6. According to the bank manager, the application had to arrive before the end of the month. _____

7. Tommy reached for the letter. _____

8. "Tommy put letter in mailbox!" he begged. _____

9. Because of his charming smile, Sarah agreed and put the letter in his right hand. _____

10. Sarah lifted Tommy, who was still chewing the apple he held in his left hand. _____

11. Holding Tommy with one arm, she propped the mailbox open with her other hand. _____

(12) Tommy dropped the apple in the mailbox! _____

(13) Tears fell from his eyes, and he wailed in frustration. _____

(14) "Want apple!" he screamed in his loudest voice. _____

(15) Sarah went to the post office to report the accident and to mail her letter.
_____

You also need to recognize prepositions when your sentence contains pronouns because the object of a preposition must be an object pronoun, not a subject pronoun. You give money for the book to *me*, not to *I*, because *to* is a preposition and *me* is the object. (Check out Chapter 2 for more on subject and object pronouns.)

Q. Select the correct pronoun from the pair in parentheses and write it in the blank. To make these questions harder, some of the blanks require subject pronouns, and some require object pronouns to act as the object of a preposition.

One day, the animal rescue squad brought a cat and a dog to (I, me).

A. **me.** The object pronoun *me* fits the role as the object of the prepositon *for*.

(16) Fifi, you're a cat, not a dog! Give the dog food to _____ (I, me).

(17) Don't even think about Spot's food because it belongs to _____ (he, him).

(18) Between you and _____ (I, me), Fifi should eat less food.

(19) The vet said that _____ (she, her) should weigh five pounds less.

(20) The diet _____ (he, him) recommended is not acceptable to _____ (I, me) because it is very expensive.

When you select a preposition, you have to be sure it fits your meaning. This task can sometimes be hard for those who are in the process of learning English. With practice, though, you'll always land on the right one.

Try your hand at selecting prepositions. I've provided context clues in each sentence so you know what meaning the sentence should express.

Q. Select the appropriate preposition from the parentheses and write it in the blank.

Billy shouted _____ (at, to) me when I broke his computer; it took him ten minutes to calm down.

A. **at.** Billy's anger is key here. He's yelling, so the best choice is *shouted at me*. If he *shouted to me*, he raised his voice so that I could hear his message from some distance away.

21. Go _____ (in to, into, by) the store and buy some notebooks and a pen.

22. Teachers and students are frantic _____ (in, at) autumn as the end of vacation nears.

23. I like to buy school supplies _____ (on, by, in) Smith's Stationery _____ (on, at, in) Fifth Avenue.

24. There's no public transportation _____ (to, for) the mall, so everyone goes _____ (in, by) car.

25. At the store, teachers talked _____ (about, around) their new students.

Connecting with Conjunctions

Recently, a toddler told me about her day: "I went to school <u>and</u> I played with blocks <u>and</u> I had a snack <u>but</u> I didn't like it <u>and</u> I ate another snack at home." The underlined words are *conjunctions*, the part of speech that connects ideas. With practice, my young friend will learn to use conjunctions more effectively. So will you, if you complete the exercises in this section.

Here are some guidelines for this part of speech:

>> **Be sure the conjunction you select matches the message you're giving.** *And* adds. ("I worked all day <u>and</u> then cooked your dinner.") *Because* introduces a reason. ("You have to clean your room now <u>because</u> I said so.") Other conjunctions (*when, after, since, until*) create a timeline. ("<u>Before</u> you go out, you must do your homework.") Some conjunctions reveal objections or problems. ("You can go out with your friends, <u>but</u> schoolwork comes first.") A conjunction may show a condition. ("<u>If</u> you don't do your homework, I will take away your phone.") Other conjunctions indicate choice. ("You <u>or</u> your brother can fold the laundry. <u>Neither</u> your teacher <u>nor</u> I believe that the dog ate your homework.")

TIP

Some words may act as conjunctions in some sentences and prepositions in others.

Take a rest *after* you finish your chores. (*after* = conjunction)

I exercise *after* lunch. (*after* = preposition)

I explain what you need to know about prepositions in "Pinning Down Prepositions" earlier in the chapter.

>> **Some conjunctions work in pairs.** *Either/or* and *neither/nor* are the most common paired conjunctions, though *or* and *nor* may show up alone.

>> **Connect matching grammatical elements.** Conjunctions may tie nouns together. They also string together a bunch of descriptions. They may attach one subject-verb statement

to another. (Chapters 3 and 7 tell you more about subjects and verbs.) In Standard English, though, what conjunctions can't do is connect mismatched elements like *reading* and *to dance*. Most of the time, your "ear" will tell you whether grammatical elements match.

TIP

Be extra careful about where you place each half of a conjunction pair because it's easy to mismatch the elements that the conjunctions connect. In this sentence, the elements the pair connects are underlined. Can you spot the problem?

Either <u>Lupita should analyze the data</u> or <u>you</u>.

This sentence makes sense only if Lupita is a psychologist who analyzes patients, and she might analyze *you*. Here's the correction:

Either <u>Lupita</u> or <u>you</u> should analyze the data.

Now, you have to analyze the data, or Lupita does.

Identify the conjunction in each sentence. Underline what the conjunction connects.

YOUR TURN

Q. Daniel baked the cake and iced it.

A. and. <u>baked the cake</u>↔<u>iced it</u>.

26 Daniel wants to work in a bakery or restaurant.

27 Liza and Belle prefer less messy jobs.

28 Belle studies art, although she doesn't like the smell of paint.

29 Liza will look for a job in marketing after she graduates.

30 Either her father or her uncle will hire her.

31 They are looking for workers who are smart, energetic, and creative.

32 Sayed studies history, yet he is more interested in chemistry.

33 He should be a teacher because he explains things very well.

34 Gina devotes most of her time to her favorite activities: the school newspaper, the chess team, and student government.

35 Aliyah plans on a career in government, for she is very patriotic.

Interjections Are Simple!

I lied a little in the heading of this section, but not much. An *interjection*, the part of speech that often shows strong emotion, isn't connected grammatically to the sentence. Instead, the interjection comments on the content of the sentence. You may find interjections before, within, or after the sentence. They're always separated from the sentence by punctuation — normally a comma or an exclamation point. Take a look at these examples; the interjections are italicized:

> *Yes!* My team won the division championship.

> *Ouch,* my arms hurt. Be more careful with your baseball bat.

> You got tickets to the World Series? *Awesome!*

If you try really hard, you can manage to make an error with an interjection. For example, you may forget to use a comma or an exclamation point to separate the interjection from the sentence it comments on. You may also mistake an interjection for a subject. In the second sample sentence, you'd be wrong to match the verb *hurt* with *ouch*, a word that appears to be singular instead of the real subject, *arms*, which is plural. Finally, on social media or in texts, many people pile on exclamation points after interjections to indicate strong emotion. In formal English, though, one exclamation point is enough.

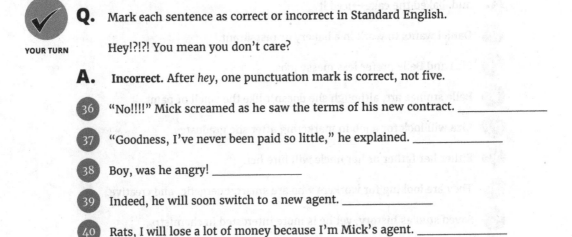

Q. Mark each sentence as correct or incorrect in Standard English.

Hey!?!?! You mean you don't care?

A. **Incorrect.** After *hey*, one punctuation mark is correct, not five.

36 "No!!!!" Mick screamed as he saw the terms of his new contract. _____

37 "Goodness, I've never been paid so little," he explained. _____

38 Boy, was he angry! _____

39 Indeed, he will soon switch to a new agent. _____

40 Rats, I will lose a lot of money because I'm Mick's agent. _____

Calling All Overachievers: Extra Practice with Prepositions, Conjunctions, and Interjections

Read this letter from a prisoner to his girlfriend. Look at the underlined parts. If everything is okay, mark it correct. If you find a mistake, correct it.

Dear Gertrude,

Oh!! I wish I were with you in this cold, cold day. The prison

bars on my cell have not stopped me from dreaming and to hope I will

see you someday. I close my eyes, but I pretend I am in the beach with

you. Between you and I, there may be a way to escape. Indeed I really

think so. I will explain my plan at you. Hank, the guard, loves cake.

When you come to visit, bring a cake with a file baked in side. Offer a

slice both to him and to the other guards. Handle it in care! Be sure not

to cut at the side of the cake with the file in it. When the guards leave,

I will file down the bars and come at you. We will be free but happy

together.

Love,
Otto

Answers to Prepositions, Conjunctions, and Interjections Questions

Will it be "Hooray! I got them all right" or "Bummer, I got some wrong"? Check to see how you did.

1. **block, son. One day, Sarah walked <u>around the block with her young son</u>.** The object of the preposition *around* is *block*, and the object of *with* is *son*.

2. **hand. Tommy held an apple <u>in his hand</u>.** Find the object by asking *whom? what?* after the preposition: *in what? in his hand.*

3. **corner, mailbox. <u>At the corner</u>, Sarah stopped <u>near a mailbox</u>.** Notice that you have two prepositional phrases here, each giving information about where *Sarah stopped*.

4. **pocket, corner, envelope. She took a letter <u>from her pocket</u> and placed a stamp <u>on the corner of the envelope</u>.** Ask *from what?* and the answer is *pocket. Pocket* is the object of the preposition *from.* Ask *on what?* The answer, *corner*, is the object of the preposition *on.* Ask *of what?* and you see that *envelope* is the object of the preposition *of.*

5. **bank, application. The letter <u>to Sarah's bank about her loan application</u> was important.** In this sentence, one prepositional phrase follows another. Each has its own object. Ask *to what? to Sarah's bank.* Ask *about what? about application.* Did you include descriptions (*Sarah's bank, her loan application*) in your answer? Only the most important word, the noun, is the object, but I won't mind if you mark your answer correct.

6. **manager, end, month. <u>According to the bank manager</u>, the application had to arrive <u>before the end of the month</u>.** Three prepositional phrases are tucked into this sentence. The first begins with a two-word preposition, *according to.* The last two phrases express one idea, but they each have a preposition and an object. Did I catch you with *to arrive?* In some sentences, *to* may act as a preposition, but here it's part of a verb form (*an infinitive*), not a prepositional phrase.

7. **letter. Tommy reached <u>for the letter</u>.** Ask *for what? for the letter. Letter* is the object of the preposition *for.*

8. **mailbox. "Tommy put letter <u>in mailbox</u>!"** An adult would say, "in the mailbox." Tommy talks like a toddler, but he already knows how to add an object (*mailbox*) to a preposition (*in*).

9. **smile, hand. Because of his charming smile, Sarah agreed and put the letter in his right hand.** *Because of* is a two-word preposition. When you ask *because of what?* you see that the object is *smile.* When you ask *in what?* you discover that *hand* is the object of the preposition *in.*

10. **hand. Sarah lifted Tommy, who was still chewing the apple he held <u>in his left hand</u>.** Ask *in what?* and you see that *hand* is the object of the preposition *in.*

11. **arm, hand. Holding Tommy <u>with one arm</u>, she propped the mailbox open <u>with her other hand</u>.** Both prepositional phrases begin with the preposition *with.* Each has its own object.

12. **mailbox. Tommy dropped the apple <u>in the mailbox</u>!** Ask *in what? in the mailbox.*

13. **eyes, frustration. Tears fell <u>from his eyes</u>, and he wailed <u>in frustration</u>.** Ask *from what?* and you discover the object, *eyes.* Ask *in what?* and you land on the object, *frustration.*

14. **voice. "Want apple!" he screamed <u>in his loudest voice</u>.** Did you select *loudest voice* as the object? The noun, *voice*, is the true object of the preposition. *Loudest* is a description.

(15) **office. Sarah went <u>to the post office</u> to report the accident and to mail her letter.** Did you underline *to report* and *to mail*? Those are verb forms. *To* may act as a preposition, but in that role, it needs a noun or a pronoun as an object, not an action word.

(16) **me.** The object of the preposition *to* is the object pronoun *me*.

(17) **him.** The object of the preposition *to* is the object pronoun *him*.

(18) **me.** The phrase *between you and I* has become more common lately, but *me*, the object pronoun, is proper. *I* has not yet been accepted by most grammarians.

(19) **she.** Did I fool you? In this sentence, *she* is not the object of a preposition. It's the subject of the verb *should weigh*.

(20) **he, me.** First up is a subject pronoun, *he*, which you need for the verb *recommended*. Next is an object pronoun, *me*, for the preposition *to*.

(21) **into.** In Standard English, you go *into a store*, not *in to* or *by*.

(22) **in.** When you state an exact time (say, 12:30 a.m.) you use the preposition *at*. When you refer to a longer period of time, such as a season, *in* is better.

(23) **in, on.** You go into the store and buy *in* the store. When you give a general location, *on* works best. For a specific address (say, 600 Fifth Avenue), use *at*.

(24) **to, by.** The standard phrases are *to the mall* and *by car*. If you insert *a* into that last phrase, you can go *in a car*.

(25) **about.** *About* means "concerning, on the topic of." *Around* may refer to every side of something (*around the block)*, or it may express an estimate (*around 2:30)*.

(26) **or. Bakery ↔ restaurant** The conjunction *or* connects two nouns.

(27) **and. Liza ↔ Belle** The conjunction *and* connects two nouns.

(28) **although. Belle studies art ↔ she doesn't like the smell of paint.** The conjunction *although* connects two subject-verb statements.

(29) **after. Liza will look for a job in marketing ↔ she graduates** The conjunction *after* connects two subject-verb statements.

(30) **Either/or father ↔ uncle** This pair of conjunctions, *either/or*, connects two nouns.

(31) **and. smart ↔ energetic ↔ creative** The conjunction *and* connects three descriptions. The conjunction appears before the last item — the normal spot for a conjunction in a list.

(32) **yet. Sayed studies history ↔ he is more interested in chemistry** The conjunction *yet* connects two subject-verb statements.

(33) **because. He should be a teacher ↔ he explains things very well** The conjunction *because* connects one subject-verb statement to another.

(34) **and.school newspaper ↔ chess team ↔ student government** The conjunction *and* connects the items on this list, all nouns and the descriptions attached to them.

(35) **for. Aliyah plans on a career in government ↔ she is very patriotic** Surprised? The word *for* is usually a preposition ("for your own good"). In this sentence it's a conjunction meaning "because" and connects two subject-verb statements.

(36) **Incorrect.** Four exclamation points are three too many.

(37) **Incorrect.** You need an exclamation point or a comma after *goodness.*

(38) **Correct.** No problems with the interjection, *boy.*

(39) **Correct.** This sentence correctly places and punctuates *indeed.*

(40) **Correct.** The financial situation may be bad, but the sentence is fine.

Answers to the "Overachievers" section

(1) **Incorrect.** In Standard English, one exclamation point is enough.

(2) **Incorrect.** *In* is wrong because you're talking about a specific, relatively short period of time. The better choice for this spot is *on.*

(3) **Incorrect.** Conjunctions should connect elements that match grammatically. *Dreaming and to hope* don't match. Change *to hope* to *hoping,* and the problem is solved.

(4) **Incorrect.** The conjunction *but* signals a change — introducing a problem or an objection. The letter writer has plenty of problems, but he's not talking about them in this sentence. Instead, the process flows smoothly from closing eyes to pretending. The conjunction you want here is *and.*

(5) **Incorrect.** In Standard English, you are *at the beach,* not *in.*

(6) **Incorrect.** *Between* is a preposition, so it should be followed by object pronouns, such as *me,* not *I.*

(7) **Incorrect.** *Indeed* is an interjection in this sentence. It should be followed by a comma.

(8) **Incorrect.** In Standard English, you explain *to,* not *at.*

(9) **Incorrect.** *Inside* is written as one word, not two.

(10) **Correct.** *Both/and* is a paired conjunction. Look at the words that follow each part of this pair: *to him, to the other guards.* These prepositional phrases match, so this one is correct.

(11) **Incorrect.** The proper expression is *with care,* not *in care.*

(12) **Incorrect.** *At* isn't needed in this spot. You *cut,* not *cut at.* Delete the preposition.

(13) **Correct.** *In* is the proper preposition here.

(14) **Incorrect.** *Come at* hints at an attack. *Come to* is neutral, showing only the direction of movement. *To* is the preposition you want.

(15) **Incorrect.** The logical connection here is *free and happy.* The conjunction *but* hints that it's hard to be happy while being *free* — not a logical statement.

2

Creating Correct Sentences

Chapter 6

Digging Deeper into Verb Tense

Doing and being: In the real world, that's a good definition of life. In grammar, it's an accurate definition of a *verb*, the part of speech that tells what's happening or what is. Like life, verbs can be complicated. Chapter 3 covers the most basic verb forms — the simple past, present, and future tenses. (*Tense* is how verbs express time.) This chapter focuses on *progressive tense* (when an *ing* form of a verb appears) and *perfect tense* (when *has* or *had* attaches to another verb). As you work through the questions in this chapter, you'll progress to a perfect understanding of these tenses.

Working with "ing" Verbs

What <u>are</u> you <u>doing</u> right now? You <u>are reading</u> this book. I hope that soon you <u>will be feeling</u> more confident about your grammar skills. I also hope I <u>was</u> not <u>boring</u> you by showing you some sentences with underlined verbs. In case you're wondering, every underlined verb is in *progressive tense*. Progressive verbs rely on two words: a form of the verb *be* (*am, is, were, will be, has been*, for example) and the *ing* form of another verb (*cooking, dealing, working, having*, and so forth). Progressive verbs communicate the same information as simple verbs, but they add a shade of meaning, spotlighting action or a state of being occurring over a span of time.

Often, you can use either the simple or the progressive tense to get your message across. In these examples, the progressive verb is underlined:

> Jaime <u>was napping</u> when I called. (past progressive)
>
> Because I <u>am</u> not <u>feeling</u> well, I would like a nap also. (present progressive)
>
> Next month, when the boss <u>will be traveling</u>, John will take a few naps under his desk. (future progressive)

Did you notice that the two parts of the verb in the second example are separated by *not*? That's the usual pattern for a negative statement, as well as for questions:

> <u>Were</u> you <u>waiting</u> for Oliver?

TIP

When you add *ing* to a verb that ends with the letter *e*, you generally drop the *e*: *bite → biting*, *love → loving*, and so forth. For more help with spelling, turn to Chapter 20.

YOUR TURN

Q. Insert the progressive form of the verb in parentheses into each blank. Note: You may have to rearrange some words when you're dealing with questions and negative statements.

I can't reach Maria, because she _____ to Florida and her phone is off. (*drive*, present progressive)

A. **is driving.** *Maria* is a singular noun, so the present-tense form *is* pairs with *driving* to create the present progressive.

1. She _____ from the cold in her hometown when she planned the trip. (*shiver*, past progressive)

2. _____ you _____ too? (*freeze*, present progressive)

3. My dog and I _____ to join her as soon as possible. (*plan*, past progressive)

4. However, you _____ for exams next week, and I want to be here to reassure you. (*study*, future progressive)

5. I know you _____ about the exams, but I am sure you will do well. (*worry*, present progressive)

6. Doug, on the other hand, _____ for the tests. (*prepare*, present progressive, negative)

7. Yesterday, he and his friend Marco _____ video games all day! (*play*, past progressive)

8. _____ Doug _____ to college next year? (*apply*, future progressive)

9. His teachers _____ him, but most likely, he won't earn higher than a D average. (*help*, present progressive)

10. The temperature _____ below zero now. I've changed my mind. I'll join Maria in Florida. Good luck on your exams! (*drop*, present progressive)

Putting Perfect Tenses in the Spotlight

The perfect tenses attach *has, have,* or *had* to a verb form in order to create a timeline. Each perfect tense — past perfect, present perfect, and future perfect — also has a progressive form, which includes an *ing* verb. The difference between plain perfect tense and progressive perfect is small. The progressive perfect is a bit more immediate than the plain form. It refers to something that's ongoing or takes place over a span of time. In many sentences, the plain and progressive forms may be interchanged. Here's the lowdown on the perfect tenses:

>> **Past perfect and past perfect progressive place one event in the past before another event in the past.** This tense adds *had* to a verb describing the earlier event. Suppose you're dealing with two events: (1) a son dumping his laundry in his mother's basement and (2) the mother changing the front-door lock. *Had* tells you which event comes first:

> Mike <u>had been dumping</u> his dirty laundry in his mom's basement every Tuesday, but then Mom changed the front-door lock.

> <u>Had</u> Mike <u>avoided</u> chores before he moved out?

> Mike <u>had</u> not <u>paid</u> attention when his mother tried to teach him how to do his own laundry.

In the first example, *had been dumping* is in past perfect progressive tense. Dumping the laundry occurred over a span of time. Then, Mom rebelled and changed the lock. The second example is a question, so *Mike* appears between the two parts of the verb — the usual question pattern. The third example is a negative statement, so *had paid* is separated by *not.*

WARNING

Don't overuse the past perfect tense. If you're just listing a number of things that happened and the order doesn't matter, use the simple past tense: "When I was on vacation, I swam, sunbathed, and shopped for souvenirs."

>> **Present perfect links the past and the present.** With this tense, an action starts in the past and continues in the present. Form the present perfect tense by adding *has* (singular) or *have* (plural) to a form of the main verb. (What form? The past participle. You don't need to remember that term, just that it's the *ed* form of the verb — if the verb is regular! I explain everything you need to know about participles in the next section, where I also show you some common irregulars.) Form the present perfect progressive by adding *has been* or *have been* to the *ing* form of the main verb.

> Nessie <u>has lived</u> in Scotland since April 1, 2010.

> She <u>has been explaining</u> that her name has no connection to the Loch Ness Monster since April 2, 2010.

> Nessie <u>has</u> not <u>succeeded</u> in her efforts to distance herself from the famous monster.

> <u>Has</u> the monster <u>ignored</u> Nessie?

In the first example, *has lived* is in present perfect tense. Nessie's time in Scotland began in the past and continues in the present. In the second example, *has been explaining* is in present perfect progressive tense. The explaining started in the past and continues in the present. The verb emphasizes the span of time that Nessie has been talking about the Loch

Ness Monster. The third example makes a negative statement. Following the usual pattern, *not* appears between parts of the verb. The last example is a question, which also separates parts of the verb.

>> **Future perfect deals with a deadline sometime in the future.** The future perfect tense tacks on *will have* to a form of the main verb (the participle). Add *will have been* to the *ing* form of the main verb to create the future perfect progressive.

> Before sundown, Diego <u>will have grilled</u> several dozen burgers.

> When his guests arrive, Diego <u>will have been cooking</u> for several hours and <u>will</u> not <u>have rested</u> at all.

> <u>Will</u> his guests <u>have been warned</u> of Diego's poor cooking skills?

The verb in the first example is in future perfect tense. The sun hasn't gone down, and Diego hasn't yet completed his grilling work. The first verb in the second example (*will have been cooking*) is in future perfect progressive tense. The second verb in that sentence makes a negative statement, so the word *not* appears between *will* and *have rested*. The guests' arrival, Diego's cooking session, and his failure to rest all take place in the future. The guests' arrival is the last event. The last example is a question, so the people concerned (*guests*) separate *will* and the rest of the verb (*have been warned*). In this example, only one event appears, but another (their arrival) is understood.

YOUR TURN

Practice, especially with these verbs, makes perfect. (Perfect tense, get it?) Try this example and then keep going. The verb you're working on appears in parentheses at the end of the sentence. Using the time clues in the sentence, write the correct form of the verb in the blank.

Q. Although Antoine _____ a speech, the teacher asked Hanna to report instead. (*prepare*)

A. **had prepared.** With two events in the past, the *had* signals the earlier event. The preparing of the speech took place before the teacher's request, so *had prepared* is the form you want.

11. Mike _____ on thin ice for two hours when he heard the first crack. (*skate*)

12. Aliyah _____ Mike for years about his skating habits, but he doesn't listen. (*warn*)

13. _____ Mike ever _____ to anyone, now or in the past? (*listen*)

14. Mike _____ not _____ the weather forecast before he decided to skate. (*check*)

15. _____ Aliyah _____ Mike's health insurance every year, including this one? (*renew*)

16. After Mike _____ an hour in the emergency room, the doctor examined him. (*wait*)

17. By the time Mike is finished at the hospital, Aliyah _____ _____ countless outdated magazines in the waiting room. (*scan*)

18. Graciela _____ to speak to Mike ever since he declared that "a little thin ice" shouldn't scare anyone. (*refuse*)

19. Mike angrily stated that Graciela's motorcycle _____ him more seriously than his skates. (*injure*)

20. Before the emergency room visit is over, Aliyah _____ quietly to both Mike and Graciela. (*whisper*)

21. Despite years of practice, Aliyah _____ success only on rare occasions, but she keeps trying to resolve conflicts anyway. (*achieve*)

22. Since childhood, Mike _____ arguments by stomping away. (*end*)

23. After Aliyah _____ that Graciela should "butt out of Mike's business," Graciela simply ignored her. (*declare*)

24. Graciela _____ not _____ so annoyed since Aliyah put a bee in her hat. (*be*)

25. Aliyah didn't give up; she _____ stubborn ever since she was born! (*be*)

Getting the Part(iciple): Irregular Forms

To form the present perfect, past perfect, and future tense of a regular verb, all you have to do is add *ed* to the base verb: *had walked, has* or *have walked, will have walked*. Easy, isn't it? Sadly, the English language isn't always a rule-follower. Many "combo" forms are irregular. You can't write *had goed* or *has goed* or *will have goed*, because *goed* isn't Standard English. Instead, you need *gone*. This part of a perfect-tense verb is called a *participle*. Part of a perfect-tense verb is a <u>part</u>iciple: The terms makes sense.

You can't get far without irregular participles, so here's a table of the most common forms. If you need a participle that doesn't appear in this table, check the dictionary.

Base Verb	Participle	Base Verb	Participle
become	become	begin	begun
bite	bitten	break	broken
bring	brung	catch	caught
choose	chosen	come	come
drink	drunk	eat	eaten
fall	fallen	feel	felt
fly	flown	freeze	frozen
get	gotten	go	gone
know	known	lead	led
lend	lent	lose	lost

Base Verb	Participle	Base Verb	Participle
ride	ridden	ring	rung
rise	risen	run	run
say	said	see	seen
shake	shaken	sing	sung
sit	sat	slide	slid
speak	spoken	take	taken
throw	thrown	wear	worn
win	won	write	written

 Fill in each blank with the correct form of the verb in parentheses.

YOUR TURN

Q. Oh no! The chef _____ (*leave*, present perfect) the eggs out of the refrigerator, and they _____ bad. (*go*, present perfect)

A. **has left, have gone.** *Chef* is a singular noun, which should be paired with *has left*. The pronoun *they* refers to *eggs* and is plural, so it pairs with *have gone*.

26 The cat _____ (*eat*, past perfect) almost all the party favors before we stopped him.

27 The birthday banner _____ (*fall*, future perfect) before Mom arrives because the tape holding it to the wall is peeling off.

28 The twins _____ (*see*, present perfect progressive) a party planner once a week.

29 Mom _____ (*speak*, present perfect) often of her wish to have a huge party.

30 Dad hired a choir that _____ (*sing*, present perfect, negative) in public for a year.

31 _____ the new choir director _____ (*shake*, past perfect) the group's confidence?

32 I predict that half the singers _____ (*catch*, future perfect) "a cold" before tonight's performance.

33 "We _____ (*lose*, present perfect) our voices," they will claim, falsely.

34 I _____ (*be*, present perfect, negative) worried.

35 Dad _____ (*lead*, present perfect progressive) a huge company for years, so he is more than able to take care of a party.

Calling All Overachievers: Extra Practice with Progressive and Perfect Tenses

Have you sharpened your verb skills with the exercises in this chapter? Time to find out. Read this email from a supervisor to her employees. Check each underlined verb and label it "correct" or "incorrect."

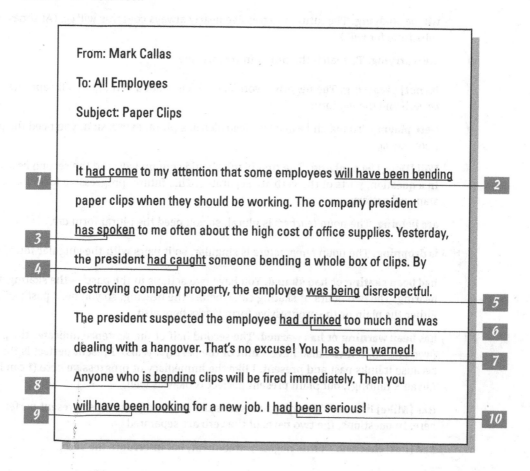

From: Mark Callas

To: All Employees

Subject: Paper Clips

1 It <u>had come</u> to my attention that some employees <u>will have been bending</u> **2** paper clips when they should be working. The company president **3** <u>has spoken</u> to me often about the high cost of office supplies. Yesterday, **4** the president <u>had caught</u> someone bending a whole box of clips. By destroying company property, the employee <u>was being</u> disrespectful. **5** The president suspected the employee <u>had drinked</u> too much and was **6** dealing with a hangover. That's no excuse! You <u>has been warned!</u> **7** **8** Anyone who <u>is bending</u> clips will be fired immediately. Then you **9** <u>will have been looking</u> for a new job. I <u>had been</u> serious! **10**

Answers to Verb Tense Questions

1. **was shivering.** The pronoun *she* pairs well with *was*, the past-tense form of *be*.

2. **are [you] freezing.** The pronoun *you* pairs with *are*, a present-tense form of *be*.

3. **were planning.** The expression *My dog and I* is plural, so the *be* verb you want is *were*.

4. **will be studying.** The future progressive nearly always contains *will be*. (At times, *shall* may substitute for *will*.)

5. **are worrying.** To match the pronoun *you*, use *are*.

6. **is [not] preparing.** The negative word *not*, which is not a verb, generally appears between the *be* verb and the *ing* form.

7. **were playing.** To match *he and his friend Marco*, a plural expression, you need the plural form *were playing*.

8. **Will [Doug] be applying.** The first blank should contain *will*, and the second *be applying*. In a question, parts of the verb are separated. This future-progressive form follows the standard pattern.

9. **are helping.** The noun *teachers* is plural, so you need the plural form *are*.

10. **is dropping.** The noun *temperature* is singular, so it pairs with the singular form, *is*.

11. **had been skating** or **had skated.** You have two actions in the past — the skating and the hearing. The two hours of skating came before the hearing, so you need past perfect tense. Either the plain or the progressive form works here also.

12. **has been warning** or **has warned.** The second half of the sentence indicates the present (*won't listen*), but you also have a hint of the past (*for years*). Present perfect is the best choice because it links past and present. I like the immediacy of progressive here (I can hear Aliyah's ranting), but plain present perfect is okay as well.

13. **Has [Mike] listened.** This question spans the past and present, so present perfect is perfect here. In questions, the two parts of the verb are separated.

14. **had [not] checked.** In this negative statement, *not* interrupts the verb.

15. **Has been renewing.** In questions, the verb parts are separated by the name of the person or thing doing the action. The sentence links past and present, so either present perfect or present perfect progressive fits. I chose present perfect progressive, but if you opted for present perfect, count yourself correct.

16. **had waited** or **had been waiting.** The waiting preceded the doctor's announcement, so you should use past perfect. Progressive adds a "you are there" feel but isn't necessary.

17. **will have scanned.** The deadline in the sentence (*the end of today's trip*) is your clue for future perfect tense.

18 **has refused.** Notice the present-past link? Mike declared, and Graciela is acting now. Hence, you need present perfect tense.

19 **had injured.** The stating and the injuring occur at two different times in the past. The injuring is first, so that verb should be in past perfect tense.

20 **will have whispered.** The future perfect needs an end point. In this sentence, it's the end of the hospital visit. The action expressed by a future perfect verb happens before the endpoint.

21 **has achieved.** Because the sentence states that she keeps trying, you have a present-past connection, a situation that requires present perfect tense.

22 **has ended or has been ending.** This sentence has a past-tense clue (*since childhood*), and Mike's habits haven't changed. Either present perfect or present perfect progressive works here.

23 **had declared.** The *after* at the beginning of the sentence is your clue that one action occurs before another. Because both are in the past, you need past perfect tense for the earlier action.

24 **had [not] been.** In this negative statement, *not* appears between *had* and *been*. The statement about her mood refers to the present time; the placement of the bee occurred earlier.

25 **has been.** This state of being began at birth and continues in the present, so present perfect is the tense you need in this sentence.

26 **had eaten.** The irregular participle *eaten* pairs with *had* to form the past perfect.

27 **will have fallen.** The irregular participle *fallen* joins with *will have* to form the future perfect.

28 **have been seeing.** The noun *twins* is plural, and the plural verb in present perfect progressive tense starts with *have been*. *Been* is an irregular participle.

29 **has spoken.** *Spoken* is irregular, but swapping *en* for *ed* is a common irregular pattern: *fallen*, *taken*, *broken*, and many others.

30 **has [not] sung.** In a negative statement, *not* appears between the two parts of the verb.

31 **Has [the choir director] shaken.** In a question, the two parts of the verb are separated by the name of the person or thing involved (*choir director*).

32 **will have caught.** This future perfect form relies on *will have* and the irregular participle *caught*.

33 **have lost.** The plural pronoun *we* requires the plural verb *have*, plus the irregular participle *lost*.

34 **have [not] been.** In a negative statement, *not* separates the two parts of the verb.

35 **has led.** The irregular participle *led* joins with the singular verb *has* to pair with *Dad*, a singular noun. If you answered with the progressive form, *has been leading*, count yourself correct.

Answers to Overachiever Verb-Tense Questions

1. **Incorrect.** *Had come* is wrong because the *had* places one action before another action in the past. The paper-clip issue is ongoing, so present perfect (*has come*) is better.

2. **Incorrect.** *Will be* places the action in the future, but the memo places the problem in the past and present. To connect these two time periods, use present perfect progressive tense, *have been bending.*

3. **Correct.** *Has spoken* is the right irregular verb to pair with *president,* a singular noun. You need the present perfect tense because the president spoke in the past and continues "often" in the present.

4. **Incorrect.** The sentence doesn't place events in order or connect two time periods, so you don't need a perfect tense. *Caught* is the simple past-tense verb form you want for this sentence.

5. **Correct.** The present progressive form describes the employee's behavior over a period of time.

6. **Incorrect.** *Had drunk* is the irregular form you need for the past perfect tense of the verb *drink.*

7. **Incorrect.** The pronoun *you* never pairs with *has.* For both singular and plural, you need *have.*

8. **Correct.** The progressive tense spotlights an ongoing action.

9. **Incorrect.** The sentence doesn't include a deadline, so future perfect tense isn't a good choice. Progressive — *will be looking* — is what you want.

10. **Incorrect.** You're not connecting present and past, so the simple present, *am,* is better for this sentence.

Chapter 7

Tackling Subjects, Objects, and Complements

Verbs, as I explain in Chapter 3, are the heart of the sentence. They express action ("Elena <u>studies</u> Dutch") or state of being ("The textbook <u>is</u> expensive"). As you surely noticed, verbs don't appear alone in these sample sentences. Someone or something does the action or exists in the state of being. That's the *subject*. Other words may add to or complete the idea begun by the subject and verb. Often, those words are *objects* or *complements*. In this chapter, you practice identifying these important elements of a sentence and using them properly.

Zeroing in on the Subject

Every sentence needs a subject, which is usually a *noun* (a word that names people, places, things, or ideas) or a *pronoun* (words such as *he, it, who,* and so forth that substitute for nouns). Locating the subject is easy. First, find the verb. (If you don't know how to find the verb, turn to Chapter 3.) Next, place *who?* or *what?* before the verb and answer the question you just created. For example, suppose the sentence is "Dad parked the car." The verb is *parked.* The subject questions are *who parked?* and *what parked?* The answer, *Dad*, is the subject. Here are a few tips for subject hunting:

>> **A sentence may have more than one subject.** Suppose the sentence is "Dad and I went to the mall." The verb is *went*. When you ask *who went? what went?* the answer is *Dad and I.* That's your subject.

>> **One subject may pair with more than one verb.** In the sentence "George sang and danced for hours," the verbs are *sang* and *danced*. *George* is the answer to *who or what sang?* and *who or what danced? George* is the subject of both verbs.

>> **The subject may appear anywhere in the sentence.** The subject usually appears before the verb, but not always. That's why you should rely on logic, not location. Ask the subject questions *who?* and *what?* before the verb. The answer is always the subject, no matter where it appears in the sentence. Suppose the sentence is "Across the field stood a house." The verb is *stood*. Now, ask *who stood? what stood?* A <u>house</u> stood. *House* is the subject of the verb *stood*.

>> ***Here*** **and** ***there*** **aren't subjects.** Once again, the questions *who?* and *what?* before the verb point you to the real subject. Look at this sentence: "Here on the desk is my favorite pencil." Locate the verb, *is*. Ask *who is? what is?* The answer is *pencil. Pencil* is the subject.

>> **In a sentence that gives a command, the subject is** ***you.*** The word *you* doesn't appear in the sentence, but it's understood. Don't believe me? Think again! Now look at the last sentence and ask yourself who is supposed to *think*. The answer is that *you* are. The subject of the verb *think* is *you.*

>> **If the sentence is a question, the subject often appears between two parts of the verb.** The easiest way to find the subject in a question is to rearrange the words so that the sentence resembles a statement. Suppose you see this sentence: "Did Abdul go to the dance?" Change it to "Abdul did go to the dance." Now follow the usual procedure. Find the verb (*did go*) and ask *who or what did go?* The answer is *Abdul,* which is the subject.

 Locate the subjects in these sentences.

YOUR TURN **Q.** Angelo raided his piggy bank because his car needed new tires.

_____

A. **Angelo, car.** In this sentence, you find two verbs, raided and needed. When you ask *who raided?* the answer is *Angelo raided. Angelo* is the subject of the verb *raided*. (You can ask *what raided?* also, but that question has no answer.) Now, ask *who needed?* You get no answer. Ask *what needed?* The answer is *car needed,* so *car* is the subject of the verb *needed.*

1 Ana and Max spend most of their free time in the library.

_____

2 In the last year, Max has grown quite tall, but he has not adjusted to his new size.

_____

3 Yesterday, he reached under a table to pick up a book Ana had dropped.

_____

4 Max stood up too quickly and smashed his head on the bottom of the table.

_____

5 There is a dent in the table now.

_____

6 Did you see a dent in Max's head?

_____

7 Max's thick hair protects him from severe head injuries.

8 His thick skull protects him also!

_____

9 When Max hit it, the table fell over.

_____

10 From under the table and out of a pile of encyclopedias crawled Ana.

_____

11 "Be more careful!" she yelled.

_____

12 The table and Ana's toe had broken with a loud snap.

_____

13 Ana was quite angry with Max.

_____

14 She had planned a vacation on a tropical island, not a trip to the emergency room.

_____

15 Can she swim with a cast on her foot?

_____

Meeting Their Match: Pairing Subjects and Verbs

Although they don't have dating apps to help them, every subject and verb must find a match. Singular subjects pair with singular verbs, and plural subjects pair with plural verbs. English teachers call this rule *agreement*. In this section, I take you through the basics of subject-verb agreement. Then, I hit you with some tricky subject-verb situations.

Boning up on the basics

The good news is that most of the time English verbs have only one form for both singular and plural. "I *burp*" and "the dinosaurs *burp*" are both correct, even though *I* is singular and *dinosaurs* is plural. You have to worry only in a few special circumstances. Here are the rules, with italicized subjects and verbs in the examples so you can locate them quickly:

>> **Talking about someone in the present tense requires different verb forms for singular and plural.** A singular verb ends in *s,* (one baby *spits*), but the plural doesn't (two babies *spit*).

>> **Verbs that include *does/do* or *has/have* change forms for singular and plural.** Singular verbs use *does* or *has.* (John *does paint* his toenails blue. He *has stated* that fact.) Plurals use *do* and *have.* (*Do* the toenails *need* more polish? No, *they have* plenty already.)

>> ***I* pairs with the plural form of most verbs.** The pronoun *I* is always singular, but "I go" is correct, not "I goes." The exception is the verb *be,* which is irregular. *I* pairs with *am.*

>> **Although *you* and *they* may be either singular or plural, these subjects always pair with plural verbs.** *You catch* a robber, whether *you* refers to one person or ten. *They,* when it's used as a gender-neutral pronoun for one person, pairs with a plural verb. (That driver is texting! *They are* going to cause an accident!)

>> **The verb *be* changes form according to the noun or pronoun paired with it.** I cover this topic in Chapter 3.

>> **Two or more singular subjects joined by *and* pair with a plural verb.** The word *and* adds, forming a plural subject. (*Sol* and *Sarah were married* yesterday.)

>> **Two or more singular subjects joined by *or* pair with a singular verb.** The logic here is that you're looking at each subject separately. (*Dana* or *John is cooking* tonight.)

>> **Ignore interrupters when matching subjects to verbs.** *Interrupters* include phrases such as "of the books" and "except for . . ." and longer expressions such as "who golfs badly" and "which takes the cake." ("*Harriet,* according to her brother, *loves* the snow.")

WARNING

Some interrupters (*as well as, in addition to*) appear to create a plural, but grammatically, they aren't part of the subject and, like all interrupters, have no effect on the singular/plural issue.

In the blank, write the correct form of the verb in parentheses.

Q. John's teacher _____ (*remain, remains*) uninterested in his excuses for missing homework.

A. **remains.** The subject, *teacher*, is singular, so the verb must also be singular. The letter *s* creates a singular verb.

16 John _____ his eyebrows when his teacher catches him in a lie. (*raises, raise*)

17 John, whose homework _____ (*has, have*) been late every day this year, says that his dog always _____ (*snacks, snack*) on his homework assignments.

18 We _____ (*does, do*) not believe his story.

19 You probably _____ (*believes, believe*) John because you _____ (*give/gives*) everyone the benefit of the doubt.

20 _____ (*Does, Do*) you think that John's friends always _____ (*tell, tells*) the truth?

21 _____ (*Has, Have*) John's excuse been accepted?

22 I never _____ (*knows, know*) when John _____ (*is lying, are lying*).

23 Sometimes, he _____ (*tells, tell*) very odd tales.

24 Why _____ (*does, do*) everyone believe him?

25 Nadine, who used to be one of John's closest friends, _____ (*scolds, scold*) John for his dishonesty.

26 John, along with some other students, _____ (*cheats, cheat*) on tests.

27 The principal, in addition to everyone else on the faculty, _____ (*has wanted, have wanted*) to expel John for years.

28 John and his brother _____ (*spends, spend*) a lot of time in detention.

29 There _____ six teachers taking turns supervising detention. (*is, are*)

30 During today's detention, John and Dana _____ (*was texting, were texting*) each other instead of studying math.

31 When he works on a math problem, John often _____ (*removes, remove*) his phone from his pocket and _____ (*searches, search*) for the correct answer.

32 "In every single one of my pockets _____ (*is, are*) a math formula," John once remarked.

33 John, as well as his friend Dana, _____ (*has failed, have failed*) math.

34 Teachers of every subject _____ (*wants, want*) John to be punished.

35 There _____ (*was, were*) a movie director and an agent in the principal's office trying to gain access to John.

36 John's offers, in addition to a "how to cheat" podcast, _____ (*includes, include*) a chance to be on a reality television show.

Taming the tough guys: Difficult subjects

A few pronouns may trip you up when you form subject-verb pairs. With a little extra attention, though, you can tame these difficult subjects. Check out these rules:

» **Pronouns ending in *one, thing,* and *body* (*everyone, something,* and *anybody,* for example) are singular.** Even though they sometimes sound plural, *everyone is* here, and *nobody needs* more grammar rules. For these singular pronouns, you need a singular verb.

» *All, some, most, none,* and *any* **can be either singular or plural.** Subjects that can be counted are plural. ("*All* of the ears *are sticking* out. *Some* of the ears *are going* to be glued flat.") A subject that can be measured but not counted is singular. ("*Most* of the sugar in his diet *comes* from doughnuts. *None* of his food *contains* any vitamins.")

» **In *either/or* and *neither/nor* sentences, match the verb to the closest subject.** Sentences with this structure have two subjects, but the two don't add up to a plural. Instead, each subject is separate. Note: If the sentence is a question, the verb may include two words. The subject near the part of the verb that changes (*has, do, does,* and so forth) is the one to match. ("Either *Josh* or his *partners are going* to jail. *Are* either his *partners* or *Josh going* to jail?")

Place the correct verb in each blank.

YOUR TURN **Q.** Neither the fire marshal nor the police officers (was/were) aware of the bowling tournament.

A. **were.** The subject *police officers* is closer to the verb than *marshal*. Because *police officers* is plural, the verb must also be plural.

37 All the dancers in Lola's musical _____ (*wears, wear*) green tap shoes.

38 Most of the principal singers _____ (*has/have*) enough talent to carry the musical.

39 Everyone _____ (*is practicing, are practicing*) daily.

40 Why _____ (*does, do*) no one understand that Lola's piano is out of tune?

41 Most of the music _____ (*is played, are played*) too loud.

42. Nobody _____ (*has heard, have heard*) them, and no one _____ (*is expecting, are expecting*) a preview.

43. Neither her co-stars nor Lola _____ (*is willing, are willing*) to guess how audiences will react.

44. Some of the reviews (has/have) the ability to make or break the production.

45. _____ (*Has, Have*) either the director or the musicians agreed on a contract?

46. Something _____ (*has soured, have soured*) in their relationship.

47. Everyone _____ (*agrees, agree*) on one thing.

48. All the fame in the world _____ (*is, are*) not as valuable as art and a big paycheck.

49. _____ (*Has, Have*) someone mentioned the Tony Awards?

50. Either Lola or her producers _____ (*was posting, were posting*) about the show on social media, but no one clicked the link to buy tickets.

Adding Meaning: Objects and Complements

Subjects and verbs give a lot of information, but most sentences tack on other elements — *direct objects, indirect objects,* and *subject complements* — to add to the meaning expressed by the subject-verb pair. To locate objects and subject complements, keep these points in mind:

>> **Verbs expressing action may direct that action to a *direct object*.** The answer to the question *whom?* or *what?* after the verb is the *direct object*. For example, in the sentence *Lulu hates sports, hates* is the action verb, and *Lulu* is the subject of *hates.* Ask *Lulu hates whom?* and you get no answer. Ask *Lulu hates what?* and the answer is *sports. Sports* is the direct object of the verb *hates.*

>> **Verbs that express action sometimes appear with a direct object and an indirect object.** In the sentence *Lulu gave me an annoyed glance,* the subject-verb combination is *Lulu gave.* The direct object of the verb *gave* is *glance,* which answers the question *Lulu gave what?* The indirect object questions are *to whom? to what?* So now you have *Lulu gave an annoyed glance to whom?* The answer is *to me,* and *me* is the indirect object. (You don't get an answer when you ask *to what.*)

>> **Verbs from the "be" family and its synonyms (*am, is, was, were, has been, seems, appears,* and so forth) need a *subject complement* to complete the idea begun by the subject-verb pair.** A subject complement may be a noun, a pronoun, or a descriptive word. In the sentence *Lulu is a terrible basketball player,* the subject-verb pair is *Lulu is.* Now, ask *Lulu is who? Lulu is what?* The answer is *a terrible basketball player.* The most important word in that answer is *player,* and *player* is the subject complement. In the sentence *The soup tastes salty,* the subject-verb pair is *soup tastes.* Ask *soup tastes who? soup tastes what?* and the answer is *salty. Salty* is the subject complement.

TIP

Most of the time, the distinction between objects and complements doesn't matter. When a pronoun completes the thought begun by the subject and verb, however, you have to be alert. In Standard English, the same type of pronoun that acts as a subject also acts as a subject complement. For more about subject pronouns, see Chapter 2.

YOUR TURN

Locate the objects and subject complements in each sentence. You may find one, more than one, or none. Underline each one and label it as a direct object (DO), an indirect object (IO), or a subject complement (SC).

Q. Lulu hates baseball, too, even though she is very athletic.

A. baseball **(DO)**, athletic **(SC)**. *Hates* is an action verb. Ask *Lulu hates whom or what?* and *baseball* pops up as the answer. *Baseball* is the direct object. *Is* is a linking verb, so when you ask, *she is who or what?* the answer, *athletic*, is a subject complement.

51 During the softball game, Fatima swung the bat with all her strength.

52 She is extremely strong because she exercises for two hours every day.

53 The bat hit the ball and lifted it over the outfield fence.

54 There was wild joy in our cheering section!

55 The applause always sounds louder when Fatima plays.

56 Compared to Fatima, the next batter seemed small and weak.

57 She is the captain of the team.

58 The pitcher tossed the captain a slow curveball.

59 Would he hit it?

60 Yes! The captain smacked the ball and gave our team another run.

Calling All Overachievers: Extra Practice with Subjects, Objects, and Complements

Take a close look at each underlined word. Label subjects with S, direct and indirect objects with O, and subject complements with SC. If the word fits none of those categories, write N.

Jenna's [1]<u>sisters</u> gave [2]<u>her</u> a [3]<u>cookbook</u>. Jenna [4]<u>loves</u> cake. [5]<u>Everyone</u> loves [6]<u>cake</u>! She [7]<u>prepared</u> the [8]<u>first</u> recipe, Chocolate Surprise. [9]<u>It</u> was [10]<u>certainly</u> a [11]<u>surprise</u>. By mistake, Jenna added [12]<u>salt</u> instead of sugar to the batter. When the cake was [13]<u>ready</u>, Jenna served each [14]<u>sister</u> a [15]<u>slice</u>. [16]<u>They</u> said [17]<u>nothing</u>. They couldn't say [18]<u>anything</u>, because when [19]<u>Jenna</u> saw that the top layer of the cake was slipping, she stirred [20]<u>glue</u> into the icing.

Answers to Subject, Object, and Complement Questions

1. **Ana, Max.** The verb in this sentence is *spend*. When you ask *who* before that verb, the answer is *Ana and Max. Ana* and *Max* are both subjects of the verb *spend*.

2. **Max, he.** Who *has grown*? *Max has grown. Max* is the subject of the verb *has grown*. Who *has adjusted*? *He has adjusted. He* is the subject of the verb has adjusted. (*Not* isn't part of the verb.)

3. **he, Ana.** Who *reached*? *He reached. He* is the subject of the verb *reached. Who had dropped*? *Ana had dropped. Ana* is the subject of the verb *had dropped*. Did I fool you with *to pick up*? True, *pick up* is an action. However, in this sentence *to pick up* isn't functioning as a verb. Instead, the phrase tells you why *he reached*, so it's a description.

4. **Max.** This sentence has two verbs, *stood* and *smashed*. When you ask *who stood*? the answer is *Max*. You get the same answer for *who smashed*? *Max* is the subject of both verbs.

5. **dent.** *There* is never a subject. Neither is *here*, which often appears in similar sentences. The real subject, which you find with the usual questions, appears after the verb. *What is*? *A dent is. Dent* is the subject of the verb *is*.

6. **you.** The verb in this sentence is *did see*. Ignore the fact that the sentence asks a question and ask the usual subject questions. *Who did see*? *You did see. You* is the subject of *did see*.

7. **hair.** When you ask *what*? before the verb *protects*, the answer is *hair. Hair* is the subject of the verb *protects*.

8. **skull.** The verb is *protects*. Ask *what protects*? and the answer is *skull*, which is the subject.

9. **Max, table.** Who *hit*? *Max hit. Max* is the subject of the verb *hit. What fell*? *The table*, which is the subject of the verb *fell*.

10. **Ana.** The verb is *crawled*. When you ask *who crawled*? the answer is *Ana. Ana* is the subject of the verb *crawled*, even though the word appears after the verb.

11. **you understood, she.** In a command sentence, the subject is always *you*, though the word doesn't appear. Therefore, "you understood" is the subject of the command verb, *be. Yelled* is also a verb. When you ask *who yelled*? the answer is *she*, which is the subject of the verb *yelled*.

12. **table, toe.** *Had broken* is the verb. What *had broken*? Two things: *table* and *toe*, which are both subjects of the verb *had broken*.

13. **Ana.** When you ask *who was*? the answer is *Ana was. Ana* is the subject of the verb *was*.

14. **she.** The verb is *had planned*. Who *had planned*? *She. She* is the subject of the verb *had planned*.

15. **she.** If you rearrange the words, you get "she can swim with a cast on her foot." The verb is *can swim. Who can swim*? *She. She* is the subject of the verb *can swim*.

16. **raises.** The singular subject *John* matches the singular verb, *raises*.

17. **has, snacks.** The first blank requires a singular verb, *has*, to pair with the singular subject *homework*. For the second blank, you want the singular verb *snacks* to match the singular noun *dog*.

18. **do.** *We* is a plural pronoun, which is paired with *do*, a plural verb.

19. **believe, give.** Whether it's singular or plural, the pronoun *you* requires a plural verb. *Believe* and *give* are plural verbs.

20. **Do, tell.** The subject of the first verb, *do tell*, is *you*, which always requires a plural verb. For the second blank, the subject is *friends*, a plural, which must be matched with the plural verb *tell*.

21. **Has.** The subject is *excuse*, a singular noun, so *has* is the singular verb you want.

22. **know, is lying.** For the first blank, you need a verb to match the subject, *I*. That pronoun is singular, but it matches with plural verbs, except when the verb is in the *be* family. *John* is the singular subject of the singular verb *is lying*.

23. **tells.** *He* is a singular pronoun, so it matches with the singular verb *tells*.

24. **does.** The pronoun *everyone* sounds plural, but it's actually singular and a good match for the singular verb *does*.

25. **scolds.** *Nadine* is one person — and, therefore, a singular noun. Pair *Nadine* with the singular verb *scolds*.

26. **cheats.** Ignore interrupters! *Along with, in addition to,* and *as well as* appear to create a plural, but they're not relevant to the singular subject-verb pair, with is *John cheats*.

27. **has wanted.** As with the preceding sentence, pay no attention to the interrupter and focus on the singular subject-verb pair, *principal has wanted*.

28. **spend.** One (*John*) plus one (*his brother*) form a plural, for which you need the plural verb *spend*.

29. **are.** *There* isn't the subject. The plural noun *teachers* is the subject and requires the plural verb *are*.

30. **were texting.** *John and Dana* is a plural subject requiring the plural verb *were texting*.

31. **removes, searches.** The singular noun *John* is the subject of both verbs, *removes* and *searches*.

32. **is.** Did *pockets* distract you? The real subject is *formula*, which is singular and requires a singular verb.

33. **has failed.** The expression *as well as* doesn't create a plural verb. *John* is the singular subject of this sentence, and *has failed* is the singular verb.

34. **want.** Were you fooled by the singular noun *subject*? *Subject* is not the subject of this sentence. *Teachers*, a plural subject, must be paired with the plural verb *want*.

35. **were.** In a "here" or "there" sentence, the subject appears after the verb. In this case, it's two people, *director* and *agent*. They act as a plural subject, which requires the plural verb *were*.

36. **include.** The subject is *offers*, a plural, which requires the plural verb *include*.

37. **wear.** You can count *dancers*, so in this sentence, the pronoun *all* is plural and requires the plural verb *wear*.

(38) **have.** The pronoun *most* can be either singular (for measured quantities) or plural (for counted quantities). *Singers* are in the second category, so the plural verb *have* is the one you want.

(39) **is practicing.** The "ones" — *everyone, someone, anyone,* and *no one* — are singular, so you need the singular verb *is practicing* to match the singular subject *everybody.*

(40) **does.** The subject here is *no one,* a singular pronoun, which pairs with the singular verb *does.*

(41) **is played.** The subject, the pronoun *most,* can be either singular or plural. It's plural when you can count whatever it's referring to. That's not the case with *music,* so you need a singular verb, *is played.*

(42) **has heard, is expecting.** The "bodies" and the "ones" — *everybody, everyone, somebody, someone, anybody, anyone, nobody,* and *no one* — are singular, so you should match the subjects, *nobody* and *no one,* with singular verbs, *has heard* and *is expecting.*

(43) **is willing.** In an *either/or* and *neither/nor* sentence, match the verb to the closest subject. In this sentence *Lola* is closer than *co-stars,* so the verb should be singular.

(44) **have.** *Some* may be either singular or plural, depending on whether it's applied to a measurable or a countable quantity. You can count *reviews,* so a plural verb is required in this sentence.

(45) **Has.** In an *either/or* and *neither/nor* question, look at the part of the verb that changes. Which subject is closer? In this sentence, *director,* a singular noun, is closer, so you need a singular verb.

(46) **has soured.** The "things" — *everything, something, anything,* and *nothing* — are singular, so you need the singular verb *has soured* to match the subject, *nothing.*

(47) **agrees.** The "ones" — *everyone, someone, anyone,* and *no one* — are singular, so you need the singular verb *agrees* to match the singular subject *everyone.*

(48) **is.** *All* can be either singular or plural, depending on whether it's referring to a measurable or countable quantity. *Fame* can be measured, so *all* is singular and requires the singular verb, *is.*

(49) **Has.** The "ones" — *everyone, someone, anyone,* and *no one* — are singular, so you need the singular verb *has* to match the singular subject *someone.*

(50) **were posting.** The closer subject in the *either/or* sentence is *producers,* a plural, so you need the plural verb, *were posting.*

(51) **bat (DO).** The subject-verb pair is *Fatima swung.* When you ask *Fatima swung whom or what?* you get *bat,* the direct object.

(52) **strong (SC).** The answer to "she is who or what?" is *strong,* which is the subject complement. The action verb *exercises* has no object, because when you ask, *she exercises whom or what?* you get no answer. (*Two hours every day* answers *when?* or *for how long?*)

(53) **ball (DO), it (DO).** The sentence has two action verbs, *hit* and *lifted. Bat* is the subject of both verbs. Ask *bat hit whom? or what?* and you get *ball,* the direct object. Ask *bat lifted whom or what?* and you get *it,* also a direct object.

(54) **No object or complement.** The verb is *was,* and the subject is *joy.* (*There* is never a subject.) If you ask *joy is who or what?* you get no answer, so you have no object or complement. (*In our cheering section* is a description answering the question *where?*)

(55) **louder (SC).** The verb *sounds* expresses information coming from one of the five senses — in this sentence, hearing — so a subject complement follows it. The subject-verb pair is *applause sounds.* When you ask *applause sounds who or what?* the answer is *louder*, the subject complement.

(56) **small (SC), weak (SC).** *Seemed* is a synonym of *was*, a verb form from the *be* family of verbs. Its meaning is completed by a subject complement. When you ask *seemed who or what?* you get two answers, *small* and *weak.* Both are subject complements.

(57) **captain (SC).** The verb *is* takes a subject complement. In this sentence, ask *she is who? what?* The answer is *captain*, the subject complement.

(58) **captain (IO), ball (DO).** The subject-verb pair here is *pitcher tossed.* Ask *pitcher tossed whom or what?* The answer is *ball*, the direct object. Now ask *pitcher tossed ball to whom or what?* The answer is *captain*, the indirect object.

(59) **it (DO).** The subject-verb pair is *he would hit.* Ask *he would hit whom? or what?* The answer is *it*, the direct object.

(60) **ball (DO), team (IO), run (DO).** This sentence has two verbs (*smacked* and *gave*). *Captain* is the subject of both. Ask *captain smacked whom or what?* The answer is *ball*, a direct object. Ask *captain gave whom or what?* The answer is *run*, another direct object. Now, ask *captain gave run to whom or what?* The answer is *team*, the indirect object.

Answers to Overachiever Questions

(1) **S.** *Sisters* is the subject of the verb *gave*, answering the question *who gave?*

(2) **O.** *Her* is the indirect object of the verb *gave*, answering the question *sisters gave cookbook to whom?*

(3) **O.** *Cookbook* is the direct object of the verb *gave*, answering the question *sisters gave what?*

(4) **N.** *Loves* is a verb.

(5) **S.** The pronoun *everyone* is the subject of the verb *loves*, answering the question *who loves?*

(6) **O.** *Cake* is the direct object of the verb *loves*, answering the question *everyone loves what?*

(7) **N.** *Prepared* is a verb.

(8) **N.** *First* is a description, telling you which *recipe* Jenna made.

(9) **S.** The pronoun *it* is the subject of the verb *was*, answering the question *what was?*

(10) **N.** *Certainly* is a description, adding meaning to the verb, *was.*

(11) **SC.** *Surprise* is the subject complement of the verb *was*, answering the question *it was what?*

(12) **O.** *Salt* is the direct object of the verb *added*, answering the question *Jenna added what?*

(13) **SC.** *Ready* is the subject complement of the verb *was*, answering the question *cake was what?*

(14) **O.** *Sister* is the indirect object of the verb *served*, answering the question *Jenna served slice to whom?*

(15) **O.** *Slice* is the direct object of the verb *served*, answering the question *Jenna served what?*

(16) **S.** *They* is the subject of the verb *said*, answering the question *who said?*

(17) **O.** *Nothing* is the direct object of the verb *said*, answering the question *They said what?*

(18) **O.** *Anything* is the direct object of the verb *could say*, answering the question *They could say what?* Note: *Couldn't* is short for *could not. Not* is not a verb. It's a descriptive word, reversing the meaning of the verb from positive to negative.

(19) **S.** *Jenna* is the subject of the verb *saw*, answering the question *who saw?*

(20) **O.** *Glue* is the direct object of the verb *stirred*, answering the question *she stirred what?*

Chapter **8**

Having It All: Writing Complete Sentences

My friend texted her young daughter: "Let me know that you arrived safely." Her phone pinged immediately: "Here." The parent's comment is a complete and proper sentence, according to the rules of Standard English. I'm betting that her daughter thinks her answer is also complete and proper. Both are correct! The requirements of Standard English are important, but sometimes the rules bend. This chapter explains exactly what every sentence needs in order to be complete and correct in Standard English. It also discusses when an incomplete sentence is acceptable.

Examining the Essentials

According to the rules of Standard English, this trio must be present in all your sentences:

» **Subject/verb pair:** A *verb* expresses action or state of being, and a *subject* specifies who or what is acting or being. (See Chapters 2 and 7 for more on subjects and verbs.)

» **Complete thought:** You shouldn't leave the reader hanging with only half an idea. (*If it rains* is an incomplete thought. *If it rains, my paper umbrella won't protect me* is a complete thought.)

» **End mark:** The end mark may be a period, question mark, or exclamation point.

Just three requirements. That should be easy, don't you think? Luckily, determining whether a sentence is complete is usually simple. Occasionally, applying the rules can be complicated. In the following sections I take you through each rule, one at a time, so you can master every step.

Making a Match between Subjects and Verbs

You don't need a dating app to match these two elements of a sentence. First, zero in on the *verb*, the word or words expressing action or state of being. (Chapter 3 explains how to find verbs.) Next, look for the *subject*, who or what is doing the action, or exists in the state of being. (Chapter 6 tells you more about subjects.) Now, check to see that the subject and verb make sense together. Here are some proper subject–verb pairs, with the subject in italics and the verb underlined:

> *Odelia* <u>has been singing</u>
>
> the *kitten* <u>is meowing</u>
>
> that *car* <u>has gone</u>
>
> my *poodle* <u>had bitten</u>

Now examine some mismatches:

> Odelia singing
>
> kitten meowing
>
> car gone
>
> poodle bitten

Take a close look at the first two examples in each list. A verb form ending with *ing* appears, and the matching pairs have helping verbs (*has been, is*). The mismatches don't. A verb with *ing* tacked on can't function as a verb all by itself.

Now, reread the last two examples in each list. The matching pairs have helpers (*has, had*), and the mismatches don't. The mismatches — *gone, bitten* — are *irregular past participles*. They can't function as the verb in a sentence unless they have helping verbs attached. (See Chapter 6 for a list of irregular past participles.)

If you can find a verb but no matching subject, the sentence may still be complete. If the sentence gives a command (*Go home!*) the subject is always *you*, although the word *you* doesn't appear. Instead, it's understood that *you* are the person who is supposed to do whatever the commanding verb says.

TIP

In a text, you may skip the subject if you're sure that the meaning is clear without one. If I text *going home?* to you, you can easily figure out that I'm asking about your movements unless earlier texts have been discussing someone else's travel plans. (Turn to Chapter 13 for a full discussion of grammar and texting.)

Other verb forms appear without subjects because the word isn't functioning as a verb. Instead, it's acting as a description. For example, *poodle bitten* doesn't work as a subject-verb pair, but it's fine in this sentence: "The poodle, bitten in a fight with the cat, was rushed to the vet." The subject-verb pair in that sentence is *poodle was rushed. Bitten in a fight with the cat* functions as a description, telling you more about the *poodle*.

WARNING

In Standard English, *be* never works alone as the verb in a sentence that doesn't issue a command. It either changes form (*am, are, was, were*) or joins with a helper (*are being, will be, has been, could be,* and so forth). Also, *be*, by itself, can never function as a helping verb. *He be writing* isn't Standard English. *He is writing* or *he will be writing* are both correct in Standard English.

YOUR TURN

Label each as M (matching subject-verb pair) or N (not a matching subject-verb pair).

Q. Arthur sneezing

A. **N.** The *ing* form of a verb needs a helping verb. *Arthur is sneezing* or *Arthur has been sneezing* are two possible corrections.

1. Gemma sleeping

2. faucet was dripping

3. song be

4. ocean liner sunk

5. toe tapping

6. doughnut dunking

7. football thrown

8. earthquake be shaking

9. ears froze

10. wind blew

Now, practice with these slightly harder questions. Identify the subject-verb pair in these sentences. If you find no matching pair, write NP for "no pair."

YOUR TURN

Q. Some sails shook in the wind. _____

A. **sails shook.**

11. Ahmed working hard all day, cleaning the house.

12. Daniela has been napping for the last hour.

13. Daniela's cat be demanding food.

(14) Feed her now!

(15) The cat broken Daniela's peaceful sleep.

(16) Ahmed run to the store for cat treats.

(17) Then, Ahmed relaxed by watching television.

(18) He gone to bed.

(19) Too soon, the alarm rang.

(20) It was time to go to work again.

Checking for Complete Thoughts

Some subject/verb pairs form a closed circle: The thought they express is complete. You want this quality in your sentences because otherwise, your reader echoes the outlaw who, with his head in the noose, said, "Don't leave me hanging!"

Some expressions are incomplete when they're statements but complete when they're questions. To illustrate my point: "Who won the game?" makes sense, but "Who won the game" doesn't.

TIP

In informal writing, you can start a sentence with *and*, *but*, *or*, and other words that continue an idea begun in the preceding sentence. Technically, the sentence is incomplete, so avoid this pattern in formal situations.

YOUR TURN

Q. If the sentence has a complete thought, write "complete." If the reader is left in suspense, write "incomplete."

Whenever the cow jumps over the moon. _____

A. **Incomplete.** Aren't you wondering, "What happens whenever the cow jumps over the moon?" The thought is not complete.

TIP

Remember, the number of words doesn't indicate completeness. The content does.

(21) The cow, who used to work for NASA until she got a starring role in a science fiction film. _____

(22) On long-term training flights, the milking machine malfunctioned. _____

(23) Why didn't the astronauts assume responsibility for milking procedures?

_____

24 For one thing, milking, which wasn't on the to-do list but should have been, increasing the comfort level of the cow assigned to the jump. _____

25 The cow protested. _____

26 She mooed. _____

27 Because she couldn't change NASA's manual. _____

28 The author of the manual, fairly well-known in the field of rocket science and having also grown up on a farm. _____

29 NASA has reached out to the cow community and promised to review milking procedures. _____

30 Applying to NASA, her mother, when only a calf. _____

31 Quitting was not a bad decision, however. _____

32 Twenty years of moon jumping is enough for any cow.

_____

33 Unless NASA comes up with a better way to combine moon jumping and milk producing, the agency will have to work without cows. _____

34 Will NASA send a flock of sheep to the moon someday? _____

35 Perhaps someday, having heard "the sheep jumped over the moon," set to the same music. _____

Setting the Tone with End Marks

When you're speaking, the listener knows you've arrived at the end of a sentence because the thought is complete, and your tone communicates that you're done. In writing, the tone part is taken care of by a period, question mark, or exclamation point. Periods are for statements, question marks are for (surprise!) questions, and exclamation points scream at the reader. In formal, Standard English, you must have one, and only one, of these marks at the end of a sentence. On social media and in texts, where rules shatter all the time, it's common to pile on a bunch of punctuation marks to show strong emotion.

According to many grammarians, including me, it's sometimes okay to end a sentence without an end mark. When you're texting, the send button separates one idea from the next. Periods aren't necessary! If you're asking a question, though, you still need a question mark so the reader can interpret your message properly.

TIP

End marks become complicated when they tangle with quotation marks. (For tips on end mark/quotation mark interactions, check out Chapter 11.)

Write the appropriate endmark in the blank provided.

YOUR TURN

Q. Did Cameron really ride to the anti-noise protest on his motorcycle _____

A. ? (question mark). You're clearly asking a question, so the question mark fits here.

36 No, he rode his motorcycle to the mathematicians' convention _____

37 You're not serious _____

38 Yes, Cameron is a true fan of triangles _____

39 Does he bring his own triangles _____

40 I'm not sure, but I heard him say that his math colleagues always bring awesome triangles _____

41 Do you think that he really means the triangles are awful _____

42 I heard him scream that everyone loves triangles because they're the best shape in the universe _____

43 Are you going also _____

44 I'd rather have dental surgery than attend a math convention _____

45 I heard Cameron declare that geometry is his passion _____

46 Are you sure that Cameron likes only triangles ____

47 I always thought that he was fond of rectangles, too _____

48 Who in the world wants an "I love math" T-shirt _____

49 I can't believe that Cameron actually bought one _____

50 Will he give me his old "I love grammar" hat _____

Proper Sentence or Not? That Is the Question

If you've plowed your way through this entire chapter, you've practiced each sentence skill separately. But to write well, you have to do everything at once — create subject/verb pairs, finish a thought, and place the appropriate endmark. Take a test drive with the questions in this section.

Analyze each sentence and label it as follows:

» **Fragment:** If the sentence lacks a subject-verb pair or a complete thought, it's a fragment.

» **Missing endmark:** If the sentence has no endmark, choose this label.

» **Correct:** If all is well, use this label.

Q. Though the computer crashes only on Friday afternoons after the tech workers have left for the weekend.

A. **Fragment.** The statement has no complete thought. Possible correction: Omit *Though* and begin the sentence with *The.*

51 Bill's holiday concert, occurring early in October, honors the longstanding tradition of his hometown and the great Elvis Presley.

_____

52 The holiday, which is called Hound Dog Day in honor of a wonderful dog breed.

_____

53 Tradition calls for blue suede shoes.

_____

54 Having brushed the shoes carefully with a suede brush, which can be bought in any shoe store.

_____

55 The citizens lead their dogs to the town square, where Heartbreak Hotel is located.

_____

56 "Look for the ghost of Elvis," the hotel clerk tells every guest

_____

57 Elvis, ghost or not, apparently does not attend the Hound Dog Day festivities.

_____

58 Why should a ghost attend Bill's festival

_____

(59) Why do you think he's there?

_____

(60) I should have known the tourists would wear blue suede shoes.

_____

(61) Personally, I prefer green sandals

_____

(62) Don't step on them!

_____

(63) Bill told every tourist the same thing, "Stay off of my shoes!"

_____

(64) While talking about shoes, Bill, who was also creating a playlist for the Hound Dog Concert.

_____

(65) The first song is "All Shook Up."

_____

Calling All Overachievers: Extra Practice with Complete Sentences

I can't let you go without pitching one more curveball at you. Read this letter introducing a new employee to customers. Some sentences are complete and correct. Others have problems — no matching subject-verb pair, incomplete thought, or missing end mark. Label each "Complete" or "Incomplete."

To Our Valued Customers:

[1]Announcing that Abner Grey is our new Director of Customer Satisfaction.

[2]Abner brings a wealth of experience to our company. [3]He served as Assistant Vice President of marketing for Antarctic Icebergs, Inc. until last year [4]His first task, to introduce himself to every customer. [5]He try to find out what works and what must be improved. [6]Expect a phone call or a personal visit from Abner soon! [7]Recognizing that our previous director did not always meet your needs because she was distracted by lawsuits, prison, and so forth, we have told Abner to work at least 90 hours per week. [8]No more stealing from customer accounts either! [9]Abner is honest. [10]Rest assured that this Director of Customer Satisfaction will never see the inside of a jail cell,

Sincerely,

Victoria Copple

CEO of Copple Industries

Answers to Complete Sentences Questions

Following are the answers to the practice questions in this chapter.

1. **N.** The *ing* form of the verb *sleep* requires a helper to pair with *Gemma*. Possible corrections include *Gemma was sleeping*, *Gemma will be sleeping*, and *Gemma has been sleeping*.

2. **M.** Here, the *ing* form (*dripping*) has a helping verb (*was*).

3. **N.** In Standard English, *be* never stands alone as a verb.

4. **N.** *Sunk* is an irregular past participle and needs a helping verb such as *has*, *have*, or *had* in order to function as a verb.

5. **N.** The *ing* form of the verb *tap* requires a helper to pair with *toe*. Possible corrections include *toe was tapping*, *toe will be tapping*, and *toe has been tapping*.

6. **N.** The *ing* form of the verb *dunk* requires a helper such as *was*, *has been*, *had*, or *will be* to pair with *doughnut*.

7. **N.** *Thrown* is an irregular past participle and needs a helping verb such as *has*, *have*, or *had* in order to pair with the subject *football*.

8. **N.** *Be*, when it's alone, never functions as a helping verb in Standard English. Some possible corrections are *earthquake is shaking*, *earthquake has been shaking*, or *earthquake will be shaking*.

9. **M.** The verb *froze* is the simple past tense form of *freeze*. It pairs well with the subject *ears*.

10. **M.** The verb *blew* is the simple past tense form of *blow* and pairs well with the subject, *wind*.

11. **NP.** In this sentence, you see two *ing* forms, *working* and *cleaning*, but without helpers, they can't pair with the subject, *Ahmed*.

12. **Daniela has been napping.** Do you notice that the *ing* form of the verb *nap* has helping verbs, *has been*? *Has been napping* pairs well with the subject, *Daniela*.

13. **NP.** *Be demanding* isn't Standard English. Change it to *is demanding* and you have a good match for the subject, *cat*.

14. **[you understood] Feed.** This sentence gives a command (*Feed*) to *you*, although *you* doesn't appear in the sentence. It's understood.

15. **NP.** *Cat broken* isn't a proper subject-verb pair. Change it to *cat broke* or *cat has broken* or something similar.

16. **NP.** The subject, *Ahmed*, can pair with *has run*, *is running*, *ran*, and other forms, but not with *run* alone.

17. **Ahmed relaxed.** Here the subject, *Ahmed*, pairs well with *relaxed*, the verb.

18. **NP.** The irregular past participle *gone* needs a helping verb. *He has gone* is correct in Standard English, but *he gone* is not.

19. **alarm rang.** The subject *alarm* pairs perfectly with the verb, *rang*.

(20) **It was.** Did you choose *to go* or *to work?* A verb form with *to* in front never functions as a verb. In this sentence these phrases are descriptions, telling more about *time.*

(21) **Incomplete.** In this one, you have a subject *(cow)* and a description of the subject *(who used to work for NASA until she got a starring role in a science fiction film).* You're waiting to hear what the cow did — quit? write a memoir? donate her spacesuit to a museum? Because the sentence leaves you wondering, it's an incomplete thought.

(22) **Complete.** The sentence tells you everything you need to know, so it's complete.

(23) **Complete.** The question makes sense, so the sentence is complete.

(24) **Incomplete.** The statement gives you an idea — *milking* — and some descriptions, but it never delivers a complete thought about milking.

(25) **Complete.** This sentence is short, but you have everything you need to know about what the *cow* did. She *protested.*

(26) **Complete.** This sentence is even shorter than the one in the preceding question, but it still delivers its complete message.

(27) **Incomplete.** The word *because* introduces a reason, but the sentence doesn't state what situation requires a reason. The reader is left with questions: Did she quit because she could change the manual? Did she write her own manual because she couldn't change NASA's manual? The sentence doesn't supply all the needed information.

(28) **Incomplete.** This one piles on descriptions of the author. However, it never delivers the punch line. What's *the author* doing? Or, what state of being is *the author* in? The sentence doesn't tell you, so it's incomplete.

(29) **Complete.** You know what NASA is doing, so this sentence is complete.

(30) **Incomplete.** What did the mama cow do when she was only a calf? The sentence doesn't actually say, so it's incomplete.

(31) **Complete.** This sentence makes a complete and forceful statement about quitting.

(32) **Complete.** All you need to know about moon jumping (that it's enough for any cow) is in the sentence.

(33) **Complete.** This sentence contains a complete statement about NASA.

(34) **Complete.** This question makes sense as is. You may wonder what NASA will do, but you won't wonder what's being asked here because the question — and the sentence — is complete.

(35) **Incomplete.** The statement contains several descriptions but no complete thought.

(36) **. (period).** Because this sentence makes a statement, a period is the appropriate end mark.

(37) **! (exclamation point).** These words may also form a question or a statement, but an exclamation point is certainly appropriate because the speaker may be expressing amazement.

(38) **. (period).** Another statement, another period.

(39) **? (question mark).** The *does* in this sentence signals a question, so you need a question mark.

(40) **. (period).** The period is the end mark for this statement.

(41) **? (question mark).** Here, the question mark signals a request for information.

(42) **. (period).** This statement calls for a period.

(43) **? (question mark).** This sentence requests information, so place the question mark at the end.

(44) **! (exclamation point).** A period would do fine here, but an exclamation point adds extra emphasis.

(45) **. (period).** This statement needs a period as an end mark.

(46) **? (question mark).** The sentence requests information, so a question mark is the end mark you want.

(47) **. (period).** I've chosen a period, but if you're bursting with emotion, opt for the exclamation point instead.

(48) **? (question mark).** I see this one as a true inquiry, but you can also interpret it as a scream of disbelief, in which case an exclamation point works well.

(49) **! (exclamation point).** I hear this one as a strong blast of surprise, suitable for an exclamation point. If you selected a period, though, count yourself correct.

(50) **? (question mark).** If you're asking for information, you need a question mark.

(51) **Correct.** This one has everything: subject-verb pair *(concert, honors)*, complete thought, and an end mark. One description *(occurring early in October)* is properly tucked into the sentence near the word it describes *(concert)*.

(52) **Fragment.** The sentence is incorrect because it gives you a subject *(the holiday)* and a long description *(which is called Hound Dog Day in honor of a wonderful dog breed)* but doesn't pair any verb with *holiday*. Several corrections are possible. Here's one: Drop the word *which* and leave the rest as it is. Problem solved!

(53) **Correct.** You have a subject-verb pair *(tradition, calls)*, a complete thought, and an end mark. No problems here!

(54) **Fragment.** This sentence has no subject. No one is doing the brushing or the buying. One possible correction: Having brushed the shoes carefully with a suede brush, which can be bought in any shoe store, Bill proudly displayed his feet.

(55) **Correct.** This sentence expresses a complete thought, and it has two proper subject-verb pairs *(citizens lead, Heartbreak Hotel is located)*. The statement ends with a period. All correct!

(56) **Missing end mark.** Take a close look at the end of the sentence. There's no punctuation! Nor is this a text in which the "send" button can conclude a thought. A period should follow *guest*.

(57) **Correct.** Here you've got everything you need: a complete thought, a subject-verb pair *(Elvis does not attend)*, and an end mark (a period).

(58) **Missing end mark.** The sentence is incorrect because it has no end mark. It needs a question mark.

(59) **Correct.** This one is a proper question, with two subject-verb pairs *(you do think, he's* — short for *he is)*, a complete thought, and a question mark.

(60) **Correct.** This sentence is a complete thought, with two matching subject-verb pairs *(I should have known, tourists would wear)*, and an end mark.

(61) **Missing endmark.** You need a period to conclude this statement.

(62) **Correct.** This sentence gives a command. The subject is *you*, even though *you* doesn't appear in the sentence.

(63) **Correct.** The sentence has two parts. In the first portion, the matching subject-verb pair is *Bill told*. The second has a command *(Stay)* with the implied subject, *you*.

(64) **Fragment.** This sentence centers on *Bill*, and it begins with a description of his action (talking about shoes). Then you see *who*, with more information attached *(also creating a playlist)*. The main idea, though, is missing. The thought is incomplete, so this is a fragment.

(65) **Correct.** The statement is complete and ends with a period. The subject-verb pair *(song is)* matches. No problems here!

Answers to "Overachievers Questions"

(1) **Incomplete.** This sentence lacks a subject/verb pair. To make the sentence correct, drop *Announcing that* or add *I am* to the beginning of the sentence.

(2) **Complete.** This sentence has a matching subject-verb pair *(Abner brings)*, a complete thought, and an end mark.

(3) **Incomplete.** The sentence needs an end mark (a period).

(4) **Incomplete.** Nothing completes the thought begun by *His first task.*

(5) **Incomplete.** *He try* is not a matching subject-verb pair in Standard English. Change it to *He will try*, and the sentence becomes complete.

(6) **Complete.** The subject, *you*, doesn't appear, but the reader understands that *you* is implied by the command *expect*.

(7) **Complete.** This sentence begins with a verb form, *recognizing*, that acts as a description of the subject, *we. We* pairs with the verb *have told*. The thought is complete, and an end mark is present.

(8) **Incomplete**. The sentence lacks a subject-verb pair.

(9) **Complete.** This short sentence has everything it needs: a subject-verb pair *(Abner is)*, a complete thought, and an end mark.

(10) **Incomplete.** Did you notice that the sentence ends with a comma? A comma doesn't function as an end mark, so this one is incomplete.

3

Perfecting Punctuation and Capitalization

Chapter 9

Catching Up on Apostrophes, Hyphens, and Dashes

The expression "little things mean a lot" applies to the punctuation marks in this chapter. They're small, but they're packed with meaning. Apostrophes are raised hooks ('). They show possession and shorten words. Hyphens are tiny horizontal lines that divide some words and weld others together. Dashes are also horizontal lines. A short dash is longer than a hyphen, and a long dash (you'll never guess!) is even longer. A short dash may show a date range or a connection. A long dash signals a break in meaning. In this chapter, you practice placing these punctuation marks in their proper spots.

Snagging Meaning with Apostrophes

Sometimes, it seems that apostrophes are more trouble than they're worth. They attract so many mistakes! Yet this punctuation mark is useful. An apostrophe tells you that something belongs to someone ("*Geraldine's* book") and shortens words, so you can save time when *you're* (instead of "you are") reading.

WARNING

The most common apostrophe mistake is to place one where it's not appropriate:

>> **Don't use an apostrophe to create a plural.** You have *one bow* and *two arrows,* not *two arrow's.* The no-apostrophe-for-plural rule holds true for names. I am one person named *Woods,* and members of my family are the *Woodses,* not the *Woods'.*

>> **Never place an apostrophe in a possessive pronoun.** Possession is built into the meaning of *my, your, his, hers, its, ours, theirs, whose,* and so on. No extra mark is necessary. (For more on pronouns, turn to Chapter 2.)

Showing who owns what: Possessives

An apostrophe allows you to turn the awkward phrase "the pen of my aunt" into "my aunt's pen." To show possession with apostrophes, keep these rules in mind:

>> **Singular owner:** Attach an apostrophe and the letter *s* (in that order) to a singular person, place, or thing to express possession ("*Ali's* tooth," "the *whale's* flipper").

>> **Plural owner:** Attach an apostrophe to a regular plural (one that ends in *s*) to express possession ("the *boys'* ties," "the *nurses'* contract").

>> **Irregular plural owner:** Add an apostrophe and the letter *s,* in that order, to an irregular plural (one that doesn't end in *s*) to express possession ("the *men's* shoe department").

>> **Joint ownership:** If two or more people own something jointly, add an apostrophe and an *s* (in that order) to the last listed owner ("*Abe and Lara's* sofa").

>> **Separate ownership:** If two or more people own things separately, everyone gets an apostrophe and an *s* ("*Jose's and Cedric's* pajamas").

>> **Hyphenated owner:** Attach the apostrophe and *s* to the end of a singular hyphenated word ("*father-in-law's* suitcase"). For plurals ending in *s,* attach the apostrophe only ("*three secretary-treasurers'* accounts").

>> **Time and money:** Time and money may be possessive in expressions such as *next week's test, two hours' homework, a day's pay,* and so forth. Follow the rules for singular and plural owners, as explained at the beginning of this bulleted list.

YOUR TURN

Turn the underlined word or words into the possessive form. Write your answers in the blanks provided.

Q. The style of this <u>year</u> sports car is <u>Jill</u> favorite.

A. **year's, Jill's.** Two singular "owners" — *Jill* (a person) and *year.* This time expression also takes an apostrophe.

① <u>Carol</u> classic car is entered in <u>tonight</u> show. _____

② She invested <u>three months</u> work in restoring the finish. _____

3. Jess and Marty tires, which they purchased a few years ago by combining their allowances, will be installed on her car today. _____

4. The boys allowance is far too generous, despite their sister-in-law objections. _____

5. Jill weekly paycheck is actually smaller than the brothers daily income. _____

6. The brothers donate a day pay from time to time to underfunded causes such as the Children Committee to Protect the Environment. _____

7. With the boys tires installed, the car gas mileage is improved. _____

8. Carol cares so much about her car that she borrowed Jess and Marty toothbrushes to clean the dashboard. _____

9. Now she needs her helpers maximum support as the final judging nears. _____.

10. She knows that the judge decision will be final, but just in case she has volunteered two thousand dollars worth of free gasoline to his favorite charity.

11. Carol success is unlikely because the court judgments can't be influenced by anything but the law. _____

12. Last week, for example, the judge ruled in favor of a developer, despite his mother-in-law plea for a different verdict. _____

13. Ten hours begging did no good at all. _____

14. Tomorrow the judge will rule on the car show effect on the native animals habitat. _____

15. The geese ecosystem is particularly sensitive to automotive exhaust. _____

Tightening up text: Contractions

Apostrophes shorten words by replacing one or more letters. The shortened word, or *contraction*, adds an informal, conversational tone to your writing.

The most frequently used contractions, paired with their long forms, include those in Table 9-1.

Table 9-1   Frequently Used Contractions

Long Form	Contraction	Long Form	Contraction	Long Form	Contraction
are not	aren't	I will	I'll	we are	we're
cannot	can't	I would	I'd	we have	we've
could have	could've	it is	it's	we will	we'll
could not	couldn't	she has	she's	were not	weren't
do not	don't	she is	she's	will not	won't
he has	he's	she will	she'll	would have	would've
he is	he's	should have	should've	would not	wouldn't
he will	he'll	should not	shouldn't	you are	you're
he would	he'd	they are	they're	you have	you've
I am	I'm	they have	they've	you will	you'll
I had	I'd	they will	they'll	you would	you'd

WARNING

A common mistake is to re-expand a contraction into something it was never meant to be. The contraction *should've*, for example, is short for *should have*, not *should of*. The expressions *should of, could of,* and *would of* aren't correct in Standard English.

You also can slice numbers out of your writing with apostrophes, especially in informal circumstances. This punctuation mark enables you to apply for a car loan in '27, drive the car until '33, and make the last payment to the bank in '40.

YOUR TURN

Change the underlined words into contractions. Place your answers in the blanks.

Q. Adam said that <u>he would</u> go to the store to buy nuts for his dinner party.

_____

A. he'd. This apostrophe is a real bargain. With it, you save four letters.

16 "Peanuts <u>are not</u> the best choice for tonight's dinner because of my allergies," commented Pam. _____

17 "<u>I am</u> sure that <u>you will</u> choose a better appetizer," she added. _____
_____

18 <u>You are</u> not a good host if you <u>will not</u> provide delicious food. _____

19 "Adam <u>would have</u> bought grapes, but I <u>would not</u> serve fruit before the main course," commented Pam. _____

20 "You <u>cannot</u> have a meal without fruit," countered Adam. "<u>What is</u> for dessert?"
_____ _____

21 Adam usually recommends a fancy dessert, but <u>he is</u> currently on a diet.

_____

22 Adam is planning to serve a special dessert wine, Chateau Adam <u>1999</u>, to his guests.

_____

23 He always provides wine when the class of <u>2006</u> gets together for a reunion.

_____

24 <u>We are</u> planning to attend the party, but <u>we will</u> bring our own refreshments!

_____

Lining Up Hyphens and Dashes

Hyphens and dashes float inside words, phrases, and sentences. The length of these horizontal lines determines their meaning. Hyphens are the shortest. Dashes are longer than hyphens and come in short and long lengths.

Hyphens

Hyphens can connect or separate. Here are a hyphen's main jobs:

>> **Hyphens cut words that don't fit on a line.** When you're writing on a computer, tablet, or phone, the device usually moves a word that's too long to the next line or, in some cases, chops the word into pieces and inserts the hyphen automatically. If you're writing by hand, you may need to insert a hyphen if you reach the end of a line without completing a word. In that situation, break the word between syllables. Insert a hyphen at the end of a syllable and continue on the next line. _Picnic,_ for example, breaks this way: _pic- nic,_ with _pic-_ appearing at the end of the line and _nic_ on the next line.

TIP

If you're not sure what the syllables are, check the dictionary.

>> **Hyphens create compounds.** Where would the world be without _well-meaning mothers-in-law?_ The hyphens turn two words into one description _(well-meaning)_ and three words into one noun _(mothers-in-law)._

>> **Hyphens clarify numbers.** If you're writing numerals, you don't have to worry about hyphens. (Most of the time, you should be writing numerals, especially for large amounts.) If you have to express an amount in words, hyphenate all numbers from _twenty-one to ninety-nine,_ except for those that are written as one word _(thirty, forty, fifty,_ and so on). Also, hyphenate fractions that function as a description _(two-thirds full)._ Don't hyphenate a fraction used as a noun _(one third of your paycheck)._

Check the hyphens (or the lack of hyphens) in these questions. Mark each as "correct" or "incorrect."

Q. line 1: ap-

line 2: ology

A. **Incorrect.** *Apology* has four syllables: *a pol o gy.* Break the word only at the end of a syllable. In this case, your best option is write *apol- ogy.* It's not a good idea to leave one letter alone on the first line or only two letters on the second line.

25 third base coach

26 well-planned plot

27 line 1: com-

line 2: plicated

28 attorney-general

29 top-of-the-line

30 top-of-the-line car

Dashes

Before you dash off somewhere, let me explain what these punctuation marks do:

» **Long dashes insert information.** Long dashes — what printers call *em dashes* — break into a sentence. Look back at the sentence you just read. I inserted the technical term for a long dash with two long dashes. When you break into one thought with another, you may use a long dash. Often, the inserted material is a definition or explanation, but sometimes, it reflects a small change in subject. "Terry went to the museum this morning — she loves modern art — so she couldn't babysit." The information about Terry's art preferences is only slightly related to the main idea of the sentence, which is that Terry couldn't babysit.

» **Long dashes clarify lists containing commas.** If you're dealing with two expressions, each of which contains commas, a long dash can separate them and make your meaning clear. "Jill invited the vice presidents for marketing, publicity, technology, and manufacturing — Jack, Peggy, Nguyen, and John." With a comma instead of a long dash, the reader might stumble into the list of names and wonder whether those people received invitations in addition to the vice presidents. The long dash indicates that the vice presidents' names are *Jack, Peggy, Nguyen, and John.*

» **Long dashes separate general and specific information.** The long dash may take the reader from general to specific: "Ollie has assembled all the ingredients for his favorite meatloaf — mustard, ground turkey, and lollipops." In this example, the general *(ingredients)* becomes specific *(mustard, ground turkey, and lollipops)* after the dash.

The same punctuation mark can signal a move in the other direction: "Eggs, ground beef, and bread crumbs — Ollie hated all those ingredients and refused to cook with them." Now, the details (eggs, ground beef, and bread crumbs) precede the general (ingredients).

» **Long dashes show that speech has broken off.** You see this usage often in mystery novels, when a character starts to give a vital clue and then stops because a dagger has flown through the air: "LaToya shouted, 'The codebook is in the —'"

TIP

Some writers use a long dash to join two complete sentences: "I hid my portion of meatloaf in my shoe — turkey and lollipops don't go together." This usage is fine in informal writing but not the best choice for formal work.

» **Short, or *en dashes,* show a range.** The range can be distance (the Chicago–New York train) or time (1900–2010).

» **Short dashes pair equal elements.** The short dash often signals a relationship: "Are you worried about the *pitcher–catcher* coordination on that team?"

YOUR TURN

Insert long dashes (em dashes) or short dashes (en dashes) where appropriate in these sentences.

Q. Melanie a passionate defender of animals attends veterinary school.

A. **Melanie — a passionate defender of animals — attends veterinary school.** You could surround a passionate defender of animals with commas, because that expression gives you extra information about of Melanie. (For more information on commas, see Chapter 10.) Long dashes add a bit of drama.

31 While she was waiting for a bus, Melanie took out her lunch almonds, steamed broccoli, and a hard-boiled egg.

32 Suddenly, she realized that two animals to be specific a squirrel and a pigeon were staring at her.

33 The Bronx Manhattan express bus was late.

34 "Well," thought Melanie, "I'll wait for two four minutes and then leave if it doesn't show up."

35 She searched for the bus Melanie has good eyesight and thought about the squirrel and the pigeon.

36 The human animal bond is amazing.

37 Who can imagine what questions go through the mind of a squirrel where's the food supply, how's my tail doing, why's that human looking at me, or something else!

38. Xander Hicks (1802 1888) theorized that squirrels spend most of the day sleeping, not thinking.

39. Will an actual descendent of Xander Hicks Melanie prove him right or wrong?

40. Will Melanie can Melanie analyze squirrel psychology?

Calling All Overachievers: Extra Practice with Apostrophes, Hyphens, and Dashes

Marty's to-do list, shown in the following figure, needs some serious editing. Check the apostrophes, hyphens, and dashes. Some appear where they shouldn't. Delete them! Some are missing. Insert them!

Thing's to Do This Week

A. Call the painters assistant and ask him to suggest a very-deep shade of yellow, because the one we selected doesnt work with the orange curtains.

B. Check last weeks design to see whether any other color's are trending.

C. Ask the secretary—treasurer for budget approval.

D. Tell the president that the project should be completed in the winter of 2027 2028.

E. Talk to the office-workers about their' rodent problems.

F. Find out why the carpenter could'nt complete this project of our's.

G. Suggest that the carpenters' four hour lunches interfere with her work.

H. Order supplies, lumber, wallpaper, nine paint brushes, and three weeks worth of paint.

I. Write you're speech for your father-in-laws birthday.

J. Buy Ellen and Greg's tickets for the Boston—New York train.

Answers to Apostrophe, Hyphen, and Dash Questions

Did you get caught on any of the punctuation questions in this chapter? Check your answers to see how you did.

1. **Carol's, tonight's.** Carol owns the car, so you just need to attach an apostrophe and an *s* to a singular form to create a singular possessive. The second answer illustrates a time/money possessive expression.

2. **three months'.** The value of time and money can be expressed with a possessive form. Because you're talking about *months*, a plural, the apostrophe goes after the *s*.

3. **Jess and Marty's.** The sentence tells you that the boys own the tires together, so only one apostrophe is needed. It's placed after the last listed owner's name. The possessive pronoun *her*, like all possessive pronouns, has no apostrophe.

4. **boys', sister-in-law's.** The plural possessive just tacks an apostrophe onto the *s* in regular, end-in-*s* plurals. Hyphenated forms are easy, too; just attach the apostrophe and an *s* to the end.

5. **Jill's, brothers'.** The first form is singular, so you add an apostrophe and an *s*. The second form is a regular plural, so you just add the apostrophe.

6. **a day's, Children's.** The first form falls into the time/money category, and because *day* is singular, you add an apostrophe and an *s*. The second is an irregular plural (not ending in *s*), so you tack on an apostrophe and an *s*.

7. **boys', car's.** A regular plural possessive form calls for an apostrophe after the *s*. The second form is singular, so you add an apostrophe and an *s*.

8. **Jess's and Marty's.** The brothers are close, but they draw the line at shared toothbrushes. Each owns a separate brush, so each name needs an apostrophe.

TIP

If a word ends in *s* (*Jess*, for example), some writers add only an apostrophe to create a possessive. That's generally accepted in all but the most formal situations or if a reader might misunderstand the meaning. For example, my last name ends in *s*. If I make it possessive by adding only an apostrophe (*Woods'*), a reader may think that the word is a plural possessive referring to a group of people named *Wood*. When in doubt, follow the rule: add *'s* to a singular noun to make a singular possessive, even if the singular form ends in the letter *s*.

9. **helpers'.** To create a plural possessive of a word ending in *s*, just attach an apostrophe.

10. **judge's, two thousand dollars'.** The first answer is a simple, singular possessive, so an apostrophe and an *s* do the trick. The second is a time/money possessive, and *two thousand dollars* is plural, so just an apostrophe is needed.

11. **Carol's, court's.** These two words are singular, so only an apostrophe and the letter *s* are needed to make each possessive.

12. **mother-in-law's.** The apostrophe and the letter *s* follow the last word of the hyphenated term.

(13) **Ten hours'.** The apostrophe creates an expression meaning *ten hours of begging*. Because *hours* is plural, only an apostrophe is added.

(14) **car show's, animals'.** The first is a singular possessive, and the second is plural.

(15) **geese's.** The word *geese* is an irregular plural, so an apostrophe and the letter *s* are added.

(16) **aren't.** The contraction drops the letter *o* and substitutes an apostrophe.

(17) **I'm, you'll.** In the first contraction, the apostrophe replaces the letter *a*. In the second, it replaces two letters, *w* and *i*.

(18) **you're, won't.** The second contraction is irregular because you can't make an apostrophe-letter swap. Illogical though it may seem, *won't* is the contraction of *will not*.

(19) **would've, wouldn't.** The first contraction cuts two letters, and the second cuts one letter.

(20) **can't, What's.** Did you know that *cannot* is written as one word? The contraction also is one word, with an apostrophe knocking out an *n* and an *o*. The second contraction combines two sounds ('What is') into one.

(21) **he's.** This contraction drops one letter.

(22) **'99.** A date may be shortened, especially if you're out with Adam. Just be sure that the context of the sentence doesn't lead the reader to imagine a different century (2099, perhaps). This one is fairly clear, given that we're nowhere near 2099 or 1899.

(23) **'06.** Not much chance of readers misunderstanding which numbers are missing here (unless they're really old)!

(24) **We're, we'll.** The apostrophes replace the letters *a* and *wi*.

(25) **Incorrect.** The expression *third base coach* is confusing. Are you talking about the baseball coach who stands near third base (the *third-base coach*) or the third person to hold that position this season (*the third base-coach*). Without a hyphen, your reader may not understand your meaning.

(26) **Correct.** The two words, *well* and *planned*, function as one description, so a hyphen should link them. If the same two words appear after the word they refer to (*plot*), the grammar changes. If you write, "The plot was well planned," *well* describes *planned*, which is part of the verb *was planned*. No hyphen is needed.

(27) **Correct.** *Complicated* breaks into four syllables: *com pli ca ted*. The hyphen properly separates the first syllable from the next three.

(28) **Correct.** This title, like many others, is hyphenated. If you're not sure about a particular title, check your dictionary.

(29) **Incorrect.** Creating one description such as *top-of-the-line* is correct only when you're describing something. In this expression, you're not.

(30) **Correct.** Now *top-of-the-line* does describe something *(car)*.

(31) **While she was waiting for a bus, Melanie took out her lunch — almonds, steamed broccoli, and a hard-boiled egg.** The long dash separates a general term, *lunch*, from the components of lunch *(almonds, steamed broccoli, and a hard-boiled egg)*. Parentheses could replace the long dash, as it is in the preceding explanation sentence. It can't be replaced by a comma, though, because the commas that separate each item in Melanie's lunch would seem to be part of a series starting with *lunch*.

(32) **Suddenly, she realized that two animals — to be specific, a squirrel and a pigeon — were staring at her.** As in the previous question, long dashes are better than simple commas here, because the expression *to be specific, a squirrel and a pigeon* already has a comma. Parentheses, however, would also be fine in this sentence.

(33) **The Bronx–Manhattan express bus was late.** The short dash shows a range. The bus travels between the *Bronx* and *Manhattan*.

(34) **"Well," thought Melanie, "I'll wait for two–four minutes and then leave if it doesn't show up."** The short dash in this sentence shows a range of time.

(35) **She searched for the bus — Melanie has good eyesight — and thought about the squirrel and the pigeon.** Here the comment about Melanie's eyesight interrupts the statement *She searched for the bus and thought about the squirrel and the pigeon.* Two long dashes mark the interruption.

(36) **The human–animal bond is amazing.** A short dash shows a relationship between two categories, *human* and *animal*.

(37) **Who can imagine what questions go through the mind of a squirrel — where's the food supply, how's my tail doing, why's that human looking at me, or something else!** The long dash signals the shift from general *(questions)* to specific (the content of those questions).

(38) **Xander Hicksom (1802–1888) theorized that squirrels spend most of the day sleeping, not thinking.** The short dash connects two dates here, the years of birth and death.

(39) **Will an actual descendent of Xander Hicks — Melanie — prove him right or wrong?** Simple commas would also do the job here, much less dramatically.

(40) **Will Melanie — can Melanie — analyze squirrel psychology?** The long dashes emphasize the real question, which is whether Melanie *can* figure out what a squirrel thinks. The dash gives the first question, *will she*, less importance.

Answers to "Overachievers Questions"

***Things** to Do This Week*

A. Call the **painter's** assistant and ask him to suggest a **very deep** shade of yellow, because the one we selected **doesn't** work with the orange curtains.

B. Check last **week's** design magazine to see whether any other **colors** are trending.

C. Ask the **secretary-treasurer** for budget approval.

D. Tell the president that the project should be completed in the winter of **2027– 2028**.

E. Talk to the **office workers** about **their** rodent problems.

F. Find out why the carpenter **couldn't** complete this project of **ours**.

G. Suggest that the **carpenter's four-hour** lunches interfere with her work.

H. Order **supplies** — lumber, wallpaper, nine paint brushes, and **three weeks'** worth of paint.

I. Write **your** speech for your **father-in-law's** birthday.

J. Buy **Ellen's** and Greg's tickets for the **Boston–New York** train.

(1) **Things** Plural words that aren't possessive need no apostrophes, so remove the apostrophe from *Things*.

(2) **painter's** The apostrophe shows that the assistant "belongs" to (works for) *the painter*.

(3) **very deep** The first word (*very*) describes the second (*deep*), so the phrase isn't hyphenated.

(4) **doesn't** Be sure to place the apostrophe in the right spot in this contraction of *does not*.

(5) **week's** This is a possessive time expression. The word *week* is singular, so you add an apostrophe and an *s*.

(6) **colors** No apostrophe is needed in this plural.

(7) **secretary-treasurer** One person holds two jobs, so the title is hyphenated.

8) **2027–2028** Use a short dash for a time range.

9) **office workers** The main word here is *workers*. *Office* is a description telling what kind of *workers*. No hyphen is needed.

10) **their** No apostrophe should appear in a possessive pronoun.

11) **couldn't** An apostrophe takes the place of the letter *o* in this contraction of *could not*.

12) **ours** No apostrophe should appear in a possessive pronoun.

13) **carpenter's** This singular possessive form adds an *s* and an apostrophe to *carpenter*.

14) **four-hour** In this sentence, two words combine, with the help of a hyphen, to make one description.

15) **supplies** — A long dash introduces this list.

16) **three weeks'** The plural time possessive form is appropriate here.

17) **your** No apostrophe should appear in a possessive pronoun. (*You're* is a contraction of "you are.")

18) **father-in-law's** Add an apostrophe to the end of this hyphenated word to show possession.

19) **Ellen's and Greg's** They have separate tickets, so they have separate apostrophes.

20) **Boston–New York** The short dash shows a connection between places.

IN THIS CHAPTER

» **Separating items in a list with punctuation**

» **Placing commas in combined sentences**

» **Changing the meaning of descriptions with commas**

» **Inserting commas when interrupting and introducing sentences**

» **Using commas to indicate direct address**

» **Inserting commas into dates**

Chapter **10**

Pausing to Consider the Comma

When you're speaking, you separate ideas with bits of silence: sometimes a long pause (a period, written as a dot) and sometimes a short pause (a comma, written as a curved hook extending below the line). Commas nearly always have an important effect on the meaning of a sentence. They can indicate relationships between items or people, keep words and numbers from running together, and sometimes change the meaning of a sentence. In this chapter, you practice inserting and deleting commas so that your writing is always clear and accurate.

Keeping Lists in Order with Commas

When you're writing a list that's not in a sentence, line breaks signal when one item in a list ends and another begins. Commas do the same thing in sentences. For example, suppose Professor DuBois wants you to do the following:

» Go online.

» Locate the origin of the handheld meat patty.

» Write a paper about hamburger history.

Inserted into a sentence, the line breaks in the preceding list turn into commas:

> Professor DuBois wants you to go online, locate the origin of the handheld meat patty, and write a paper about hamburger history.

Notice that a comma doesn't precede the first item and that the last two items are separated by *and*, which has a comma in front of it. The last comma is a style issue, not a grammatical necessity. In Standard American English, most people insert a comma before the *and* or whatever word joins the last two items of the list. In Britain, most writers don't. My advice is to do what you wish, so long as you always insert a comma when someone might misunderstand the meaning. For example, suppose you write, "I wish to thank my parents, Abe Lincoln and Jane Austen." If your readers lack knowledge of history and literature, they may think that your parents are Abe and Jane. A comma before *and* indicates that the writer is thanking four people — two parents, a president, and a novelist.

TIP

If the list is very long (and *long* is a judgment call), it may be preceded by a colon (one dot atop another). The words before the colon should be a complete thought. Here's an example:

> Ms. Meanie required the following for every homework assignment: green ink, a plastic cover, at least two illustrations, a minimum of three quotations, and a list of sources.

TIP

If any item in a list has a comma *within* it, you can insert a semicolon (a dot atop a comma) to separate the list items:

> Because he has only one extra ticket to the magic show, Daniel will invite Peter McKinney, the mayor; Agnes Hutton; or Jeannie Battle, magic expert.

Or, you can make a bulleted list:

> Because he has only one extra ticket to the magic show, Daniel will invite one of these people:

» Peter McKinney, the mayor

» Agnes Hutton

» Jeannie Battle, magic expert

YOUR TURN In this exercise, supply the beginning of a sentence and a list. Insert the list into the sentence and punctuate it properly. Note: I use numbers to separate items on the list. Don't use numbers in your answer sentence.

Q. List of things to buy at the pharmacy: **(1)** toenail clippers **(2)** green shoe polish **(3)** earwax remover

Getting ready for his big date, Rob went to the pharmacy to buy

A. **Getting ready for his big date, Rob went to the pharmacy to buy toenail clippers, green shoe polish, and earwax remover.** You have three items and two commas; no comma is needed before the first item on the list.

1 Supermarket shopping list: **(1)** pitted dates **(2)** chocolate-covered mushrooms **(3)** anchovies **(4)** pickles

Rob planned to serve a tasteful selection of

_____

_____

2 Guests: **(1)** Helen Ogee, tech billionaire **(2)** Natasha Smith, Olympic medalist **(3)** Blair Berry, auto dealer **(4)** Hannah Bridge, punctuation expert **(5)** Jane Fine, veterinarian

Rob's guest list is heavily tilted toward women he would like to date:

_____

_____

3 Activities: **(1)** juggling cabbages **(2)** pinning a tail on the donkey **(3)** playing double solitaire

After everyone arrives, Rob plans an evening of

_____

_____

4 Goals: **(1)** get three phone numbers **(2)** arrange at least one future date **(3)** avoid a visit from the police

Rob will consider his party a success if he can

_____

_____

5 Results: **(1)** the police arrived at 10:00, 11:00, and 11:30 p.m. **(2)** no one gave out any phone numbers **(3)** everyone thought the host's name was Bob

Rob didn't meet his goals:

_____

_____

Placing Commas in Combined Sentences

Certain words — *and*, *but*, *or*, *nor*, and *for* — are like officials who perform weddings. They link two equals. (Always a good idea in a marriage, don't you think?) These powerful words are *conjunctions*. Forget the grammar term! Just remember to place a comma before the conjunction when you're combining two complete sentences. Here are some examples:

> The wedding cake was pink, and the bride's nose was purple.

> A wedding in the middle of an ice rink is festive, but the air is chilly.

> The bride's nose began to run, for she had forgotten her heated veil.

You get the idea. A complete sentence and a comma precede each conjunction. Another complete sentence follows the conjunction. (See Chapter 8 for more information on complete sentences.)

WARNING

You don't need a comma when one of these conjunctions links anything other than a complete sentence (say, two descriptions).

YOUR TURN

Time to scatter commas around these sentences, starting with this example. If no comma is needed, write "no comma" in the margin.

Q. The groom skated to the center of the rink and waited for his shivering bride.

A. **No comma.** The words in front of the conjunction (*The groom skated to the center of the rink*) are a complete sentence, but the words after the conjunction (*waited for his shivering bride*) aren't. Because the conjunction *and* links two verbs (*skated* and *waited*), as well as words that describe those verbs, no comma is called for.

6 The best man held onto the railing for he was afraid of slipping on the ice.

7 The beautiful flowers and the colorful spotlights impressed the guests.

8 One of the bridesmaids whispered that her own wedding would be on a beach or in a tropical forest.

9 The guests sipped hot chocolate but they were still cold.

10 The ice-dancing during the reception made them sweat and then the temperature seemed fine.

11 Do you know who is in charge of the gifts or who is paying the orchestra?

12 I'd like to swipe a present for my blender is broken.

13 I don't need an icemaker but I'll take one anyway.

14 The happy couple drove away in a sled and never came back.

Punctuating Descriptions

Life would be much simpler for the comma-inserter if nobody ever described anything. However, descriptions are a part of life, so you need to know these punctuation rules:

>> **For descriptions that come before the word being described, place commas only when you have a list of two or more descriptions of the same type and importance.** You can tell when two or more descriptions are equally important; they can be written in a different order without changing the meaning of the sentence. For example, "the *tan, dusty* dictionary" and "the *dusty, tan* dictionary" have the same meaning, so you need a comma between the descriptions. However, "*two dusty* dictionaries" is different. One description is a number, and one is a condition. You can't reverse them: "*dusty two* dictionaries" doesn't work in Standard English. Because the descriptions aren't the same type, you don't insert commas.

>> **If the description *follows* the word being described, you must determine how important the information is before you decide whether or not to place commas around it.** If a description supplies essential, identifying material, don't set it apart with commas. If the description falls into the "nice to know, but I didn't really need it" (extra) category, surround it with commas. For example, in the sentence "The dictionary *on the table* is dusty," the description in italics is necessary because it tells which dictionary is dusty. In the sentence "Charlie's dictionary, *which is on the table,* is dusty," the description in italics is set off by commas because you already know *Charlie's dictionary* is the one being discussed. The part about the table is extra information.

Think of the commas surrounding a description as little handles that allow you to lift the description out of the sentence. If the remaining words are clear and complete, the commas are correct. If the meaning is unclear, remove the commas.

>> **When descriptions containing verb forms introduce a sentence, they are always set off from the rest of the sentence by commas.** An example: Sighing into his handkerchief, Charlie looked for a dust cloth. The description, *sighing into his handkerchief,* has a verb form (*sighing*) and thus is set off by a comma from the rest of the sentence.

YOUR TURN Got the idea? Now try your comma skills on the following sentences. If the italicized words need to be set off, add the commas. If no commas are called for, write "correct" in the margin. Note: Some sentences present you with more than one group of italicized words, separated by a nonitalicized word or words. Treat each group of italicized words as a separate task.

Q. Henry took the ruffled striped shirt to the closest dry cleaner Fleur and Sons.

A. **Henry took the ruffled, striped shirt to the closest dry cleaner, Fleur and Sons.** The first two descriptions precede the word being described (*shirt*), and either description can come first. For these reasons, a comma is needed between them. The second description names the closest dry cleaner. In grammar terms, it's an appositive. Don't worry about the name. Focus on its effect on the sentence. Fleur and Sons follows what's being described (*the closest dry cleaner*). Because there can only be one closest dry cleaner, the name is extra, not essential identifying information, and it's set off by commas.

(15) *Oscar's favorite* food *which he cooks every Saturday night* is hot dogs.

(16) The place *where he feels most comfortable during the cooking process* is next to his *huge brick* barbecue.

(17) Oscar stores *his wheat* buns in a *large plastic* tub *that used to belong to his grandpa.*

(18) One of the horses *that lives in Oscar's barn* often sniffs around *Oscar's lucky* horseshoe *which Oscar found while playing tag.*

(19) Oscar rode *his three favorite* horses in a race *honoring the Barbecue King and Queen.*

(20) Oscar *who is an animal lover* will never sell one of his horses.

(21) *Being sentimental* Oscar dedicated a song to the horse *that was born on his birthday.*

(22) The jockeys *who were trying to prepare for the big race* became annoyed by Oscar's song, but the jockeys *who had already raced* didn't mind Oscar's music.

(23) The *deep horrible* secret is that Oscar can't stay in tune *when he sings.*

(24) His guitar *a Gibson* is also missing *two important* strings.

Inserting Extras with Commas: Introductions and Interruptions

An introductory expression makes a comment on the rest of the sentence or adds a bit of extra information. An introductory statement is usually separated from the rest of the sentence by a comma. Check out the italicized portion of each of these sentences for examples of introductory expressions:

Creeping through the tunnel, Brad thought about potential book deals.

No, Brad wasn't worried that the bank guards would discover the robbery.

While he was cracking the safe, he called his agent.

You don't need commas for short introductory expressions unless you want to emphasize them. For example, "In the morning Brad drank 12 cups of coffee" needs no comma to separate *In the morning* from the rest of the sentence. (If you want to make a big deal out of the time of day, you can insert a comma after *morning.*)

Interrupters show up inside — not in front of — a sentence. They function the same way as introductory expressions. They comment on or otherwise interrupt the main idea of the sentence. Therefore, they are set off by commas. Check out these italicized interrupters:

Ghada, *carrying the loot,* thought that a Hollywood director should make a film about her adventures.

There was no guarantee, *of course,* that Ghada would make it out alive.

Up for some practice? Insert commas where needed and resist the temptation to insert them where they're not required in these sentences.

Q. Tired after a long day delivering pizza Elsie was in no mood for fireworks.

A. **Tired after a long day delivering pizza, Elsie was in no mood for fireworks.** The comma sets off the introductory expression, Tired after a long day delivering pizza. Notice how that information applies to Elsie? She's the subject of the sentence.

25 In desperate need of a pizza fix Brad turned to his cellphone.

26 Ghada on the other hand wasn't hungry.

27 Yes pizza was an excellent idea.

28 The toppings by the way proved to be a problem.

29 Finally Brad selected pepperoni as guards searched for him.

30 Ghada wondered how Brad given his low-fat diet could consider pepperoni.

31 Frozen with indecision Brad decided to call the pizzeria to request the cheapest pie.

32 Ghada on a tight budget wanted to redeem her coupons.

33 To demand fast delivery was Brad's priority.

34 Lighting a match and holding it in his trembling hand Brad realized that time was almost up.

35 Worrying about toppings had used up too many minutes.

36 Well the robbers wasted too much time.

37 Of course the guards caught Brad and Ghada.

38 As the guards chomped on the pepperoni pizza Brad had ordered he and Ghada slipped away.

39 Brad and Ghada celebrated their escape I believe by ordering another pizza.

40 Although she prefers pineapple Ghada ate all the pepperoni.

Directly Addressing the Listener or Reader

A "direct address" situation occurs when you write or speak directly to a person, and the person's name or title appears in the sentence. Direct-address expressions should be separated from everything else in the sentence. Commas do the job if the direct address appears at the beginning or in the middle of a sentence. If the direct address is at the end of the sentence, place a comma before it and the proper end mark (a period, question mark, or exclamation point) after it. Take a look at these examples. *Travis* is being addressed:

> Travis, you can have the tennis court at 10 a.m.
>
> When you hit the ball, Travis, avoid using too much force.
>
> Don't cheat, Travis!

The most common direct-address mistake is to send one comma to do a two-comma job. In the second example, two commas surround *Travis*.

Can you insert commas to highlight the direct-address name in these sentences?

YOUR TURN

Q. Listen Champ I think you need to get a new pair of boxing gloves.

A. **Listen, Champ, I think you need to get a new pair of boxing gloves.** In this example, you're talking to *Champ*, a title that's substituting for the actual name. Direct-address expressions don't have to be proper names, though they frequently are.

41 Ladies and Gentlemen I present the Fifth Annual Elbox Championships.

42 I know Mort that you are an undefeated Elbox competitor. Would you tell our audience about the sport?

43 Elboxing is about 5,000 years old Chester. It originated in ancient Egypt.

44 Really? Man I can't believe you knew that!

45 Yes Chester the sport grew out of the natural movement of the elbow when someone tried to cut ahead in line by "elbowing."

46 Excuse me a moment. The reigning champion has decided to pay us a visit. Miss William could you tell us how you feel about the upcoming match?

47 Certainly Sir. I am confident that my new training routine will pay off.

48 Mort I can't wait to see the match.

Punctuating Dates

When are you reading this book? On 12 September 2026 or on September 12, 2026? Your answer depends on style, and to some extent, on your reader. In recent years, the rules for placing commas in dates have changed quite a bit. To make things more complicated, standard American English punctuation sometimes differs from the format used in other parts of the English-speaking world. Here are the basics of the American system, with international variations noted:

» If the date is alone on a line (say, at the top of a letter), insert a comma after the day of the month: September 12, 2026. Also correct for a date appearing on a separate line, and popular abroad, is a comma-free form: 12 September 2026. A correct but informal version slashes out the comma: 9/21/26 (in the U.S., where the month precedes the day), 21/9/26 (outside the U.S., where the month follows the day).

» If the date appears inside a sentence, a comma traditionally follows the year if the sentence continues: "Mark started school on September 12, 2022, and graduated four years later." Also correct but not traditional: "Mark started school on 12 September 2022 and graduated four years later."

» If no year appears, no comma appears: "Mark started his summer vacation on June 12th."

» In a month-year situation, traditionalists insert a comma between the two (June, 2026). More modern writers omit the comma (June 2026).

TIP

With several possible correct formats, what should you do? Check with the Authority Figure who will read your work, or take a look at how other writers producing the same sort of material handle dates.

YOUR TURN

Which of these is correct? Choose one, more than one, or none. To help you decide, I give you the context.

Q. Alone on a line

  I.   March 9 2026

  II. March, 9, 2026

  III. March 9, 2026

A. III. A comma should separate the day and the year but not the month and the day.

49 at the end of a sentence

  I.   14 May 2027.

  II. 2027, May 14.

  III. May 14th.

50 in the middle of a sentence

  I.   20 July 1940

  II. July 20, 1940,

  III. July, 20, 1940

51 alone on a line

  I.   October 16, 1999

  II. 10/16/99

  III. 16 October 1999

52 in the middle of a sentence

  I.   June 20, 1901,

  II. June, 1901,

  III. 1901 June

53 in the middle of a sentence

 I. 1920 June

 II. June 1920

 III. June, 1920,

Calling All Overachievers: Extra Practice with Commas

YOUR TURN The following figure shows an employee self-evaluation with some serious problems, a few of which concern commas. (The rest deal with the truly bad idea of being honest with your boss.) Forget about the content errors and concentrate on commas. Insert them where they are needed and delete them where they should not appear.

Annual Self-Evaluation — October 1, 2027

(1) Well, Ms. **(2) Kwame,** that time of year has arrived again. **(3) I,** must think about my strengths and weaknesses as an **(4) employee,** of NewGramm International. First and **(5) foremost,** let me say that I love working for NewGramm. When I applied for the **(6) job,** I never dreamed how much fun I would have taking **(7) two** long lunches a day. Sneaking out the back **(8) door,** is not my idea of fun. Because no one ever watches what I am doing at **(9) NewGramm,** I can leave by the front door without worrying.

(10) Also, **(11) Ms. Kwame,** I confess that I do almost no work at all. Upon transferring to the office in **(12) Idaho,** I immediately claimed a privilege given only to the most **(13) experienced,** most **(14) skilled,** employees and started to take **(15) two** extra weeks of vacation. I have only one more thing to say. May I have a raise?

Answers to Comma Questions

Check your answers to this chapter's problems against the following solutions.

(1) **Rob planned to serve a tasteful selection of pitted dates, chocolate-covered mushrooms, anchovies, and pickles.** Each item on Rob's list is separated from the next by a comma. No comma comes before the first item, *pitted dates*. The comma before the *and* is optional.

(2) **Rob's guest list is heavily tilted toward women he would like to date: Helen Ogee, tech billionaire; Natasha Smith, Olympic medalist; Blair Berry, auto dealer; Hannah Bridge, punctuation expert; and Jane Fine, veterinarian.**

Or

Rob's guest list is heavily tilted toward women he would like to date:

- **Helen Ogee, tech billionaire**
- **Natasha Smith, Olympic medalist**
- **Blair Berry, auto dealer**
- **Hannah Bridge, punctuation expert**
- **Jane Fine, veterinarian**

The commas within each item of Rob's dream-date list make it impossible to distinguish between one dream date and another with a simple comma. Semicolons or a bulleted list do the trick. Also, I hope you noticed that this rather long list begins with a colon.

(3) **After everyone arrives, Rob plans an evening of juggling cabbages, pinning a tail on the donkey, and playing double solitaire.** Fun guy, huh? I can't imagine why he has so much trouble getting dates. I hope you didn't have any trouble separating these thrilling activities with commas. The comma before *and* is optional.

(4) **Rob will consider his party a success if he can get three phone numbers, arrange at least one future date, and avoid a visit from the police.** All you have to do is place a comma between each item. Add a comma before *and* if you wish.

(5) **Rob didn't meet his goals: The police arrived at 10:00, 11:00, and 11:30 p.m.; no one gave out any phone numbers; and everyone thought his name was Bob.**

Or

Rob didn't meet his goals:

- **The police arrived at 10:00, 11:00, and 11:30 p.m.**
- **No one gave out any phone numbers.**
- **Everyone thought his name was Bob.**

In the first version, a semicolon signals where one item ends and another begins. In the second version, bullet points separate items. You need one of these formats because the first item on the list contains commas, so a plain comma isn't enough to separate the list items.

(6) **The best man held onto the railing, for he was afraid of slipping on the ice.** The conjunction (*for*) joins two complete sentences, so a comma precedes it.

7 **No comma.** Read the words preceding the conjunction (*and*). They don't make sense by themselves, so you don't have a complete sentence and don't need a comma before the conjunction.

8 **No comma.** Read the words after the conjunction (*or*). You have a description (*in a tropical forest*) but not a complete sentence. Therefore, you don't need a comma before *or*.

9 **The guests sipped hot chocolate, but they were still cold.** Here, you have two complete thoughts, one before and one after the conjunction (*but*). You need a comma in front of the conjunction.

10 **The ice-dancing during the reception made them sweat, and then the temperature seemed fine.** Two complete thoughts sit in front of and after *and*, so a comma is needed.

11 **No comma.** This one is a little tricky. The conjunction *or* joins *who is in charge of the gifts* and *who is paying the orchestra*. These two questions sound like complete sentences. However, the real question here is *Do you know*. The *who* statements in this sentence are just that: statements. No complete sentence = no comma.

12 **I'd like to swipe a present, for my blender is broken.** The ideas before and after the conjunction *for* are complete, so a comma goes in front of *for*.

13 **I don't need an icemaker, but I'll take one anyway.** The two statements connected by *but* are complete sentences, so you have to insert a comma before *but*.

14 **No comma.** The words after the conjunction (*and*) don't form a complete sentence. No comma needed here!

15 **Oscar's favorite food, which he cooks every Saturday night, is hot dogs.** Two words tell you more about *food*, but one is a possessive (*Oscar's*) and the other is a description (*favorite*). Because the two descriptions aren't of the same type, they aren't separated by commas. Moving on: After you find out that the food is Oscar's favorite, you have enough identification. The information about Oscar's Saturday nights is extra and thus set off by commas.

16 **Correct.** The term *place* is quite general, so the description is an essential identifier. The two descriptions preceding *barbecue* aren't of the same type. One gives size and the other composition. You can't easily reverse them (a *brick huge barbecue* sounds funny), so don't insert a comma.

17 **Correct.** The paired descriptions (*his* and *wheat*, *large* and *plastic*) aren't of the same type. *His* is a possessive, and you should never set off a possessive with a comma. *Large* indicates size, and *plastic* refers to composition. The last description nails down which tub you're talking about, so it isn't set off by commas.

TIP In general, descriptions beginning with *which* take commas, and descriptions beginning with *that* are comma-free.

18 **One of the horses that lives in Oscar's barn often sniffs around Oscar's lucky horseshoe, which Oscar found while playing tag.** Which horses are you talking about? Without the barn information, you don't know. Identifying information doesn't take commas. The two words preceding *horseshoe* aren't equivalent. *Oscar's* is a possessive (never set off by commas), and *lucky* is a quality that we all want in our horseshoes. The last description is extra because we already know enough to identify which horseshoe is getting sniffed. Because it's extra, a comma must separate the description from the rest of the sentence.

19 **Correct.** The three descriptions preceding *horses* aren't of the same type: One (*his*) is possessive, and another (*three*) is a number. Commas never set off possessives and numbers. The second descriptive element, honoring the Barbeque King and Queen, explains which race you're talking about. Without that information, the topic could be any contest. Because it's an identifier, that phrase isn't set off by a comma.

20. **Oscar, who is an animal lover, will never sell one of his horses.** You know Oscar's name, so the information about loving animals is extra and thus set off by commas.

21. **Being sentimental, Oscar dedicated a song to the horse that was born on his birthday.** The introductory expression (which is also a description) contains a verb, so it must be followed by a comma. The second description (*that was born on his birthday*) is essential because you don't know which horse you're discussing without this information. Thus, you need no comma.

22. **The jockeys who were trying to prepare for the big race became annoyed by Oscar's song, but the jockeys who had already raced didn't mind.** In this sentence, the jockeys are divided into two groups — those who are preparing and those who are done for the day. Because the *who* statements identify each group, no commas are needed.

23. **The deep, horrible secret is that Oscar can't stay in tune when he sings.** The first two descriptions may be reversed without loss of meaning, so a comma is appropriate. The last description also gives you essential information. Without that description, you don't know whether Oscar can stay in tune when he plays the tuba, for example, but not when he sings. Essential descriptions aren't set off by commas.

24. **His guitar, a Gibson, is missing two important strings.** The *his* tells you which guitar is being discussed, so the fact that it's a Gibson is extra and should be set off by commas.

25. **In desperate need of a pizza fix, Brad turned to his cell phone.** The introductory expression here merits a comma because it's fairly long. Length doesn't always determine whether you need a comma, but in general, the longer the introduction, the more likely it is that you'll need a comma.

26. **Ghada, on the other hand, wasn't hungry.** The expression inside the commas makes a comment on the rest of the sentence, comparing Ghada to Brad. As an interrupter, it must be separated by two commas from the rest of the sentence.

27. **Yes, pizza was an excellent idea.** *Yes* and *no,* when they show up at the beginning of a sentence, take commas because they comment on the main idea.

28. **The toppings, by the way, proved to be a problem.** The expression *by the way* isn't connected to the meaning of the sentence, so it's set off by commas.

29. **No comma.** The introductory word *finally* is tied closely to the main action in the sentence, *chose*. No comma is necessary for a simple statement. However, if you want to emphasize that Brad took an unreasonable amount of time to decide, you can insert a comma after *finally*. The comma gives the word more importance by cutting it off from the rest of the sentence.

30. **Ghada wondered how Brad, given his low-fat diet, could consider pepperoni.** The expression *given his low-fat diet* interrupts the flow of the sentence and calls for two commas.

31. **Frozen with indecision, Brad decided to call the pizzeria to request the cheapest pie.** Introductory expressions with verb forms (*Frozen*) always take commas.

32. **Ghada, on a tight budget, wanted to redeem her coupons.** The phrase *on a tight budget* interrupts the flow of the sentence and comments on the main idea. That's why you need two commas.

33 **No comma.** Did I catch you here? This sentence doesn't have an introductory expression. *To demand fast delivery* is the subject of the sentence, not an extra comment. (To learn more about subjects, turn to Chapter 7.)

34 **Lighting a match and holding it in his trembling hand, Brad realized that time was almost up.** Introductory expressions containing verbs always take commas. This introductory expression has two verbs, *lighting* and *holding*.

35 **No comma.** The verb form (*Worrying about toppings*) is the subject of the sentence, not an introduction to another idea. No comma is needed.

36 **Well, the robbers wasted too much time.** Words such as *well, indeed, clearly*, and so forth take commas when they occur at the beginning of the sentence and aren't part of the main idea.

37 **Of course, the guards caught Brad and Ghada.** The phrase *of course* is a comment on the rest of the sentence, not part of its meaning. Therefore, it should be separated from the main idea by a comma.

38 **As the guards chomped on the pepperoni pizza Brad had ordered, he and Ghada slipped away.** This introductory statement has a subject and a verb and thus is followed by a comma.

39 **Brad and Ghada celebrated their escape, I believe, by ordering another pizza.** The expression *I believe* interrupts and comments on the sentence, so it should be separated from the main statement by commas.

40 **Although she prefers pineapple, Ghada ate all the pepperoni.** The introductory statement contains a verb, so it should be separated from the rest of the sentence by a comma.

41 **Ladies and Gentlemen, I present the Fifth Annual Elbox Championships.** Even though *Ladies and Gentlemen* doesn't name the members of the audience, they're still being addressed, so a comma sets off the expression from the rest of the sentence.

42 **I know, Mort, that you are an undefeated Elbox competitor. Would you tell our audience about the sport?** Here, you see the benefit of the direct-address comma. Without it, the reader thinks *I know Mort* is the beginning of the sentence and then becomes confused. When *Mort* is cut away with two commas, the sentence is clear.

43 **Elboxing is about 5,000 years old, Chester. It originated in ancient Egypt.** You're talking to Chester, so his name needs to be set off by a comma.

44 **Really? Man, I can't believe you knew that!** *Man* is sometimes simply an exclamation of feeling, not a true address. But *man* can be a form of address, and in this sentence, it is. Hence, the comma slices it away from the rest of the sentence.

45 **Yes, Chester, the sport grew out of the natural movement of the elbow when someone tried to but ahead in line by "elbowing."** Chester is being addressed directly, so you need to surround the name with commas.

46 **Excuse me a moment. The reigning champion has decided to pay us a visit. Miss William, could you tell us how you feel about the upcoming match?** Here, the person being addressed is Miss William.

47 **Certainly, Sir. I am confident that my new training routine will pay off.** The very polite Miss William talks to *Sir* in this sentence, so that term is set off by a comma.

48 **Mort, I can't wait to see the match.** Because Mort is being addressed, his name is followed by a comma.

(49) **I and III.** At the end of a sentence, day-month-year or month-day is acceptable. The year never appears first, so II is not correct. The end of a sentence needs an end mark. In these answers, that mark is a period.

(50) **I and II.** In the first correct answer, commas disappear. In the second, commas separate the day from the year and the year from the rest of the sentence.

(51) **I, II, and III.** All three dates are in acceptable formats. Note: A year has only 12 months, so no reader will misunderstand the date in the format illustrated by II. If the day might be misread as a month (4 might be the day or the month of April, for example), it's wise to select a different format.

(52) **I and II.** A comma separates the year from the rest of the sentence, so the first option is correct. Traditionally, a comma separates the month and year if no day is specified, so II is okay. Because the year should not come before the month, III isn't correct.

(53) **II and III.** In the first correct answer, no commas appear. In the second, a comma separates the month and year and the year from the rest of the sentence. Choice I is wrong because the year shouldn't precede the month.

Answers to "Overachievers Questions"

Annual Self-Evaluation — October 1, 2027

Well,[1] Ms. Kwame,[2] that time of year has arrived again. I[3] must think about my strengths and weaknesses as an **employee**[4] of NewGramm International. First and **foremost**,[5] let me say that I love working for NewGramm.

When I applied for the **job**,[6] I never dreamed how much fun I would have taking **two**[7] long lunches a day. Sneaking out the back **door**[8] is not my idea of fun. Because no one ever watches what I am doing at **NewGramm**,[9] I can leave by the front door without worrying. **Also**,[10] **Ms. Kwame**,[11] I confess that I do almost no work at all. Upon transferring to the office in **Idaho**,[12] I immediately claimed a privilege given only to the most **experienced**,[13] most **skilled**[14] employees and started to take **two**[15] extra weeks of vacation.

I have only one more thing to say. May I have a raise?

---

1. **Well,** An introductory word should be followed by a comma.

2. **Ms. Kwame,** Commas surround *Ms. Kwame* because she's being directly addressed in this sentence. (The first comma follows the introductory word *well*. The second follows *Ms. Kwame*.

3. **I** The pronoun *I* is part of the main idea of the sentence, not an introductory expression. No comma should separate it from the rest of the sentence.

4. **employee** The phrase *of NewGramm* is an essential identifier of the type of employee being discussed. No comma should separate it from the word it describes *(employee)*.

5. **foremost,** A comma follows the introductory expression, *First and foremost.*

6. **job,** The introductory expression *When I applied for the job* should be separated from the rest of the sentence by a comma.

7. **two long** Two descriptions are attached to *lunches* — *two* and *long*. These descriptions aren't of the same type. *Two* is a number, and *long* is a measure of time. Also, numbers are never separated from other descriptions by a comma. The verdict: Delete the comma after *two*.

8. **door** In this sentence, the expression *Sneaking out the back door* isn't an introductory element. It's the subject of the sentence, and it shouldn't be separated from the verb *(is)* by a comma.

9. **NewGramm,** The introductory expression *Because no one ever watches what I am doing at NewGramm* should be separated from the rest of the sentence by a comma.

10. **Also,** *Also* is an introduction to the sentence. Slice it off with a comma.

11. **Ms. Kwame,** A comma follows *Ms. Kwame* because the name is a direct address.

12. **Idaho,** A comma follows the introductory statement.

13. **most experienced, most skilled** Two descriptions are attached to *employees: most experienced* and *most skilled*. Because these descriptions are more or less interchangeable, a comma separates them from each other. No comma separates *skilled* from the word it describes, *employees.*

14. **skilled** No comma ever separates the last description from what it describes, so the comma before *employees* has to go.

15. **Two extra** Two descriptions (in this case, *two* and *extra*) aren't separated by commas when one of the descriptions is a number.

Chapter **11**

"Can I Quote You on That?" Quotation Marks

Quotation marks (" ") come in pairs. They surround words that someone spoke or wrote. In a novel or a short story, they let the reader know that a character is speaking. They don't belong in a sentence that summarizes — not repeats — the actual words someone wrote or said. Sometimes, quotation marks enclose slang expressions or tell the reader that the writer doesn't agree with the words inside the quotation marks. Quotation marks also punctuate the titles of certain types of literary or other artworks.

Many — too many! — rules come into play when you're dealing with quotation marks. Because the rules for quotation marks are rooted in custom, not logic, they can be hard to remember. You may be tempted to scrap this punctuation entirely. Resist the temptation! Instead, work through the exercises in this chapter. If you do so, you'll be sure to employ quotation marks correctly every time.

Quoting and Paraphrasing: What's the Difference?

I have something to tell you: I love Jane Austen's novels and read all six once a year. If you want someone to know that fact about me, you have two choices:

> "I love Jane Austen's novels and read all six once a year," wrote Woods.

> Woods explained that she enjoys Jane Austen's writing and works her way through Austen's six novels every year.

The first example is a *direct quotation*. My exact words are inside the quotation marks. The second example is a *paraphrase*. The sense of what I wrote is there, but the words are slightly different. You don't have to know these terms. You do have to know that quotations must be set off by quotation marks, as you see in the first example. Paraphrases shouldn't be enclosed by quotation marks, as you see in the second example.

WARNING Even when you're paraphrasing, you still have to cite sources for information and ideas that aren't the product of your own brain. Citation format changes from field to field. A citation in a science paper isn't the same as one in a literary essay, for example. A number of handy computer programs format citations automatically. You type in the source information, and the citation pops up, perfectly formatted. If that option isn't available to you, consult the style manual that your teacher or supervisor prefers.

YOUR TURN Can you tell the difference between quotations and paraphrases? Below is a short paragraph from an imaginary news article. Following the story are sentences about something in the paragraph. Based on the paragraph, write "Quotation" if all or part of the sentence is quoted. Write "Paraphrase" if no quotation appears. Note: I haven't inserted quotation marks any-where in the questions. In real writing, the quotation marks would be present.

> The annual report from Hoops International is due tomorrow. According to inside sources who wish to remain anonymous, the company will announce that profits have nearly doubled in the last year. The increase is credited to the company's newest prod-uct, the Talking Hoop. Buyers moving the hoop around their hips hear a drill sergeant screaming commands as they exercise. Company officials have high hopes for their next product, Musical Hoops.

Q. The Talking Hoop has been so successful that the company has made twice as much money this year as it did last year. _____

A. **Paraphrase.** The information is from the paragraph, but the wording is different.

1 Hoops International plans to market a hoop with musical tones. _____

2 The company is doing well, and profits have nearly doubled in the last year. _____

3 Go faster, Private! is what you hear when you're playing with the Talking Hoop.
_____

4. The annual report should give shareholders cause for celebration. _____

5. Our best-selling product is the Talking Hoop, said Max Hippo, the president of the company. _____

6. The Talking Hoop is used for exercise. _____

Giving Voice to Direct Quotations

The basic rule governing quotation marks is simple: Place quotation marks around words drawn directly from someone else's speech or writing, or, if you're writing what is sure to be a best-selling novel, place quotation marks around dialogue. The tricky part is that quotation marks are in a sentence with other punctuation, such as commas, periods, and the like. These rules explain what goes where when the sentence labels the speaker with a tag (*he murmured, she screams*, and so forth):

>> **The speaker tag should be separated from the quotation by a comma.**

- If the speaker tag is **before** the quotation, the comma comes *before* the opening quotation mark: *Sharon sneezed and then said, "I hate hay fever season."*

- If the speaker tag is **after** the quotation, the comma goes *inside* the closing quotation mark: *"What a large nose you have," whispered Joe lovingly.*

- If the speaker tag appears **in the middle** of a quotation, a comma is placed before the first closing quotation mark and immediately after the tag: *"Here's the handkerchief," said Joe, "that I borrowed last week."*

>> **If the quotation ends the sentence, the period goes *inside* the closing quotation mark.**

>> *Joe added, "I would like to kiss your giant nose."*

>> **If the quotation is a question or an exclamation, the question mark or the exclamation point goes inside the closing quotation mark.** *"Why did you slap me?" asked Joe. "I was complimenting you!"*

>> Question marks and exclamation points serve as sentence-ending punctuation, so you don't need to add a period after the quotation marks.

>> **If the quotation is neither a question nor an exclamation, but the sentence in which the quotation appears is, the question mark or exclamation point goes outside the closing quotation mark.** *I can't believe that Joe said he's "a world-class lover"! Do you think Sharon will ever get over his "compliments"?*

TIP

Sometimes, a quotation is tucked into the sentence without a speaker tag. You see examples in the previous two bullet points. With no speaker tag, no comma separates the quotation from the rest of the sentence. Nor does the quotation begin with a capital letter unless you need one for another reason (a name, for example). Quotations with speaker tags, on the other hand, always begin with a capital letter, regardless of where the speaker tag falls. In an interrupted quotation (speaker tag in the middle), the first word of the first half of the quotation is capitalized, but the first word of the second half isn't unless it's a proper name. (For more information about capitalization, turn to Chapter 12.)

Now that you know the rules, it's time to apply your knowledge. Your job is to identify the direct quotation and fill in the proper punctuation, in the proper order, in the proper places. To help you, I added information in parentheses at the end of some sentences and underlined the quoted words. To make your life harder, I omit end marks (periods, question marks, and exclamation points).

Q. The annual company softball game is tomorrow declared Becky

A. **"The annual company softball game is tomorrow," declared Becky.** Don't count yourself right unless you placed the comma *inside* the closing quotation mark.

(7) I plan to pitch added Becky, who once tried out for the Olympics

(8) Andy interrupted As usual, I will play third base

(9) No one knew how to answer Andy, who in the past has been called overly sensitive

(10) Finally, Gus said No one wants Andy at third base

(11) Who wants to win asked the boss in a commanding, take-no-prisoners tone

(12) Did she mean it when she said that we were not hard-boiled enough to play decently

(13) Sarah screamed You can't bench Andy (The statement Sarah is making is an exclamation.)

(14) The opposing team, everyone knows, is first in the league and our toughest opponent (The whole statement about the opposing team is an exclamation.)

(15) The odds favor the other team sighed Becky but I will not give up

(16) The league has ruled that all decisions regarding player placement are subject to the umpire's approval

(17) The umpire has been known to label us out-of-shape players who think they belong in the Major Leagues (The label is a direct quotation.)

(18) Do you think there will be a rain delay inquired Harry, the team's trainer

(19) He asked Has anyone checked Sue's shoes to make sure that she hasn't sharpened her spikes again

(20) Surely the umpire doesn't think that Sue would ignore the rule that fair play is essential at all times (Imagine that the writer of this sentence is exclaiming.)

(21) Sue has been known to cork her bat commented Harry

(22) The corking muttered Sue has never been proved

Punctuating Titles

Punctuating titles is easy, especially if you're a sports fan. Imagine a basketball player, one who tops seven feet. Next to him, place a jockey; most jockeys hover around five feet. Got the picture? Good. When you're deciding how to punctuate a title, figure out whether you're dealing with an NBA player or a Derby rider using these rules:

>> **Titles of full-length works are italicized or underlined.** The basketball player represents full-length works — novels, magazines, television series, plays, epic poems, websites, films, and the like. The titles of those works can be italicized (on a computer) or underlined (for handwritten works).

>> **Titles of shorter works are placed in quotation marks.** The jockey, on the other hand, represents smaller works or parts of a whole — a poem, a short story, one post on a website, a single episode of a television show, a song, an article — you get the idea. The titles of these little guys aren't italicized or underlined; they're placed in quotation marks.

TIP

These rules apply to titles that are tucked into sentences. Centered titles, all alone at the top of a page, don't get any special treatment: no italics, no underlining, and no quotation marks.

When a title in quotation marks is part of a sentence, it sometimes tangles with other punctuation marks. If the title is the last element of the sentence, the rules of American English call for any commas or periods following the title to be placed inside the quotation marks. (In Britain, commas and periods that follow the title should be placed outside the quotation marks.) Question marks and exclamation points, on the other hand, don't go inside the quotation marks unless they're actually part of the title.

TIP

If a title that ends with a question mark is the last thing in a sentence, the question mark ends the sentence. Don't place both a period and a question mark at the end of the same sentence.

YOUR TURN

All set for a practice lap around the track? Check out the titles in this series of sentences. Place quotation marks around the title if necessary, adding endmarks where needed; otherwise, underline the title. Here and there, you find parentheses at the end of a sentence, in which I add some information to help you.

Q. Have you read Sarah's latest poem, Sonnet for the Tax Assessor (The sentence is a question, but the title isn't.)

A. **Have you read Sarah's latest poem, "Sonnet for the Tax Collector"?** The title of a poem takes quotation marks. Question marks never go inside the quotation marks unless the title itself is a question.

23 Sarah's poem will be published in a collection entitled Tax Day Blues

24 Mary's fifth bestseller, Publish Your Poetry Now, inspired Sarah.

25 Some of us wish that Sarah had read the recent newspaper article, Forget About Writing Poetry

26. Julie, an accomplished violinist, has turned Sarah's poem into a song, although she changed the name to Sonata Taxiana

27. She's including it on her next album, Songs of April

28. I may listen to it if I can bring myself to stop streaming my favorite series, Big Brother and Sister

29. During a recent episode titled Sister Knows Everything, the main character figured out her brother's password and checked his computer.

30. She discovered that he had written a play, Who Will Be My First Love?

Calling All Overachievers: Extra Practice with Quotation Marks

YOUR TURN

Tommy Brainfree's classic composition is reproduced in the following figure. Identify spots where a set of quotation marks needs to be inserted. Place the quotation marks correctly in relation to other punctuation in the sentence. Also, underline titles where appropriate.

My Summer Vacation

By Tommy Brainfree

This summer I went to Camp Waterbug, a famous place that was described

in a story called Campfire Blues. At Camp Waterbug I learned to paddle a canoe

without tipping it over more than twice a trip. My counselor even wrote an article

about me in the camp newsletter, Waterbug Bites. The article was called How to

Tip a Canoe. The counselor said, Brainfree is well named. I was not upset

because I believed him (eventually) when he explained that he was just kidding.

Are you sure? I asked him when I first read it.

You know, he responded quickly, that I have a lot of respect for you. I

nodded in agreement, but that night I placed a bunch of frogs under his sheets,

just in case he thought about writing How to Fool a Camper. One of the frogs had

a little label tied to his leg. It said, JUST KIDDING TOO.

Answers to Quotation Problems

It's time to see if you've mastered the use of quotation marks. I'm proud of you for tackling the tough exercises in this chapter. You can quote me on that!

1. **Paraphrase.** Nothing in the sentence repeats the exact wording in the paragraph.

2. **Quotation.** Part of the sentence is quoted. The phrase "have nearly doubled in the past year" comes directly from the text and should be enclosed in quotation marks.

3. **Quotation.** Although the paragraph doesn't tell you what the drill sergeant says, these words are described as "what you hear." That description tells you that the words are quoted. Because "Go faster, Private!" is a quotation, quotation marks should surround it.

4. **Paraphrase.** Comb through the paragraph, and you see that these words don't appear.

5. **Quotation.** The first part of the sentence, as far as the word *said*, tells you Max Hippo's exact words.

6. **Paraphrase**. The words in this sentence aren't lifted directly from the paragraph, so they're paraphrased.

7. **"I plan to pitch," added Becky, who once tried out for the Olympics.** The directly quoted words, *I plan to pitch*, are enclosed in quotation marks. The comma that sets off the speaker tag (*added Becky*) goes inside the closing quotation mark. A period ends the sentence.

8. **Andy interrupted, "As usual, I will play third base."** The speaker tag comes first in this sentence, so the comma is placed before the opening quotation mark. The period that ends the sentence goes inside the closing quotation mark.

9. **No one knew how to answer Andy, who in the past has been called "overly sensitive."** The quotation is short, but it still deserves quotation marks. The period at the end of the sentence is placed inside the closing quotation mark. Notice that this quotation doesn't have a speaker tag, so a comma doesn't precede it, and it doesn't start with a capital letter.

10. **Finally, Gus said, "No one wants Andy at third base."** A comma follows the speaker tag, and a period ends the sentence.

11. **"Who wants to win?" asked the boss in a commanding, take-no-prisoners tone.** Because the quoted words are a question, the question mark goes inside the closing quotation mark.

12. **Did she mean it when she said that we were "not hard-boiled enough to play decently"?** The quoted words aren't a question, but the entire sentence is. The question mark belongs outside the closing quotation mark.

TIP If both the sentence and the quotation are questions, the question mark belongs inside the closing quotation mark.

13. **Sarah screamed, "You can't bench Andy!"** A comma separates the speaker tag (*Sarah screamed*) from the quotation and precedes the opening quotation mark. Because the quoted words are an exclamation, the exclamation point belongs inside the closing quotation mark.

14. **The opposing team, everyone knows, is "first in the league and our toughest opponent"!** The hint in parentheses gives a logical reason for the answer. Because the whole statement is an exclamation, the exclamation point belongs outside the closing quotation mark.

15. **"The odds favor the other team," sighed Becky, "but I will not give up."** Here's an interrupted quotation with the speaker tag in the middle. This sort of interruption is perfectly proper. The quoted material makes up one sentence, so the second half begins with a lower-case letter.

16. **The league has ruled that "all decisions regarding player placement are subject to the umpire's approval."** This quotation is tucked into the sentence without a speaker tag, so it takes no comma or capital letter. The period at the end of the sentence goes inside the closing quotation mark.

17. **The umpire has been known to label us "out-of-shape players who think they belong in the Major Leagues."** This quotation is plopped into the sentence without a speaker tag, so the first word takes no capital letter and isn't preceded by a comma. It ends with a period, which is slipped inside the closing quotation mark.

18. **"Do you think there will be a rain delay?" inquired Harry, the team's trainer.** Harry's words are a question, so the question mark goes inside the closing quotation mark.

19. **He asked, "Has anyone checked Sue's shoes to make sure that she hasn't sharpened her spikes again?"** This speaker tag *He asked* begins the sentence. It's set off by a comma, which precedes the opening quotation mark. The quoted words form a question, so the question mark belongs inside the quotation marks.

20. **Surely the umpire doesn't think that Sue would violate the rule that fair play is "essential at all times"!** The information in the parentheses tells you that the writer is exclaiming. The whole sentence is an exclamation, and the quoted expression is fairly mild, so the exclamation point belongs to the sentence, not to the quotation. Place it outside the closing quotation mark. Because no speaker tag is present, the quotation begins with a lowercase letter and isn't set off by a comma.

21. **"Sue has been known to cork her bat," commented Harry.** A straightforward statement with a speaker tag (*commented Harry*) calls for a comma inside the closing quotation mark. The quotation is a complete sentence. In quoted material, the period that normally ends the sentence is replaced by a comma because the sentence continues on — in this case, with *commented Harry*. Periods don't belong in the middle of a sentence unless they're part of an abbreviation.

22. **"The corking," muttered Sue, "has never been proved."** A speaker tag breaks into this quotation and is set off by commas. The one after *corking* goes inside because when you're ending a quotation or part of a quotation, the comma or period always goes inside. The same situation appears at the end of the sentence. The period needs to be inserted inside the closing quotation mark.

23. **Tax Day Blues or *Tax Day Blues*.** If it's a collection, it's a full-length work. Full-length works are not placed in quotation marks but are underlined if you are writing by hand or italicized if you are using a computer.

24. **Publish Your Poetry Now or *Publish Your Poetry Now*.** The book title is underlined if you're writing by hand or italicized if you are writing on a computer.

25. **"Forget About Writing Poetry."** The title of an article is enclosed by quotation marks. The period following a quotation or a title in quotation marks goes inside the closing quotation mark.

26. **"Sonata Taxiana."** The period always goes inside a closing quotation mark, at least in the United States. In the United Kingdom, the period is generally outside. Quotation marks are best here because a "Sonata Taxiana" isn't a full-length work.

27) **<u>Songs of April.</u>** or *Songs of April*. A CD is a full-length work, so the title is underlined or, better yet, italicized.

28) **<u>Big Brother and Sister.</u>** or *Big Brother and Sister*. The title of the whole series is underlined. (You can italicize it if you're typing.) The title of an individual episode goes in quotation marks.

29) **"Sister Knows Everything,"** The episode title belongs in quotation marks. The series title gets italicized (or underlined, if you're writing with a pen). The comma around this introductory expression sits inside the quotation marks.

30) **<u>Who Will Be My First Love?</u>** or *Who Will Be My First Love?* A question mark is part of the title, which is underlined or italicized because a play is a full-length work.

Answers to "Overachievers Questions"

My Summer Vacation

By Tommy Brainfree

This summer I went to Camp Waterbug, a famous place that was described in a story called (1) "Campfire Blues." At Camp Waterbug I learned to paddle a canoe without tipping it over more than twice a trip. My counselor even wrote an article about me in the camp newsletter, (2) <u>Waterbug Bites.</u> The article was called (3) "How to Tip a Canoe." In it the counselor wrote, (4) "Brainfree is well named." I was not upset because I believed him (eventually) when he explained that he was just kidding.

(5) "Are you sure?" I asked him when I first read it.

(6) "You know," he responded quickly, (7) "that I have a lot of respect for you." I nodded in agreement, but that night I placed a bunch of frogs under his sheets, just in case he thought about writing (8) "How to Fool a Camper." One of the frogs had a little label tied to his leg. It said, (9) "JUST KIDDING TOO." Someday, I'm going to write a book and call it (10) <u>Don't Send Your Kid to Camp.</u>

(1) **"Campfire Blues"** Story titles belong in quotation marks.

(2) *Waterbug Bites* or **Waterbug Bites** The newsletter title should be italicized or underlined.

(3) **"How to Tip a Canoe"** An article title belongs in quotation marks. The period at the end of the sentence should be inside the closing quotation mark.

(4) **"Brainfree is well named."** Directly quoted speech belongs in quotation marks, with the period inside the closing mark.

(5) **"Are you sure?"** The quoted words are a question, so the question mark goes inside the quotation marks.

(6) **"You know,"** The interrupted quotation with an inserted speaker tag needs two sets of marks. The comma at the end of the first part of the quotation goes inside the closing mark.

(7) **"that I have a lot of respect for you."** The period at the end of the second half of the quotation goes inside the closing mark.

(8) **"How to Fool a Camper."** Another article title, another set of quotation marks. The period goes inside.

(9) **"JUST KIDDING TOO."** This quotation reproduces the exact written words and thus calls for quotation marks. The period goes inside.

(10) *Don't Send Your Kid to Camp* or **Don't Send Your Kid to Camp** The title of a book should be italicized or underlined.

Chapter **12**

Hitting the Big Time: Capital Letters

Most people know the basics of capitalization: Capital letters are needed for proper names, the personal pronoun *I*, and the first letter of a sentence. Trouble may arrive with the finer points of capital letters — titles of people and publications and abbreviations. In this chapter, you practice all these topics. I cover the capitalization of quoted material in Chapter 11. If you want to fine-tune your capitalization skills in texts, tweets, emails, and presentation slides, turn to Chapter 13.

WARNING
The major style-setters in the land of grammar (yes, grammar has style!) sometimes disagree about what should be capitalized. In this workbook, I follow the most common capitalization styles. If an authority figure — a teacher or a boss — will judge your writing, you may want to check their preferences.

Setting up Sentences and Naming Names

If I forget to capitalize the first letter of the first word of a sentence — starting this paragraph with *if*, for example — the computer automatically changes the word to *If*. Capital letters add importance, and the start of a new sentence is important information.

TIP

You can't capitalize a numeral, so avoid starting a sentence with one. You can write the number in words, but often, that solution is wordy and awkward. It's better to revise the sentence. Suppose you want to explain your career steps. Instead of writing, "2024 was when I got my first promotion," you might write, "My first promotion was in 2024."

Here are some other capitalization rules:

>> Always capitalize specific names (Jamal, Walmart, Alps, Cheerios).

>> Capitalize terms that refer to a shared cultural identity or origin (White, Black, Pakistani, European).

>> Geographical areas are capitalized (the Midwest, Southern Italy).

>> Directions (east, north) are not capitalized.

>> General terms (boy, company, mountain, cereal) aren't capitalized.

YOUR TURN

Questions 1–15: This paragraph is written without capital letters. Some words are underlined. Write "C" if the underlined word should be capitalized. Write "NC" if the underlined word should not be capitalized.

(1) sports fans who live in **(2)** seattle are excited because today their **(3)** city will host a **(4)** marathon sponsored by **(5)** microdadda, a local technology **(6)** company with headquarters in the **(7)** cascade mountains. Because my **(8)** friend **(9)** josh and **(10)** i have run in the **(11)** park every **(12)** day since **(13)** april, we feel prepared. **(14)** the race is one of the most important in the **(15)** northwest.

Awarding Titles

Which titles apply to you — *doctor, head dog groomer, vice president, Ms.* or *Mr.* or something else? Everyone has a few titles, so it's good to know when titles require capital letters. Follow these guidelines:

>> **A title preceding and attached to a name is capitalized** (*Mr. Smith, Professor Wiley*). Small, unimportant words in titles (*a, the, of,* and the like) are never capitalized (*Head of School Abdullah*).

>> **Titles written after or without a name are generally not capitalized** (*the treasurer; a mayor; George Wiley, professor of psychology*).

>> **Titles of national or international importance may be capitalized even when used alone** (*President, Prime Minister, Secretary-General*). Some style manuals opt for lowercase, regardless of rank.

>> **Family relationships are capitalized when they are used in place of a name** ("Did you know *Mom* designed that building?" but "My *mother* is an architect").

YOUR TURN

In the following sentences, add capital letters where needed. Cross out incorrect capitals and substitute the lowercase (noncapitalized) form.

Q. The reverend archie smith, Chief Executive of the city council, has invited senator Bickford to next month's fundraiser.

A. **Reverend, Archie, Smith, chief, executive, Senator.** Personal names are always capitalized, so *Archie Smith* needs capitals. *Reverend* and *Senator* precede the names (*Archie Smith* and *Bickford*) and act as part of the person's name, not just as a description of their jobs. They should be capitalized. The title *chief executive* follows the name and isn't capitalized.

16   Yesterday mayor victoria johnson ordered all public servants in her town to conserve sticky tape.

17   Herman harris, chief city engineer, has promised to hold the line on tape spending.

18   However, the Municipal Dogcatcher, Agnes e. Bark, insists on taping reward signs to every tree.

19   My Sister says that the signs placed by dogcatcher Bark seldom fall far from the tree.

20   Did you ask mom whether ms. Bark's paper signs will last until December?

21   Few Dogcatchers care as much as agnes about rounding up lost dogs.

22   The recent dog-show champion, BooBoo, bit uncle Lou last week.

23   My Brother thinks that no one would have been hurt had Agnes found BooBoo first.

24   The Mayor's Cousin, who owns a thumbtack company, prefers to substitute tacks for tape.

25   Until the issue is resolved, Agnes, herself the chief executive of Sticking, Inc., will continue to tape her signs.

Capitalizing Titles of Literary and Media Works

If you write a poem about your boss or a scientific study on the biological effects of too many final exams, how do you capitalize the title? The answer depends on the style you're following:

>> **In the United States, the titles of literary, creative, and general-interest works are capitalized in "headline style."** Headline style specifies capital letters for the first and last word of the title and subtitle, in addition to all nouns, verbs, descriptive words, and any other words that require emphasis. Articles (*a, an, the*) and short prepositions (*at, by, to,* and the like) are usually not capitalized. *For Dummies* chapter titles employ headline style, though the company capitalizes *For* in its book titles. In Britain, titles of all sorts of works often appear in sentence style, which I describe in the next bullet point.

>> **The titles of scientific works employ "sentence style,"** which calls for capital letters only for the first word of the title and subtitle and for proper nouns. Everything else is in lower-case (noncapitals). Here's the title of a scientific paper in sentence style: "Cloning fruit flies: Hazards of fly bites."

YOUR TURN The following titles are written without any capital letters at all. Insert capitals where they are needed. The style you should follow (headline or sentence) is specified in parentheses at the end of each title. By the way, titles of short works are enclosed in quotation marks. Titles of full-length works are italicized. (See Chapter 11 for more information on the punctuation of titles.)

Q. "the wonders of the workweek completed: an ode" *(headline)*

A. **"The Wonders of the Workweek Completed: An Ode"** The first word of the title and subtitle *(The, An)* are always capitalized. So are the nouns *(Wonders, Workweek, Ode)* and descriptive words *(Completed)*. The unimportant words *of* and *the* aren't capitalized.

26 moby duck: a tale of obsessive bird-watching (headline)

27 "an analysis of the *duckensis mobyous*: the consequences of pollution on population" (sentence)

28 "call me izzy smell: my life as a duck hunter" (headline)

29 the duck and i: essays on the relationship between human beings and feathered species (sentence)

30 duck and cover: a cookbook (headline)

31 "the duck stops here: political wisdom from the environmental movement" (sentence)

32 duck up: how the duck triumphed over the hunter (headline)

33 "moby duck doesn't live here anymore" (headline)

34 "population estimates of the duck pond: an inexact science" (sentence)

35 for the love of a duck: a sentimental memoir (headline)

Managing Capital Letters in Abbreviations

The world of abbreviations is prime real estate for turf wars. Some publications and institutions proudly announce that "*we* don't capitalize a.m." whereas others declare exactly the opposite, choosing "AM" instead. (Both are correct, but don't mix the forms. Notice that the capitalized version doesn't use periods.) You're wise to ask in advance about the publication's or Authority Figure's preferences. These are the general, one-size-fits-most guidelines for abbreviations:

>> **Acronyms** — forms created by the first letter of each word (*NATO, UNICEF,* and so forth) — take capitals but not periods.

>> **Initials and titles** are capitalized and take periods (*George W. Bush* and *Msgr. Sullivan,* for example). The three most common titles — Mr., Mrs., and Ms. — are always capitalized and usually written with periods.

>> **Latin abbreviations** such as *e.g.* (for example) and *ibid.* (in the same place) aren't usually capitalized but do end with a period.

>> **State abbreviations** are the two-letter, no-period, capitalized forms created by the post office *(IN* and *AL).*

>> **Abbreviations in texts or tweets to friends** may be informal, written without capitals or periods. If you've *gtg* (got to go), you probably don't have time for capitals. However, avoid these abbreviations when writing to someone you're trying to impress — a boss, client, or teacher.

>> **When an abbreviation comes at the end of a sentence,** the period for the abbreviation does double duty as an endmark.

YOUR TURN

Okay, try your hand at abbreviating. Check out the full word, which I place in lowercase letters, even when capital letters are called for. See whether you can insert the proper abbreviation or acronym for the following words, taking care to capitalize where necessary and filling in the blanks with your answers.

Q. figure _____

A. fig.

36 illustration _____

37 before common era _____

38 mister Burns _____

39 united states president _____

40 national hockey league _____

41 reverend Wong _____

42 new york _____

43 Adams boulevard _____

44 irregular _____

45 incorporated _____

Calling All Overachievers: Extra Practice with Capital Letters

Use the information in this chapter to help you find ten capitalization mistakes in the following figure, which is an excerpt from possibly the worst book report ever written.

Moby, the Life Of a Duck: A Book Report

If you are ever given a book about Ducks, take my advice and burn it. When i had to

read *Moby Duck,* the Teacher promised me that it was good. She said that

"Excitement was on every page." I don't think so! A duckling with special powers is

raised by his Grandpa. Moby actually goes to school and earns a Doctorate in bird

Science! After a really boring account of Moby's Freshman year, the book turns to

his career as a Flight Instructor. I was very happy to see him fly away at the end of

the book.

Answers to Capitalization Problems

Now that you've burned a hole through your thinking cap while answering questions about capitalization, check out the answers to see how you did.

1. **C** The first word of a sentence is capitalized.

2. **C** The name of a city is capitalized.

3. **NC** The general term *city* is not capitalized.

4. **NC** The general term *marathon* is not capitalized. The name of a specific race ("the Boston Marathon") is capitalized.

5. **C** The name of a company is capitalized.

6. **NC** The general term *company* is not capitalized.

7. **C** The name of a mountain range is always capitalized.

8. **NC** The general term *friend* is not capitalized.

9. **C** A person's name is always is capitalized.

10. **C** The personal pronoun *I* is always capitalized.

11. **NC** The general term *park* is not capitalized.

12. **NC** The general term *day* is not capitalized.

13. **C** The name of a month is capitalized.

14. **C** The first word of a sentence is capitalized.

15. **C** The name of an area of the country is capitalized.

16. **Mayor Victoria Johnson.** Titles that come before a name and proper names take capitals; common nouns, such as *servants* and *tape,* don't.

17. **Harris.** Names take capitals, but titles written after the name usually don't.

18. **municipal dogcatcher, E.** The title in this sentence isn't attached to the name; in fact, it's separated from the name by a comma. It should not be capitalized. Initials take capitals and periods.

19. **sister, Dogcatcher.** Family relationships aren't capitalized unless the relationship is used as a name. The title *Dogcatcher* is attached to the name, so it's capitalized.

20. **Mom, Ms.** The word Mom substitutes for the name here, so it's capitalized. The title *Ms.* is always capitalized, but the period is optional.

21. **dogcatchers, Agnes.** The common noun *dogcatchers* doesn't need a capital letter, but the proper name Agnes does.

(22) **Uncle.** The title uncle is capitalized if it precedes or substitutes for the name. Did I confuse you with *BooBoo*? People can spell their own names (and the names of their pets) however they want.

(23) **brother.** Family titles aren't capitalized unless they substitute for the name.

(24) **mayor's, cousin.** These titles aren't attached to or used as names, so they aren't capitalized.

(25) **Correct.** Names are always capitalized, but titles aren't, except when they precede the name.

(26) **Moby Duck: A Tale of Obsessive Bird-Watching** In headline style, the first word of the title (*Moby*) and subtitle (*A*) are in caps. Nouns (*Duck, Tale*, and *Watching*) and descriptive words (*Obsessive, Bird*) are also uppercased. The short preposition *of* merits only lowercase.

(27) **"An analysis of the *Duckensis mobyous*: The consequences of pollution on population"** In sentence-style capitalization, the first words of the title and subtitle are in caps, but everything else is in lowercase, with the exception of proper names. In this title, following preferred scientific style, the names of the genus (a scientific category) and species are in italics, with only the genus name in caps.

(28) **"Call Me Izzy Smell: My Life As a Duck Hunter"** Per headline style, the article (*a*) is in lowercase. I caught you on *As*, didn't I? It's short, but it's not an article or a preposition, so it rates a capital letter.

(29) **The duck and I: Essays on the relationship between human beings and feathered species** Sentence style titles take caps for the first word of the title and subtitle. The personal pronoun *I* is always capitalized.

(30) **Duck and Cover: A Cookbook** Headline style calls for capitals for the first word of the title and subtitle and all other nouns. The joining word *and* is lowercase in headline style, unless it begins a title or subtitle.

(31) **"The duck stops here: Political wisdom from the environmental movement"** Sentence style gives you two capitals in this title — the first word of the title and subtitle.

(32) **Duck Up: How the Duck Triumphed over the Hunter** Because this title is in headline style, everything is in caps except articles (*the*) and prepositions (*over*).

(33) **"Moby Duck Doesn't Live Here Anymore"** Headline style gives capital letters for all the words here because this title contains no articles or prepositions.

(34) **"Population estimates of the duck pond: An inexact science"** Sentence style calls for capital letters at the beginning of the title and subtitle. The term *duck* isn't the name of a genus, so it's written in lowercase.

(35) **For the Love of a Duck: A Sentimental Memoir** Headline style mandates lowercase for articles (*the, a*) and prepositions (*of*). The first words of the title and subtitle, even if they're articles or prepositions, merit capital letters.

(36) **illus.**

(37) **BCE** The Latin expression Anno Domini — abbreviated A D — means "in the year of our Lord" and is used with dates that aren't BC, or before Christ. To make this term more universal, historians often substitute CE or Common Era for AD and BCE or Before the Common Era for BC.

38 **Mr. Burns**

39 **U.S. Pres.**

40 **NHL** This is the acronym for the National Hockey League.

41 **Rev. Wong**

42 **NY** (postal abbreviation) **or N.Y.** (traditional form)

43 **Adams Blvd.**

44 **irreg.**

45 **Inc.**

Answers to "Overachievers Questions"

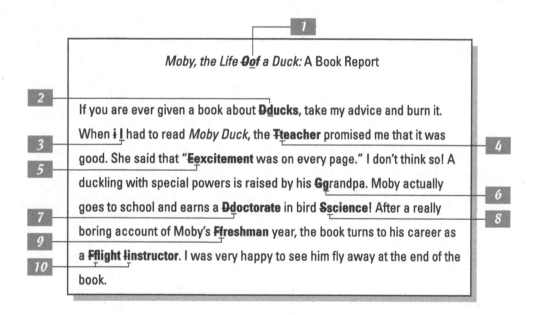

Moby, the Life ~~O~~of a Duck: A Book Report

If you are ever given a book about ~~D~~ducks, take my advice and burn it. When ~~i~~ I had to read *Moby Duck*, the ~~T~~teacher promised me that it was good. She said that "~~E~~excitement was on every page." I don't think so! A duckling with special powers is raised by his ~~G~~grandpa. Moby actually goes to school and earns a ~~D~~doctorate in bird ~~S~~science! After a really boring account of Moby's ~~F~~freshman year, the book turns to his career as a ~~F~~flight ~~I~~instructor. I was very happy to see him fly away at the end of the book.

1 In a headline-style title, prepositions aren't capitalized.

2 An ordinary term for animals, in this case, *ducks,* is lowercase.

3 The personal pronoun *I* is always capitalized.

4 The name of the teacher isn't given, just the term *teacher,* which should be lowercase.

5 When a quotation is written without a speaker tag, the first word isn't capitalized.

(6) Family relationships are capitalized only when they serve as a name.

(7) Most academic degrees are lowercase.

(8) Most school subjects are written in lowercase. (I must point out that *English* is in caps because it's so important. Okay, I'm lying. It's in caps because it's the name of a language.)

(9) School years are in lowercase too.

(10) Job titles, when they aren't attached to the beginning of a name, are in lowercase.

4

Grammar in Action

Chapter **13**

Texting, Emailing, and Posting

Does grammar matter when you text, email, or post? The answer is a definite *maybe*. These formats have bent some traditional grammar rules and broken more than a few. In the process, a new set of rules has been created. In this chapter I don't deal with the grammar "rules" for texting or other communication with friends. You already know them (the rules *and* the friends). Instead, I concentrate on other settings — work or school, for instance — that call for more formal writing.

Perfecting Your Texts

You're typing on a keyboard the size of a low-calorie cookie. You want to get the message out with the fewest possible thumbstrokes. Texts are *not* the medium for measured, formal, follow-every-grammar-rule-ever-invented communication. In a text, you may drop some words and most punctuation marks and skip most capital letters. Especially when you're writing to people who spend a lot of time with you (coworkers, for example), you assume that the person reading your text will grasp what you're trying to say. And you're probably right! However, one rule is unbreakable: If the slightest chance of being misunderstood exists, reword your text. Clarity is more important than avoiding extra strain on your thumb muscles.

WARNING

When your communication travels upward on the power ladder — texts to your boss, teacher, parole board, whoever — you can break some rules of Standard English. But be careful. Your friends and relatives already know how smart and accomplished you are, and they're likely to see nonstandard writing as friendly and relaxed. Unfortunately, people outside your inner circle may view you as uneducated or sloppy if your writing doesn't fit their definition of "proper English." (For more about adjusting your level of formality to suit your audience, see Chapter 1.)

Here are some guidelines for texting at work and at school:

>> **Use only words that appear in the dictionary.** Some abbreviations are fine (see the next bullet point), but alerting a teacher that your homework will arrive "L8t" instead of "late" is not a good idea.

>> **Use abbreviations carefully.** Abbreviations that are commonly known, such as *FYI* for "for your information," are fine. Others (*F2F* for "face to face," perhaps) may stump readers who don't frequent social networking sites. Think about your reader as you type an abbreviation. When in doubt, write the whole word.

>> **In general, you should capitalize the personal pronoun *I* and proper names, especially if the names may be read as words.** If you're a carpenter and you're texting the word "woods," will the reader wonder whether you're talking about maple, teak, or me? If the last option is the one you want, the capital letter will make your text easier to decode. Most other words may be lowercase.

>> **You can omit some words.** When you're texting, you don't always need to include the *subject* — who or what you're talking about. (See Chapter 7 for more information on subjects.) If I text "attended meeting," you can probably figure out that *I* attended the meeting. If someone else went, you should include the name ("Bob attended meeting") unless the reader already knows that you're writing about *Bob*. Feel free to chop *a, an,* and *the* from your texts because these words are seldom important.

>> **Numerals and common symbols may sometimes substitute for words.** Time, money, and measurements are in this category. It's fine to write *$8* instead of "eight dollars" and *10″* instead of "ten inches."

>> **You don't need to end a sentence with a period.** A period tells the reader that your thought is complete. Hitting "send" does the same thing. You can include a period if you wish, but be aware that some readers see that little dot as overkill. To them, hitting "send" closes a door gently; adding a period slams it shut.

>> **Never drop punctuation that adds meaning.** If you type *deal?* when you're negotiating, you're asking someone to commit. That's different from *deal*, which suggests that you're giving information ("I agree to your terms") or a command ("deal with it"). The question mark makes a difference. Apostrophes may matter, too. Texting "students dance" is not the same as "students' dance." The first is an action; the second is an event.

WARNING

Before you hit "send," look at the words on your screen. Autocorrect (a function of most texting apps) guesses what you're trying to type and may change a word automatically. That's fine when "ehr" becomes "her" but not fine when "switch" turns into "witch."

The following questions are based on an imaginary text exchange between two coaches. They know each other, but not too well. In these questions, narrow your focus to the aspect of the text appearing in parentheses after each question. Can you make some cuts? Write a new text or "no cuts" if you can't make a change without puzzling the person receiving the text.

Q. I talked to my principal about scheduling (subject)

A. **talked to my principal about scheduling** Without another subject, readers assume that the subject is *I*, so you don't have to include the word.

1. the basketball team has practice today (unimportant words)

2. I can't go (subject)

3. Can Lola attend? (capitalization)

4. She has a chess match tomorrow. (subject)

5. When is the match? (unnecessary words)

6. at half past three o'clock in the afternoon (unnecessary words)

7. do you need a ride? (unnecessary words)

8. Lola is our best player. (punctuation)

9. Who is the best player on your team? (unnecessary words)

10. Jordana is the best player on our team. (unnecessary words)

When you're texting, of course, you want to broaden your vision to include the entire conversation. Some texts make sense in context, though not when they're read individually. That's fine. You can pare down a text if an earlier exchange makes the meaning clear.

Here's a conversation between two people with ties to Henry, a motorcycle rider who forgot to tuck his license into his pocket when he left the house. Each question in this section begins with the intended meaning of the text. Then you see three choices. Which ones are clear? You may select one, more than one, or none.

Q. Henry is in jail for driving without a license and needs ten thousand dollars for bail money.

I. 10K H in jail help license

II. Henry jail license 10000 needed now

III. Henry driving w/o license. Needs 10K bail. Help!

A. III. Choices I and II don't work because "K," the standard abbreviation for "thousand," isn't identified as bail. Even if the reader knows who "H" is, the texts contain too little information. Choice III includes a common abbreviation, *w/o* (without). Because *bail* appears in the text, the reader can figure out that Henry is in jail.

11   His lawyer is hopeful that Henry will be sentenced to probation and community service.

I.   hope prob and cs

II. lawyer hopeful for probation + community service

III. sentence probation and community serv fingers Xd lawyer

12   Lulu will visit Henry as soon as possible. Lulu will probably arrive at the jail around noon.

I.   12 L to H

II. Lulu > Henry asap 12ish

III. Lulu to visit Henry asap, 12 pm?

13   The bad news for Henry is that the judge, Larry Saunders, is very strict about traffic violations.

I.   superstrict judge Saunders

II. Saunders judge, strict traffic violations

III. Saunders = judge strict on traffic violations

14   The judge was once hit by a motorcycle. He will probably give Henry the maximum penalty because Henry was riding a motorcycle when he was arrested.

I.   Judge Saunders bad news for Henry b/c accident. Top penalty probable for H's motorcycle arrest.

II. JS = bad news hates cycles top penalty

III. S not good motorcycle accident jail

15   Henry claimed that his license had been shredded when he washed his jeans.

I.   Henry claimed license shredded in wash

II. license shredded wash

III. claimed license shredded in washing machine

16   Will you attend the press conference when Henry is released?

I.   press conference?

II. attend press conference on release?

III. You going to press conference on H's release?

Brushing Up on Email Etiquette

A recent study estimates that there are almost four-and-a-half billion email accounts. Chances are, at least one of those email accounts is yours. That's why you should brush up on your email etiquette with grammar in mind.

Emails are generally a bit less formal than letters on paper, but they're more formal than texts. For one thing, emails never really go away; even if you delete one, it remains on a server somewhere. It's part of history — and part of an official record if whatever you're writing about ever becomes a legal matter.

TIP

As with all your writing, consider the purpose and audience before deciding exactly how much you can relax the rules of Standard English grammar. (Chapter 1 goes into more depth on this topic.)

Here's each element of an email, along with the rules that apply to it:

>> **Sender's address** That's your own email address. The computer slots it in automatically, so you don't have any decisions to make about this part of an email except for one: the email name you select when you open an account. Other people will see your email address, so choose something you don't mind sharing. In a work or school situation, stay within the bounds of respectability. An email like ihateteachers@email.com is *not* a good idea!

>> **Recipient's address** This is the "to" line. You may type in the address or select it from your contact list. Once again, you've got no decisions and no problems as long as the name you've attached to the email is accurate (no one likes to see their name misspelled) and presentable. I once sent an email to a neighbor I'd labeled "lindafromninthfloor" in my contact list. She was quite surprised to see this "name" on the email and a little offended that I knew where she lived but not her last name.

>> **Subject line** What's in this email, and why should I open it? Aim for a short phrase that answers those questions for the reader. Capitalize the subject line in either headline or sentence style. (The rules for each appear in Chapter 12.)

>> **Greeting** In a formal letter, you might start with *Dear Mr. Antoine* or something similar, followed by a comma. (Some writers substitute a colon for the comma. That's fine.) This greeting appears alone on the first line. You can do the same thing in an email, but most people don't bother. *Hello, Ms. Woods* (if, for example, you're writing to me), or *Hi, everyone* (to a group) is fine. End a "hello" greeting with a period, and start the message on the same line. The comma between *hello* or *hi* and the name is traditional, but these days, most people omit it. You may also skip the greeting entirely or insert the person's name and a comma (*Boris,*) before beginning your message on the next line.

>> **Body** This is your message. Decide how formal you want to be. (Chapter 1 helps with this.) It's fine to drop a word or two in order to achieve a conversational tone, but apart from that, follow the rules of Standard English for punctuation, capitalization, verb tense, and everything else.

TIP

Readers don't expect to spend a half hour reading an email. Share links or files that give more details and invite follow-up questions or comments. If the message is long, consider condensing the important points and formatting them as bullet points. (More on bulleted lists appears in Chapter 14.)

>> **Closing** In traditional, printed letters, a phrase such as "Sincerely," "Best," or "Regards" appears on the line above your signature. You can follow this custom in emails, too, but you can also skip the closing entirely or substitute a final message such as "Thanks" or "See you soon." Follow the closing phrase with a comma and place your name on the next line. If the closing contains more than one word, only the first is capitalized.

YOUR TURN

Check your email etiquette. Decide whether each of the elements in these questions is correct or incorrect.

Q. Hello (subject line)

A. **Incorrect** With this subject line, the person receiving the email has no idea what's in it.

17 Very Truly Yours, (closing)

18 Inability to meet deadline for the paper due on July 16, 2026 (subject line)

19 Hi Professor Morales! (greeting)

20 Professor M I want to tell you that my paper may be late. (greeting and first line of the message)

21 Later, (closing)

22 Renovation Time Frame and Estimated Cost (subject line)

23 Renovation time frame and estimated cost (subject line)

24 Best regards, (closing)

25 annoyingcustomer (recipient's name)

Posting Without Stamps

Do you belong to a group? Classmates, colleagues, hobbyists, activists, or something else? Then you have —or could join — the group's website and share documents, add to their wiki, or make comments. Perhaps you've created your own site where you blog about your favorite topic. The internet has given everyone the opportunity to write and be read. In this section, you practice polishing your posts before you click "upload."

Which grammar rules apply when you're posting? The answer depends on your audience and purpose. Here are some questions to ask yourself before you write:

>> **Who's reading this?** On a site where computer techs evaluate new technology, you can use terms like "neural processing unit" and "HDR-compatible 4K TV." For a site aimed at general readers, stick to plain language or define any specialized vocabulary you use. If you abbreviate, consider whether readers can decode your meaning. For example, in my school 11th-grade students write a *JRP*. I can use that abbreviation on the student's website, but on the parents' page I have to write "junior research paper."

>> **Why am I writing this?** Do you want to come across as an informed professional with a serious purpose? In that case, follow the Standard English rules for verb tense, pronoun case, punctuation, and so forth. If your goal is to engage and amuse your readers, you can

write half sentences, omit some words or coin new ones, and throw in some slang. Just be sure that your readers are likely to grasp your meaning.

» **Does my post match the site's style?** Compare your post to others on the website. Do they sound similar in terms of vocabulary and tone? If you've used abbreviations and slang and no one else has, consider revising.

YOUR TURN

Each question begins with an excerpt from a post on a fictional website, which is identified in parentheses. Read the sentence following the excerpt, which represents a sentence from a reader's post on the site. If the style is similar, write "correct." If you detect a mismatch, write "incorrect."

Q. Voters must notify the State Board of Elections of any change of name or address at least 180 days before an election. (government website)

Notification may be made online at mystatevotes.org.

A. **Correct.** The original sentence is formal, obeying all the rules of Standard English. You see the same style in the proposed addition.

26 I cooked three chickens from Hall Oakly's new recipe collection, *How to Better the Bird.* One was good, one was so-so, and the last . . . let's just say that no one should put a sardine near a chicken. (cooking blog)

You can so put a sardine near a chicken! I did, and I loved the result. The recipe's in *How to Better the Bird with Butter.* Enjoy!

27 Clients are more likely to commit if shipping costs are included in the price. (article in the business section of a newspaper)

Clients are in if the shipping is, and out if the shipping's extra.

28 Tell your representative to vote no on the bill to ban sugary toothpaste. Defy the dental lobby! (activist website)

The dental lobby is, it must be said, sadly mistaken in its expressed belief that sugar and tooth decay are unquestionably linked.

29 Evidence, that's what you want here. Hit the internet and find some. (comment on a shared document on a class website)

I've got a couple of websites for you to look at. I'll text the URLs.

30 Few mountainous regions have been adequately explored, but archaeologists believe they have found a potentially important site near Sashee Lake. (magazine for general readers)

The horizontal strips of some metallic substance and the marks of a crude pickax show that this was probably a prehistoric mine.

Calling All Overachievers: Extra Practice with Texts, Emails, and Posts

Are your grammar muscles as strong as you typing muscles? Tone up both with this exercise in texting, emailing, and posting.

YOUR TURN Fire in the popcorn factory! That's big news, and everyone in town has something to say about it. Below is an email the town's fire inspector sent to residents, a text to an editor from an off-duty reporter who happened to be on scene, and a comment from a citizen posted on the town's website. Check each underlined spot. Mark it "correct" or "incorrect." Note: None of the information below is based on real people or places. I invented everything, including the email addresses.

Email

From: Inspector Anton Rodic

To: **(1)** <u>Citizens@inourtown.gov</u>

Subject: **(2)** <u>why you should never plug in too many electrical devices</u>

Dear **(3)** <u>Citizens</u>

Yesterday the town fire department responded to a call at the popcorn factory. Despite our best efforts, the building was severely damaged. Fortunately, no lives were lost, though 15 people were taken to the hospital to be treated for **(4)** <u>SPI</u>. The fire was likely caused by an overloaded electrical outlet. Under no circumstances should anyone plug 10 industrial-strength poppers into one power strip.

(5) <u>Very truly yours</u>,

Anton Rodic

Text

(6) <u>at</u> popcorn (7) <u>fire massive</u> piles of popped kernels! (8) <u>unpopped</u>

kernels hit me. (9) <u>video team</u> (10) <u>asap</u>

Posted comment

(11) <u>I can't describe how awful the fire was.</u> (12) <u>people</u> were buried in

piles of popcorn (13) <u>III</u> (14) <u>we</u> need to shut down all industrial poppers

and make popcorn at home the old-fashioned (15) <u>way</u>

Answers to Texting, Emailing, and Posting Questions

1. **basketball practice today** You don't need *The* or *has*. The meaning comes through fine without them.

2. **can't go** Readers assume a missing subject is *I*, so you can drop the word from the text. You don't need a capital letter for *can't* if you're writing to someone of equal power (one coach to another, for instance), but if you wish, you may capitalize the word.

3. **can Lola attend?** *Lola* is a name, so it's polite to capitalize it. Capitals are optional for the other words.

4. **has a chess match tomorrow** Because the question was about *Lola*, the reader knows the answer will be about her.

5. **when?** The word *when* is all you need for this question.

6. **3:30** Numerals do the job here. You don't need *p.m.* Readers aren't mind readers, but they are residents of the real world and know that teams don't practice in the middle of the night.

7. **need ride?** Unless you specify another name, *you* is always the person you're addressing.

8. **Lola is our best player** Hitting "send" is the equivalent of a period. You don't need to include this punctuation mark. (You can, if you wish.)

9. **best player on your team?** This version of the text is shorter but just as clear.

10. **Jordana** One word says it all.

11. **II.** Choice II gets the job done. Options I and III aren't clear. What's *cs*? *Prob*? I made up the abbreviations, so anyone receiving this message isn't likely to understand. The role of the lawyer is also murky in the too-short versions.

12. **III.** Choice III is short but not too short. The standard abbreviation for "as soon as possible" is *ASAP*, but you don't really need capital letters in a text. One standard abbreviation for "afternoon" is *p.m.* Writing it without periods is unlikely to confuse the reader. Choice I is vague, and II uses the "greater than" math symbol in an attempt to show that Lulu's going to Henry. Not many readers would catch that meaning.

13. **III.** Choice III has all the necessary information. The equal sign is easily recognizable, and the judge is accurately described. Choices I and II may be interpreted to mean that the judge rules harshly in all cases or has traffic violations.

14. **None.** All the choices need CIA code-breakers, and even they might be confused. Choice I is wordy, but *accident* is vague. Who had the accident? Henry? The judge? Choice II, in the same way, makes the reader guess about *top penalty*. Did the judge get the *top penalty*? Choice II doesn't tell you. Is the situation *not good*, or is the *judge not good*? You can't tell from option III.

15   **I.** Isn't it fun to put your sentences on a diet? (Much more enjoyable than the other sort of diet.) In Choice I, you have all the information you need at half the length. Choice II has shed too many words. Choice III is tempting, and if you know your reader really well, it might be fine. Because three people are involved in the story (the judge, Henry, and the texter), I prefer option I, which names Henry.

16   **III.** Choice I is unclear. Is the texter asking whether a press conference will be held, or is it a question about attendance? Choice II doesn't work because three people (the judge, Henry, and the texter) are possibilities. Only III supplies enough words to clarify the situation.

17   **Incorrect.** This closing is a bit old-fashioned, and it has too many capital letters. In a multi-word closing, only the first word is capitalized.

18   **Incorrect.** The subject line should be short, and this one is way too long. "Late Paper" would be better. The rest of the information, including the reason for lateness, belongs in the message itself.

19   **Correct.** Unless the professor is unbelievably stuffy, this friendly greeting is fine.

20   **Incorrect.** The greeting should be separated from the message by a comma. Also, why announce *I want to tell you* something? Just tell it!

21   **Incorrect.** *Later,* is informal, more suitable in a text to a friend than in an email.

22   **Correct.** This subject line alerts the recipient to the content. It's correctly capitalized in headline style.

23   **Correct.** Once again, the subject line tells the recipient what to expect. It's correctly capitalized in sentence style.

24   **Correct.** This closing is little formal, but perfectly correct.

25   **Incorrect.** Would you want to receive an email with this name? The *annoyingcustomer* would immediately turn into the *formercustomer* because no one likes being insulted.

26   **Correct.** The original has a breezy, informal tone with the ellipses (three dots) and the cozy *let's just say.* It ends with humor (*no one should put a sardine near a chicken*). The possible addition also employs informal wording. (*You can so put a sardine near a chicken!*)

27   **Incorrect.** The original sentence is formal, breaking no grammar rules. The possible addition is more informal, with shortened words (*shipping's* instead of "shipping is" and some wordplay in the first portion of the sentence.

28   **Incorrect.** The possible addition is much more formal than the sample sentence.

29   **Correct.** Comments on a shared document may be informal, so long as they're respectful. The possible addition is clear and takes the same tone as the original.

30   **Correct.** Both the original and the possible addition follow the rules of Standard English, expressing ideas in a way that nonspecialists can grasp. They make a good match.

Answers to "Overachievers Questions"

(1) Correct Structurally and grammatically, this fictional email address is correct.

(2) Incorrect The subject line is too long, and it's not capitalized.

(3) Incorrect Punctuation should follow this greeting. Insert a comma or a colon after *Citizens*.

(4) Incorrect *SPI* is a term I invented. It stands for *Severe Popping Injuries*. Don't shorten terms in an email unless you're sure the people reading it will understand what you mean.

(5) Correct In a multi-word closing, only the first word should be capitalized, as it is here.

(6) Correct You don't need to capitalize the first word of a text unless it's a proper name or the personal pronoun *I*.

(7) Incorrect Is the *popcorn fire massive* or is the texter referring to *massive piles?* The text is unclear. Punctuation would help here — a dash, period, or a comma. Or, the texter could hit "send" after typing *fire* and then continue the message in another text.

(8) Correct No capital is needed for the first word of this sentence.

(9) Incorrect The meaning isn't clear. Is the video team on the scene or is the texter requesting their presence?

(10) Correct No capital letters or additional explanation is needed for this common abbreviation of "as soon as possible."

(11) Correct This comment starts off fine with a complete, grammatically correct sentence.

(12) Incorrect The first word of this sentence should be capitalized.

(13) Incorrect Multiple exclamation points aren't appropriate for a comment directed to strangers.

(14) Incorrect The first word of this sentence should be capitalized.

(15) Incorrect The sentence requires an end mark.

Chapter **14**

Stacking Ideas: Numbered Steps and Bulleted Lists

Would you rather read a list or a paragraph? Both have roles to play when you're explaining something, but if you can learn the same thing from either format, I'm guessing you'd prefer a list. Short bursts of information save time and are easier to comprehend. That's why numbered steps and bullet points are so popular. (That's also why Dummies books use them!) The same grammar rules apply to all lists, whether they appear on a presentation slide, in an email or report, or in some other document. In this chapter, I explain how to write, capitalize, and punctuate when you're writing in this format.

Introducing the Ingredients of Steps and Bulleted Lists

Numbered steps take you through a process, from the beginning (step 1) through to the end (last step). You've probably followed numbered steps to set up a new kitchen appliance, cook your favorite recipe, and do other things that require a series of actions, in order. *Bulleted lists* present ideas grouped by topic but in no special order. Bulleted lists appear in every chapter of this book.

Regardless of where they appear (on screen or on paper), numbered steps and bulleted lists follow the same rules.

Introductory element

Your audience needs to know what the bullet points or numbered steps are about. That's the job of the introductory element. Here are the rules:

>> **If the introductory element is a complete sentence, place a colon (one dot atop another) at the end.** (*Applicants must submit these documents:*)

>> **If the introductory element begins a thought that the bullet points or numbered steps complete, don't place a colon or any other punctuation at the end.** (*Management will* or *Successful applicants are*)

>> **If the introductory element functions as a title (*Required Documents*) you may center and position it above the bullets or steps without punctuation. You can also place it at the lefthand margin and follow it with a colon.** (*Required documents:*)

>> **Never place a period at the end of an introductory element.**

TIP

Introductory elements ending with a form of the verb *be* are always incomplete thoughts and never end with punctuation.

YOUR TURN

Take a look at each introductory element. Is it correctly punctuated and capitalized? If so, write "correct." If not, revise it.

Q. Anita is responsible for these decorations

A. **Anita is responsible for these decorations:** This introduction is a full sentence and should be followed by a colon.

1. Yoshi and Abe are:

2. Charlotte requests that

3. Party supplies:

4. To set up the coffeemaker, follow these steps,

5. In the past, guests have been:

6. If the party is a success, we will make these changes next year.

7. the last person to leave the party will:

8. Social Media Publicity

Numbered steps and bullet points

Numbered steps are (you'll never guess) steps listed below an introductory element. Each set of steps is numbered, starting with one. *Bullet points* get their name from their most common form, a dot that resembles a bullet hole. Symbols such as arrows, stars, checkmarks, and other symbols are also fine. Here's what you need to know in order to format steps and bullet points correctly:

» **Every step in a numbered list should be a complete sentence.** Write the step as a command and place a period at the end. Start each step on a new line. Use numerals, not words, for the step numbers. Take a look at this example — three steps in a fictional recipe for peanut butter ravioli:

1. Defrost one container of ready-made pasta dough.

2. Boil six quarts of lightly salted water.

3. Stir the peanut butter for ten minutes.

» **If a bullet point is a complete sentence, capitalize the first word and use an endmark (period, question mark, exclamation point).** The bullet points in this list are complete sentences, so they follow this rule.

» **If the bullet point isn't a complete sentence, you generally don't capitalize the first word unless it's a proper name.** This rule is a matter of style, not grammar, so you have some leeway here. Dummies style, for example, calls for capital letters for bullet points even when they aren't complete sentences.

» **If the bullet point isn't a complete sentence, don't include an end mark.**

» **Grammatically, every bullet point should match.** If one bullet point is a complete sentence, all the bullet points should be complete sentences. Or, all the bullet points may be phrases.

TIP

You can usually hear whether bullet points match, even if you don't know which grammar term applies. *To buy, to sell,* and *to get a refund* match. *Buying, selling,* and *to get a refund* don't match.

YOUR TURN

Read these numbered steps and bullet points. If everything is as it should be, write *correct*. If not, revise.

Q. bullet point from a list of marketing ideas

email blasts

A. **Correct.** Bullet points that are not complete sentences do not have to be capitalized and should not end with a punctuation mark.

⑨ numbered step from a recipe

6. Cut the dough into four-inch squares.

⑩ bullet points naming states that were surveyed

California.

New Mexico.

Colorado.

(11) bullet point from a list of park rules

No pot-bellied pigs are allowed.

(12) numbered step in a recipe

Ten. Boil the ravioli until they are soft.

(13) bullet points from a list of chores

returning library books

picking up dry cleaning

to clean the house

(14) numbered step from user manual

3. Insert tab A into slot B.

(15) bullet points explaining why a teen may not buy a used car

opposition from parents

failed driving test

The teen has $4.78 in the bank, and the car costs $5000.

(16) numbered step from an instruction book

7. Placing the yarn directly on the loom.

Putting It All Together in Presentation Slides

Presentation slides rely on numbered steps and bulleted lists. When you're making a presentation, no matter how interesting you are and how interested in the topic your audience may be, someone's attention will drift. It might be yours! Public speaking can be scary, and it's easy to lose track or fumble for words. Listeners can fade away, too. Presentation slides help by thumb-tacking everyone's attention to the topic. Here are some guidelines for presentation slides:

>> **Most presentations begin with a title slide identifying the topic and the presenter.**

>> **Background music and art may accompany the numbered steps or bullet points in your presentation.** These add-ins don't change the grammar rules for the written portion of each slide.

>> **If you include graphs, tables, charts, or other visual elements, be sure to label them.** Follow the capitalization rules for titles I explain in Chapter 12.

Here are some sample "slides" from a presentation without capital letters or punctuation. Underneath each slide is a list of corrections. Select all the corrections needed to create a grammatically correct slide.

YOUR TURN

Q.

---

parakeet hobbies

- bowling
- they like to toss seeds
- hang-gliding

I.   Capitalize *Parakeet.*

II. Capitalize *Hobbies.*

III. Change second bullet to *toss seeds.*

IV. Change second bullet to *seed-tossing.*

A. **I, II, IV.** Capitalize both words of the title. The second bullet doesn't match the other two. Of the two possible changes, IV is better because it matches the *-ing* verb form of the other two bullets.

---

parakeets need the following items for bowling

- three-toed bowling shoes
- beak-adapted bowling balls
- featherweight pins

 I.   Capitalize *Parakeets.*

II. Place a comma at the end of the first line of the slide.

III. Place a colon at the end of the first line of the slide.

IV. Place a period at the end of each bullet point.

the best-selling bowling shoes for parakeets have

- they have room for overgrown claws

- most are in brightly colors

- many include a complimentary seed stick

- they have clips rather than laces

 I. Capitalize *The*.

II. Place a colon at the end of the first line.

III. Place a period at the end of each bullet point.

IV. Change bullet points to *room for overgrown claws, bright colors, complimentary seed stick, and clips rather than laces.*

most prominent parakeet bowlers are

- able to think on their feet (claws)

- sponsored by well-known pet food companies

- active only for five or six years

 I. Capitalize *Most*.

II. Place a colon after *are*.

III. Capitalize the first word of each bullet point.

IV. Place a period at the end of each bullet point.

> **history of parakeet bowling**
>
> - the sport began in the 15th century
>
> - early bowlers used apples to knock down corn stalks
>
> - first professional tour — 1932

I. Capitalize every word in the title except for *of*.

II. Capitalize the first word in each bullet point.

III. Place a period at the end of each bullet point.

IV. Change the last bullet point to *The first professional tour took place in 1932.*

Calling All Overachievers: Extra Practice with Presentation Slides

YOUR TURN

The employee who created the slide presentation in the following figure slept through every single grammar lesson she ever had. Now, it's up to you to correct her errors. You should find ten mistakes.

Best careers for Parakeets; paper Shredder

- Every bird earns a good salary
- excellent working conditions
- Each bird has an assistant and
- the veterinary insurance plan has a low deductible
- Seed breaks once an hour.

Answers to Numbered Steps and Bulleted List Questions

1. **Yoshi and Abe are** An introductory element that ends with a form of the verb *be* — in this case, *are* — never ends with a punctuation mark.

2. **Correct.** This introductory element is the beginning of a thought, which the bullet points complete. Therefore, no punctuation should separate it from the bullet points.

3. **Correct.** This is a title, which may be followed by a colon if it appears at the lefthand margin.

4. **To set up the coffeemaker, follow these steps:** The introductory element is a complete sentence, so you need a colon, not a comma, at the end.

5. **In the past, guests have been** The verb *have been* is a form of verb *be*, so no punctuation should separate it from the list.

6. **If the party is a success, we will make these changes next year:** No period should appear at the end of an introductory element.

7. **The last person to leave the party will** The introductory element should begin with a capital letter. This one is an incomplete thought, so no punctuation should appear at the end.

8. **Correct.** This introductory element is a title. You can center it above the list or place it on the lefthand margin and follow it with a colon.

9. **Correct.** The step is a complete sentence and ends with a period. The first word is properly capitalized.

10. **Incorrect.** The bullet points are not complete sentences and should not be followed by end marks. Here's how the list should look:

    California

    New Mexico

    Colorado

11. **Correct.** This complete sentence properly begins with a capital letter and ends with a period.

12. **10. Boil the ravioli until they are soft.** A numbered step should begin with a numeral, not with a number written as a word.

13.
    - **returning library books**
    - **picking up dry cleaning**
    - **cleaning the house**

    Items in a bulleted list should match grammatically. In this list, the first two bullet points begin with *ing* verb forms, but the last does not. The simplest correction is to change the third bullet point to an *ing* form also.

14. **Correct.** This numbered step is a complete sentence and properly begins with a capital letter and ends with a period.

(15)
- **opposition from parents**
- **failed driving test**
- **lack of funds**

Bullet points should match, grammatically. In the original list, the first two items aren't complete sentences, but the last is. Note: I chose nouns with attached descriptions, but you could also make each bullet point into a complete sentence.

(16) **7. Place the yarn directly on the loom.** A numbered step should be a complete sentence. (For more on what makes a sentence complete, turn to Chapter 8.)

(17) **I and III.** Because the introductory statement is a complete sentence, it should begin with a capital letter (Choice I) and end with a colon, which indicates that a list follows (Choice III). A comma shouldn't introduce a bulleted list. The bullet points aren't complete sentences, so no periods are necessary.

(18) **I, IV.** The first word of the introductory statement needs a capital letter (Choice I). No punctuation follows *have* because the statement isn't a complete sentence (Choices II and III). In the original list, the bullet points are complete sentences, so they don't combine well with the introductory statement. *The best bowling shoes for parakeets have they have room . . .* nope, I don't think so. The bullets should be *room for overgrown claws*, *bright colors*, *complimentary seed sticks*, and *clips rather than laces* (Choice IV).

(19) **I.** Did I catch you with this one? No punctuation is needed in the first line because *are* doesn't complete the introductory sentence. Nor should you capitalize any of the bullet points, as they complete the sentence begun by the introductory statement. Choice IV is tempting, but you've got three half sentences, one in each bullet point, all connected to the introductory line. Placing three periods doesn't make sense. The only change is a capital *M* for the first word in the introductory sentence (Choice I).

(20) **I, II, III, IV.** This slide has a title, and titles need capital letters. The first two bullet points are complete sentences, so the third should match.

Answers to "Overachievers Questions"

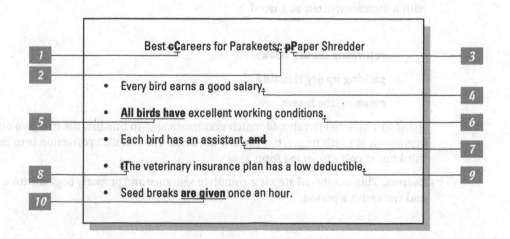

Best ~c~Careers for Parakeets~,~: ~p~Paper Shredder
- Every bird earns a good salary.
- **All birds have** excellent working conditions.
- Each bird has an assistant. ~and~
- ~t~The veterinary insurance plan has a low deductible.
- Seed breaks **are given** once an hour.

1. Capitalize the important words in a title. (See Chapter 12 for details.)

2. Separate a title from a subtitle with a colon (:).

3. Capitalize the first word of a subtitle.

4. Always place an end mark after a full-sentence bullet point; here, a period is best.

5. The first bullet point is a complete sentence, so all the bullet points should also be complete sentences. (Alternative correction: Change all the bullet points to phrases.)

6. A complete sentence that makes a statement ends with a period.

7. One bullet point should not continue on to the next. Delete *and* and place a period at the end of this sentence.

8. This bullet point is a complete sentence, so it should begin with a capital letter.

9. This complete sentence needs an end mark — specifically, a period.

10. The original bullet point was not a complete sentence. To make everything match, change this bullet point to a complete sentence by adding a verb.

Chapter **15**

Writing at School and at Work

D o you have a desk in a classroom or in an office? If so, chances are you write reports, letters, or other assignments for a teacher or a boss. With correct grammar, you're more likely to receive higher grades and better pay. In this chapter, you practice polishing your writing so that it meets academic and professional standards.

Writing on the A-Plus level

At school, you have to obey the rules. So does your writing! It's important, therefore, to know the conventions of Standard English, as well as each subject area's traditions. Here are the principles governing academic writing:

» **Use formal language.** Academic writing is no place for slang, half-sentences, and a friend-to-friend tone.

» **Identify sources of information.** Stealing is never acceptable, whether it's a wallet or an idea. Looking up something on the internet or questioning a friend or relative is fine unless your teacher has told you not to do so. If you use information from any source other than your own mind, however, you must give credit. Sometimes, you can do so in the text, inserting *according to, as reported by,* or a similar phrase. You can also attach a *citation* — an identifying tag. Depending on the field (science, history, the arts, or so forth), the citation may appear in parentheses within a sentence or as a footnote or an endnote.

TIP

Be sure you know which system of citation your teacher prefers because formats differ. Once you've identified which system you should use, check the internet or a style manual to find out where to place each element (title, author, date, publisher, page). You can also download a computer program or go to a website that formats citations for you.

» **Place quotation marks around words that are not your own.** This is another way of giving credit where credit is due. Chapter 11 goes into detail on punctuating quotations.

» **Pay attention to titles.** Very short pieces of writing don't need titles, and your teacher may not require one even for a longer work. However, creating a title helps you focus your ideas. The title of a long paper may appear on a separate page, centered about a third of the way down from the top. For shorter works, center the title on the top line. Don't place quotation marks around titles in these spots. If you refer to a title within a paragraph or in a list of sources, place quotation marks around the title of a short work (an article, poem, song, story, and so forth). Italicize or underline titles of longer works (books, films, television series, albums, and so forth). Check Chapter 11 for more information on quotation marks or italics in titles.

» **Choose the right system for capitalizing titles.** STEM fields (science, technology, engineering, and math), use *sentence style* capitalization. In sentence style, only proper names and the first word of the title and subtitle appear in caps. English, history, and the arts generally prefer *headline style.* In this style, all the important words are capitalized. (Chapter 12 goes into detail on the rules for both styles.)

» **Choose verb tense carefully.** *Tense* is the quality of a verb that expresses time. If you're writing about something that already happened — a historical event or a science experiment — past tense is best. If you're writing about a creative work — literature, visual arts, or a musical composition — present tense is generally the best choice. The logic is that the audience experiences an artistic work in the moment, so the work always exists in the present.

» **In STEM writing, format dates in day-month-year order, without commas.** In a science paper, you might refer to 20 September 2026. If you're writing only the month and year, put them in that order, again without commas (September 2026). You can use the same system for non-STEM papers, or you can write the date in this order: month, day, year, with a comma between the day and the year (September 20, 2026).

WARNING

Don't use a numeral to represent a month, regardless of the subject matter. In some countries, the day comes before the month. In other countries, the day appears after the month. You don't want your reader to wonder whether 9/4 is September 4th or April 9th.

» **Don't insert yourself into the paper.** Unless the teacher has asked for personal reflection, write about the subject matter, not about yourself. Phrases such as "in my opinion" and "I think" are necessary only if you're comparing your view of an issue with someone else's.

» **In a science paper, write in passive voice.** *Passive voice* focuses on the result (*The mixture was heated*), not on the person achieving that result. (*Ms. Jones heated the mixture.*) Chapter 18 goes into detail on passive voice.

» **Be sure abbreviations and acronyms are clear.** An *abbreviation* is a shortened form (*kg* for kilogram, for example). An *acronym* is a word created from the first letter of each word in a name (*NASA* for the National Aeronautics and Space Administration). For anything that might be unfamiliar, define the term in parentheses the first time you use it.

» **Capitalize and punctuate abbreviations correctly.** Most metric abbreviations (*m* for meter, *kg* for kilogram, and so forth) aren't capitalized and don't contain periods. Other abbreviations (such as the military rank *Capt.* or the identifier *Jr.* in a name) have both capitals and periods. Still others have one but not both (*NYC, sq. ft.*). Don't bother memorizing abbreviations except those you use often. Instead, check the dictionary.

» **Present statistics in an easily understood format.** Science depends on data, and numbers appearing in a sentence may confuse readers. Consider tables, graphs, and charts. Label each with an identifier (*Table 2*) and a title (*Growth patterns*).

YOUR TURN

Q. Below are sample bits of school assignments. Label them "acceptable" or "unacceptable."

Sample	What It Is	Acceptable or Unacceptable?
"The Easter Rising: An Oral History"	title of a history paper, centered alone on a title page	

A. **Unacceptable.** A centered title should not be enclosed in quotation marks.

Question Number	Sample	What It Is	Acceptable or Unacceptable?
1	"Friendship in the Novels of Toni Morrison"	title, alone on a title page	
2	The temperature was recorded at five-minute intervals.	science lab report	
3	Political cartoons In France, 1914–1920	title of a history essay, alone on the first line of the paper	
4	Juliet's death is, in my opinion, unnecessary.	sentence from a paper about Shakespeare's *Romeo and Juliet*	
5	The average completion rate was 60%.	sentence from a description of a psychological experiment	
6	In Rembrandt's painting, Aristotle rests his hand on a statue of the Greek poet Homer.	sentence from an essay about a famous painting	
7	The plants watered daily had way more leaves than the plants watered weekly.	sentence from a science lab report	
8	The first trade was made at 6:00 a.m. in the morning on 7/2/2020.	sentence from a research paper	
9	Dr. Martin Luther King, jr gave his famous "I Have a Dream" speech in 1963.	sentence from a history essay	

10	In the second movement, the tempo changes.	analysis of a musical composition	
11	"Mercury pollution in Lake Yary"	title page of a science research paper	
12	Jane Austen drew on her experiences in polite society for her novel *Pride and Prejudice.*	sentence from an essay written for English class	
13	Ronald Reagan said trust but verify.	sentence from a political science paper	
14	Ronald Reagan spoke about the importance of trusting the government of another country, but he stressed the need to check that promises were kept.	sentence from a political science paper	
15	The virus can be really, really dangerous to newborns.	sentence from a science report	

Writing in the Working World

Not long ago, a friend told me that a machine would soon take over my job as a writer. I believe (well, I hope) he's wrong. It's true that computer programs can compose memos, reports, and emails. AI (artificial intelligence) is getting smarter every day. However, no matter how carefully I define what I want AI to create, the result is never quite right. Small differences are unimportant, but sometimes, the meaning changes in ways that really matter. I suspect you agree with me. After all, you're reading this book because you want to express yourself in your own words, clearly and correctly.

TIP

Companies often maintain their own list of rules for work communications within the company and between the company and its clients. Some (Microsoft, Walmart, and Burger King, to name just three) publish their own writing manuals that explain their preferred tone, capitalization style, and so forth. If your company has a manual, read the parts that relate to your work. If it doesn't, use your coworkers' writing as a model.

In general, workplace writing follows these rules:

>> **In business, be businesslike.** Your coworkers may be your friends outside of work, but on the job, treat them as professionals. Also, remember that emails and memos aren't private. Write as if the boss is reading your work because that might be true.

>> **Be polite.** Take the time to check the reader's name and title. Spell both correctly! If you're writing to a customer, don't address the reader by first name. Instead, use the last name preceded by *Mr., Ms., Mx.* (nongendered term), *Dr., Judge,* and so forth.

>> **Use templates to save yourself some time.** *Templates* are fill-in-the-blank models available in word-processing programs. If you click on a memo template, for instance, you see spaces for the date, the subject, and the name of the writer and reader. All you have to do is type the details.

>> **Remember that your reader is busy.** If you're reading for fun, you probably don't mind a leisurely pace. At work, your reader expects you to get to the point. Anything that saves time, such as a bulleted list, is a plus. (Chapter 14 explains how to format a bulleted list.)

>> **Let the reader know what to expect.** In an email or a memo, the subject line alerts the reader to the content. If it's too general ("Information") or too long ("How We Think Model 2.5 of the Xtray Will Sell"), the reader may not actually read the message. Your goal is to be specific and short: "Xtray Sales Projections."

>> **Include the date.** The timing may matter, especially if the reader has an overloaded inbox! Follow your company's preferred style.

>> **In a business letter, include a greeting and a closing.** The greeting (*Dear Ms. Foley,* for example) should be on a separate line before the body of the letter. Follow the greeting with a colon (one dot atop another). The closing is a phrase, such as *Best* or *Sincerely*, followed by your name and title (if you have one) on separate lines. If the closing contains more than one word (*Sincerely yours,* perhaps), capitalize only the first word.

Avoid old-fashioned phrases such as *To Whom It May Concern* or *Yours faithfully.*

>> **Consider using graphics to get your point across.** Well-placed tables, charts, and similar visual aids can reduce word count without sacrificing meaning.

When you're writing a business report, follow the same general guidelines outlined in the preceding section, "Writing on the A–Plus Level."

Q. Below are sample bits of business writing. Label them "acceptable" or "unacceptable."

Sample	What It Is	Acceptable or Unacceptable?
Dear Oscar:	greeting in a business letter to a potential client	

A. **Unacceptable.** A business letter should be formal. Using a first name (*Oscar*) strikes the wrong tone.

Question Number	Sample	What It Is	Acceptable or Unacceptable
16	It is on this date (January 15th) that I will be able to meet with you about the agenda.	sentence from a memo to a coworker	
17	Very Truly Yours,	closing of a business letter	
18	The online meeting is scheduled for 2/3/2026.	sentence from an email to coworkers in several different countries	
19	Hannah Nguyen

Marketing Director | last two lines of a business letter | |
| 20 | To: Ali El-Amin | line from an email to a coworker | |

21	Take advantage of our mega discount!	sentence from a memo to an attorney's client	
22	Growth rates were 5% in May, 2% in June, 8% in July, 5% in August, and 6% in September.	sentence from a report on sales	
23	From: Mr. Carmen	email to a supervisor	
24	July 1, 2027	date of a memo	
25	Hi	subject line of an email	
26	Table 1: 2029 Marketing Budget	title of a table in a business report	
27	As per our agreement, you will ship three dozen cars soonest.	sentence in a business letter	
28	See the figure on the last page of this report.	sentence from a business report	
29	Dear Ms. Amati,	greeting in the message portion of a memo to a coworker	
30	Please reply by February 26, 2027.	sentence from an email to a client	

Calling All Overachievers: Extra Practice with School and Work Writing

Look at the underlined portions of these documents carefully. Are they acceptable or unacceptable? The first is a paragraph from a student's science report. The second is a letter from a business owner to a customer. Note: the student, the business, and the snakes are not real. I made everything up!

Student report

The Duncehead snake is native to the island of Viper Grande off the coast of Chile. (1) The snake is ugly but not poisonous! (2) People think that one bite can be fatal, said Augusto Rodrigo, head of the Viper Grande Zoo. (3) He explained that two species, the Duncehead and the Duncetail, are very similar in appearance. The Duncetail has slightly larger teeth than the Duncehead. (4) A person bitten by a Duncetail dies in minutes. A person bitten by a Duncehead feels only an annoying sting. Because these snakes are hard to tell apart, (5) in my opinion people should be careful to avoid contact with either of them.

Business letter

Pontia Pets: Your Source for Lovable Animals

5673 Fishbowl Road

Pontia, WA 98000

206-555-5555

Dr. Albert Llewelyn

87 Main Avenue West

(6) <u>Pontia, WA 98001</u>

(7) <u>June</u>

(8) <u>Dear Dr. Llewelyn:</u>

On (9) <u>Thursday, May 26, 2026</u>, your son David Llewelyn entered my pet shop,

which was very busy at the time. He released five snakes from their cages,

attempting to measure their teeth. He screamed, "That's a Duncetail! It bit me!

It's poisonous! I'm going to die!" Although I explained that it was a harmless

Duncehead, the police did not believe me. You will hear from my lawyer shortly.

(10) <u>Your friend,</u>

Peter Piper

Store Manager

Answers to School and Work Questions

1. **Unacceptable.** The title of a paper presented alone on a page should not be enclosed in quotation marks.

2. **Acceptable.** Science lab reports focus on process and result, not on the scientist. Therefore, passive voice (*was monitored*) is a good choice.

3. **Unacceptable.** History papers generally follow the headline style of capitalization. The correct version capitalizes *Political*, *Cartoons*, and *France*, but not *in*.

4. **Unacceptable.** The reader understands that the writer is presenting an opinion about Juliet's death. The phrase *in my opinion* should be deleted.

5. **Acceptable.** The language is appropriately formal. Because the experiment took place in the past, the past-tense verb *was* is correct.

6. **Acceptable.** Because this sentence discusses a work of art, the present-tense verb (*rests*) is correct.

7. **Unacceptable.** *Way more* is too informal for a school assignment. Also, science reports should be specific. Instead of a general assessment, the writer should say how many leaves grew on each plant.

8. **Unacceptable.** You don't need to write both *a.m.* and *in the morning*, because they give the same information. Also, is the writer referring to July 2nd or February 7th? The date may be interpreted either way, depending on the reader's nationality.

9. **Unacceptable.** The abbreviation should be *Jr.*, not *jr* written without a period.

10. **Acceptable.** Writing about an artistic work — in this case, a musical work — requires present tense.

11. **Unacceptable.** A title presented alone on a title page should not be enclosed in quotation marks.

12. **Acceptable.** The past-tense verb *drew* is acceptable here because the sentence discusses the act of writing, which took place in the past.

13. **Unacceptable.** Quoted words (*trust but verify*) should be enclosed in quotation marks.

14. **Acceptable.** This sentence refers to but doesn't quote Ronald Reagan's words, so no quotation marks are needed.

15. **Unacceptable.** Repeating *really* isn't necessary and creates too informal a tone for a school report.

16. **Unacceptable.** *It is on this date that* is too wordy. Change it to *On January 15*th.

17. **Unacceptable.** In a multi-word closing, capitalize only the first word. Also, the closing is a bit old-fashioned.

18. **Unacceptable.** In some countries, the month comes before the day. In others, the reverse is true. Because this email is going to more than one country, the date format may be misunderstood. Identify the month with a word, not a numeral.

19. **Acceptable.** The name and title should be capitalized at the end of a business letter.

(20) **Acceptable.** The *To* line of an email should contain the full name of the person you're writing to, properly capitalized, as it is here. The name of the person receiving the email comes from the sender's contact list and appears automatically, so any unacceptable capitalization should be corrected there.

(21) **Unacceptable.** Letters to a client should be formal, so the slang term *mega* is out of place here.

(22) **Unacceptable.** This sentence isn't terrible, but the information would be easier to grasp if the numbers were presented in a chart or a table.

(23) **Unacceptable.** The *From* line of an email should contain the full name of the person writing it. *Mr.* is not a substitute for the writer's first name. The name of the sender comes from the formatting the sender set up for that email account. Any corrections should be made there.

(24) **Acceptable.** The order (month, day, year) is fine, and a comma appropriately separates the day from the year.

(25) **Unacceptable.** What is this email about? *Hi* is a friendly way to say hello, not a subject.

(26) **Acceptable.** A label for a chart, table, or graph should be capitalized and include a title, as this one does.

(27) **Unacceptable.** The language here is old-fashioned, even stuffy. Change *as per our agreement* to *as agreed* or something similar. Change *soonest* to an exact date or to *as soon as possible*.

(28) **Unacceptable.** Visual elements of a report should be numbered. Instead of *the figure on the last page of this report*, substitute the figure's number (*Figure* 22, for example).

(29) **Unacceptable.** A memo has a heading with *From* and *To* lines, as well as a date and subject line. The body of the memo doesn't need a greeting.

(30) **Unacceptable.** The date should have a comma between the day and the year.

Answers to Overachiever School and Work Writing Questions

(1) **Unacceptable.** The wording of this sentence is too casual for a school report. Exclamation points are not acceptable in a science assignment.

(2) **Unacceptable.** When you are quoting someone, their words should be enclosed by quotation marks.

(3) **Acceptable.** No quotation marks are necessary here because the writer is not reproducing the exact words.

(4) **Acceptable.** This sentence has correct grammar and a suitably formal tone.

(5) **Unacceptable.** "In my opinion" is needed only when the writer is comparing views, which is not the case here. This phrase should be deleted.

(6) **Acceptable.** This address is correctly formatted.

(7) **Unacceptable.** The date should specify the day and year, as well as the month.

(8) **Acceptable.** The greeting uses the title (*Dr.*) and last name and ends with a colon, as it should.

(9) **Acceptable.** Here, the entire date appears correctly formatted.

(10) **Unacceptable.** This is a business letter, and clearly, the writer is not friends with Dr. Llewelyn. *Your friend* should be changed to *Sincerely* or something similar.

5

Getting the Details Right

Chapter **16**

Taming Tricky Words

Have you ever struggled to decide whether to write *there*, *their*, or *they're*? How about *affect* or *effect*? Will you spend *anytime* or *any time* reading this chapter? I hope so because here you find answers to these questions and many more as you tame tricky words and expressions.

Telling Word-Twins Apart

Some human twins look like each other but have completely different personalities. In the same way, some words sound the same but have unrelated definitions. This section helps you employ word-twins (and some triplets) properly. Take a look:

» **Your and you're.** *Your* shows possession: *Your* foot is on my seat. *You're* is short for "you are": *You're* very rude.

» **Hear and here.** *Hear* means "to detect sound," and *here* refers to a place: Sit *here*, where you'll be close enough to *hear* the music.

» **By, buy, and bye.** *By* means "near" or "beside," as descriptions of location and "past" as a description of movement. It may also identify a creator: I walked *by* the fireplace, where I found a book *by* Zora Neale Hurston. *Buy* means "to purchase": I want to *buy* more of her books. *Bye* is a farewell: I'm going home now. *Bye!*

» **Its and it's.** *Its* shows possession: The table fell when *its* legs snapped. *It's* is short for "it is": *It's* at the repair shop now.

>> **Principle and principal:** A *principle* is a basic belief: Lying is against his *principles,* so he always tells the truth. A *principal* is a person with authority: Think of the *principal* of your school as your pal.

>> **Whose and who's.** *Whose* shows possession: The clerk *whose* line is longest is the slowest worker in the office. *Who's* is short for "who is" or "who has": *Who's* going to fire that clerk and hire someone faster?

>> **Brake and break.** *Brake* is "to cause to slow down": Pat *braked* when the deer ran into the road. *Break* is "to crack or split": That bowl will *break* if you handle it carelessly.

>> **Past and passed.** *Past* refers to the point in time before now: Historians study the *past. Past* may also mean "in front of" or "beyond": The car sped *past* the exit. *Passed* means "went by" or "made into law": The senators *passed* in front of me as they exited the Capitol. They had just *passed* three laws.

>> **Their, they're, and there.** *Their* shows possession: The clients took *their* business elsewhere. *They're* is short for "they are": *They're* tired of waiting. *There* is a place: The clients found a more efficient office and went *there.*

>> **Whether and weather.** *Whether* signals a choice: I can't decide *whether* to go or stay home. *Weather* is what forecasts predict: The *weather* is perfect for our picnic, with sunny skies and comfortable temperatures.

>> **Vane, vain, and vein.** A *vane* shows which way the wind is blowing: It was so windy that the *vane* on top of the barn blew off. *Vain* people are overly concerned with their appearance: Leslie was so *vain* about her hair that she went hatless even when it was freezing. A *vein* carries blood throughout the body: The doctor inserted the needle into a *vein* in the patient's arm.

>> **Two, to, and too.** *Two* is a number: You have *two* hands. *To* may attach to a verb, creating an infinitive: Mom wants you *to* make dinner. *To* may also show movement toward something or someone: Go *to* the kitchen now and get started. *Too* means "also" or "more than enough": Michael will cook *too,* because there is *too* much work for one person.

Choose the correct word and write it in the blank.

YOUR TURN **Q.** Don't judge a book by _____ (its, it's) cover unless _____ (your, you're) buying a text for art class.

A. **its, you're.** In the first blank, you want a possessive form. In the second, *you are buying* is the meaning you need.

1. "_____ (Whose, Who's) _____ (your, you're) professor?" asked Mandy.

2. "I heard the teacher is also the _____ (principle, principal) of the school," she added.

3. "Is he the _____ (vane, vain, vein) guy who combs his hair ten times a day?" Andy asked. "He looks in the mirror so often it will probably _____ (brake, break) from overuse."

4. "I don't know," Mark replied. "_____ (Its, It's) a new class. I'll find out when I go _____ (their, they're, there)."

5. The friends walked _____ (past, passed) the room and peeked inside.

6. After he saw the homework posted on the wall, he wasn't sure _____ (whether, weather) or not to take the class.

7. The workload couldn't be _____ (two, to, too) intense because he had _____ (two, to, too) find a job _____ (two, to, too) help his parents pay _____ (their, they're, there) bills.

8. "I _____ (hear, here) that Professor Guleed, _____ (whose, who's) assignments look hard, is the best teacher. Plus, _____ (your, you're) in class only _____ (two, to, too) hours a week," said Mandy.

9. "Regardless of the teacher, _____ (its, it's) a tough class, with _____ (two, to, too) many facts," added Aaron "I often send letters of complaint _____ (two, to, too) the deans, but _____ (their, they're) not sympathetic."

10. "Time to go," remarked Mandy. "_____ (By, Buy, Bye) now!"

Distinguishing Between Commonly Confused Words

What a difference a letter (or a few letters) can make! The word pairs in this section are commonly confused, with one word appearing where the other is more appropriate. Take note of the difference, and use them wisely:

TIP

>> **Affect and Effect.** *Affect* is a verb meaning "to influence": Mallory's tantrum did not *affect* her mother's decision to leave the candy aisle. *Effect* is most often used as a noun, meaning "result or consequence": One *effect* of Mallory's sweet tooth was a big dental bill.

Both *affect* and *effect* may be used in other ways, though much less frequently. *Affect*, as a noun, means "the way someone displays emotions." *Effect*, as a verb, means "to bring about a change in the face of opposition."

>> **Farther and Further.** *Farther* refers to distance: Mallory runs *farther* than anyone else when a candy bar is at stake. *Further* refers to just about everything but distance (intensity, degree, time, and so forth): When Mallory thought *further* about the matter, she decided that artificial sweetener was not a good choice.

>> **Continually and Continuously.** *Continually* (and its close relative, *continual*) refers to actions that happen again and again, with little breaks between: Jamal *continually* opened the oven to check on the cake baking inside. With *continual* drafts of cold air, the oven cooled down. *Continuously* (and its relative, *continuous*) refers to a constant action that

has no gaps: Without *continuous* heat, the cake took forever to bake. Margie scolded him *continuously* until he ordered a cake from the corner bakery.

>> **Stationary and Stationery.** *Stationary* means "not moving or changing": I ride my *stationary* bike every morning. *Stationery* is school or office supplies such as paper, pens, and so forth: Just before the school year starts, *stationery* sells well.

>> **Complimentary and Complementary.** *Complimentary* means "for free": Mike received *complimentary* tickets because his brother is in the band. *Complementary* is a description of elements to go well together: Choose *complementary* colors when you buy shirts to wear with your new suit.

>> **Accept and Except.** *Accept* is "to say yes, to agree to receive": Margie, who loves sweets, *accepts* every dessert offered to her. *Except* means "everything but": Joe eats every type of dessert *except* pie, which he doesn't like.

>> **Stayed and Stood.** *Stayed* is "to remain": When I had the flu, I *stayed* home. *Stood* is the past tense of "stand": The audience *stood* for the national anthem.

 Circle the word or phrase that best fits the meaning of the sentence.

YOUR TURN **Q.** After drinking two large cups of coffee, Jake drove (farther/further) than anyone else.

A. Farther. If you're dealing with distance, *farther* is the one you want.

11 The judge insisted on (farther/further) proof that Jake had not broken the speed limit.

12 I gave the judge a letter proving that my car was (stationary/stationery), but he refused to (accept/except) it as proof that I was not moving.

13 Waving my wallet at the judge, I tried to (affect/effect) the verdict by hinting at a large bribe.

14 Judge Crater stubbornly refused to hear my side of the story and (continually/continuously) interrupted me.

15 "Don't go any (farther/further) with your testimony," he snarled and (stayed/stood) up.

16 I stopped talking because the judge said more excuses would have a negative (affect/effect) on my case.

17 The judge's words, unfortunately, were drowned out by the (continual/continuous) hammering from the construction next door, which never stopped.

18 The (affect/effect) of this noise was disastrous.

19 Nothing I could do would (affect/effect) the judge's ruling.

20 When the judge took off his robe, I noticed that his tie was patterned in (complimentary/complementary) colors.

Selecting One Word or Two

A few strange pairs are close enough to be twins when you hear them. One twin is written as a single word; the other has two words. This small change makes a big difference in meaning:

>> *All ready* means "everyone or everything completely prepared." *Already* means "before or by a particular time."

   By the time we were *all ready,* Angela had *already* left.

>> *Altogether* means "extremely, entirely." *All together* means "as one."

   Daniel was *altogether* pleased with the way the choir members were *all together* on stage.

>> *Sometime* means "at a certain point in time." *Some time* means "a period of time." *Sometimes* (with an *s*) means "from time to time, occasionally."

   Lex says that he will visit Mei *sometime,* but not now because he has to spend *some time* in the gym.

   Sometimes, Lex goes to the gym on Friday, but Monday is his usual day.

>> *Everyday* means "ordinary, common." *Every day* means "occurring daily."

   Larry loves *everyday* activities such as cooking, cleaning, and sewing.

   He performs those tasks *every day.*

>> *Anyway* means "in any event." *Any way* means "some sort of method."

   "Anyway," Mei said, "I don't think there was *any way* to avoid eating a piece of that pie without hurting the chef's feelings."

YOUR TURN

Q. Select the word or words that fits the meaning of the sentence.

This fork belongs to Lola's (everyday, every day) set of silverware.

A. **everyday** This sentence isn't about time; you need a word that means "ordinary."

21 Do you have (sometime, sometimes, some time) for basketball practice?

22 The coach told his players that he wanted them (already, all ready) to board the team bus before it arrived.

23 When he drove the bus into the parking lot, he was (altogether, all together) disappointed because only a few players were there.

24 "Is there (anyway, any way) we can win this basketball game?" he cried.

25 "I will make them practice an extra hour (everyday, every day) for the next month," he added.

26 (Sometime, Sometimes, Some time) the coach ignores his own promises, but he usually follows through.

27 When the players finally showed up, the coach would not allow them (anytime, any time) to speak.

28 "You have been (altogether, all together) irresponsible," he said.

29 Although he was angry, the coach made sure that the players knew they could ask for his help (anytime, any time).

30 The players practiced saying, "We're sorry!" (altogether, all together) in one loud shout.

Banning Bogus Expressions

English *should of* been easier. So many forms are irregular! *Being that* grammar is important, I'm going to *try and* spend more time studying it because that's what you *gotta* do. Some people think English is the *most unique* language in terms of difficulty. *Irregardless* of what they believe, many other languages are *equally as* complicated.

By now, I'm sure you've figured out that the italicized words in the preceding paragraph are all incorrect in Standard English. Here's how to correct them:

>> *Should of, could of, would of* → *should've, could've, would've* or *should have, could have, would have*

>> *Being that* → *because*

>> *Try and* → *try to*

>> *Gotta* → *got to, got a, have to,* or *have a*

>> *Most unique* → *unique* or *most unusual*

>> *Irregardless* → *regardless*

>> *Equally as* → *equally*

YOUR TURN

Identify the sentences that are correct in Standard English. You may choose one, both, or neither.

Q.

I. When you're in trouble, remember that you have a friend.

II. When you're in trouble, remember that you've gotta friend.

A. I. *Gotta* is not Standard English. Choice I eliminates that expression and substitutes *have.*

31

I. Irregardless of the teacher's views on personal technology in the classroom, Mark took notes on his phone.

II. Regardless of the teacher's views on personal technology in the classroom, Mark took notes on his phone.

32

I. Mark didn't do well on the test because he accidentally put his phone in the laundry basket.

II. Mark didn't do well on the test being that he accidentally put his phone in the laundry basket.

33

I. Now, he has to try to dry out his phone.

II. Now, he has to try and dry out his phone.

34

I. The teacher should have taken Mark's phone away.

II. The teacher should've taken Mark's phone away.

35

I. Mark thinks his method of taking notes is the most unique, but actually his teacher takes notes on her phone, too.

II. Mark thinks his method of taking notes is unique, but actually, his teacher takes notes on her phone, too.

36

I. Taking notes with a pen is equally as effective.

II. Taking notes with a pen is equally effective.

37

I. Mark could've taken excellent notes with a pencil, too.

II. Mark could of taken excellent notes with a pencil, too.

38

I. Mark claims he's gotta have his phone at all times.

II. Mark claims he has to have his phone at all times.

39

I. Because the phone isn't working, Mark will try and borrow a friend's notes.

II. Being that the phone isn't working, Mark will try to borrow a friend's notes.

I. Mark typed in nearly every word the teacher said; he's hoping someone else's notes will be equally as complete.

II. Mark typed in nearly every word the teacher said; he's hoping someone else's notes will be equally complete.

Calling All Overachievers: Extra Practice with Tricky Words

Read this exchange from the "How Can We Help?" chat box of the WeKnowEverything website. (Don't look for this website. It doesn't exist.) Applying the rules of Standard English, mark each underlined portion C for "correct" or I for "incorrect."

Agent: Thanks for reaching out. My team and I are **(1)** <u>already</u> to help you. What is the problem?

Customer: Last month's bill is incorrect. You **(2)** <u>should of</u> charged me $10, not $1000, for internet usage.

Agent: I will **(3)** <u>try to</u> help you. Please give me your account number.

Customer: I don't know my account number. Can you **(4)** <u>except</u> my name and address instead?

Agent: I can help you find your account number. Click on "bill" and scroll **(5)** <u>passed</u> the ads.

Customer: I don't know **(6)** <u>whether</u> I am looking at the right thing. I don't see anything labeled "bill."

Agent: You probably went right **(7)** <u>bye</u> it and didn't notice. Go back to the **(8)** <u>top and try again</u>.

Customer: I see it! [Types number.] I also see the problem. I was supposed to receive **(9)** <u>complementary</u> access to your streaming service.

Agent: I will deduct that charge, but free access is only for the first month. From now on, your streaming service charge will be $100 per minute. Don't watch any long films! If you need more help, please contact us **(10)** <u>any time</u>.

Answers to Tricky Word Questions

(1) **Who's, your.** In the first blank, you need "Who is." In the second, a possessive form is required.

(2) **principal.** The sentence refers to a person with authority, so *principal* is the word you want.

(3) **vain, break.** The sentence describes someone overly concerned about appearance, so *vain* fits well. Because the mirror may crack, *break* is correct.

(4) **It's, there.** In the first blank, "it is" (it's) makes sense. The second blank needs a place, *there*.

(5) **past.** They walk "in front of" the room, so *past* makes sense here.

(6) **whether.** The sentence presents a choice, not a report about temperature and the chances of rain. *Whether* expresses choice.

(7) **too, to, to, their.** In the first blank you want a word meaning "overly," which is *too*. The next two blanks require infinitives, so adding *to* is appropriate. The last blank calls for a possessive form.

(8) **hear, whose, you're, two.** The first blank refers to sound, and *hear* fits perfectly. The second blank requires a possessive, *whose*. The third needs "you are," which is *you're*. Finally, you want a number *(two)*.

(9) **it's, too, to, they're.** *It is* or *it's* fits the first blank. In the second blank, you want a sense of "more than enough," or *too*. Next up is movement, so you want *to*. For the last blank, "they are" (they're) is needed.

(10) **Bye.** The last word before leaving is *bye*.

(11) **further.** This sentence doesn't refer to distance. *Further* means "additional" and fits nicely here.

(12) **stationary, accept.** In the first blank, you need *stationary*, because the intended meaning is "not moving." In the second blank, you want a word meaning "receive," which is *accept*.

(13) **affect.** In this sentence, you want a synonym for "have influence on," which is *affect*.

(14) **continually.** The judge interrupted from time to time, so *continually* fits best.

(15) **further, stood.** In the first blank, you're not talking about distance but rather about additional speech, so *further* is the word you need. The second blank needs a word meaning "rose," which is *stood*.

(16) **effect.** Here you need a noun meaning "consequence" *(effect)*, not a verb meaning "to influence" *(affect)*.

(17) **continuous.** The hammering never stopped, so it was *continuous*.

(18) **effect.** Here, you need a synonym for "result," which is *effect*.

(19) **affect.** Nothing influenced the judge's ruling, so *affect* is your answer.

(20) **complementary.** The word *complementary* refers to the colors in that judge's tie that go well together.

(21) **some time.** The correct expression refers to a period of time.

(22) **all ready.** Every member (*all*) should be prepared (*ready*).

(23) **altogether.** You need a word that means "completely," and *altogether* means exactly that.

(24) **any way.** The coach is looking for a *way* to win.

(25) **every day.** Here, you need a word that means "each day, without exception."

(26) **Sometimes.** The sentence calls for a word meaning "from time to time."

(27) **any time.** Here you need an expression meaning "an unspecified period of time."

(28) **altogether.** In this sentence, you need a word that means "completely."

(29) **anytime.** The sentence needs the word meaning "at an unspecified point in time."

(30) **all together.** They practiced speaking with one voice, *all together*.

(31) **II.** *Irregardless* isn't correct in Standard English. Substitute *regardless*.

(32) **I.** *Being that* isn't correct in Standard English. Substitute *because*.

(33) **I.** The expression *try and* says that the speaker is going to do two things: *try* and *dry*. But the real meaning of the sentence is "try to dry."

(34) **I and II.** The expression *should of* isn't standard; the expressions *should have* and *should've* are both correct in Standard English.

(35) **II.** *Unique* means "one of a kind." Therefore, nothing can be "more unique" or "the most unique."

(36) **II.** *Equally as* isn't correct in Standard English. Drop *as*, and the sentence is fine.

(37) **I.** The contraction *could've* is the short form of *could have*. *Could of* isn't correct in Standard English.

(38) **II.** *Gotta* isn't correct in Standard English. *Has to* is a good substitute.

(39) **Neither.** In choice I, *try and* is nonstandard. Substitute *try to*. In choice II, *being that* isn't standard. It should change to *because*.

(40) **II.** The expression *equally as* isn't correct in Standard English. *Equally* does the job all by itself.

Answers to "Overachievers Questions"

(1) **I.** *Already* means "before this time." Here, you need *all ready* to show that the group is prepared.

(2) **I.** *Should of* is incorrect in Standard English. Substitute *should've* or *should have*.

(3) **C.** *Try to* is correct.

(4) **I.** The word you want here is *accept*, which means "agree to receive."

(5) **I.** This should be *past*, which means "beyond."

(6) **C.** *Whether* correctly refers to a choice between two options — "the right thing," as the customer says, or "the wrong thing," which is implied but not stated.

(7) **I.** *By* ("near" or "past") is the word you need here. *Bye* is the last word you say before leaving.

(8) **C.** The customer is being asked to do two things, *Go* and *try*. *And* is in its proper place here.

(9) **I.** The word should be *complimentary*, which means "no charge."

(10) **I.** The two-word version (*any time*) refers to a period of time. The word that fits the sentence is *anytime*, which refers to an unspecified point in time.

IN THIS CHAPTER

» **Placing descriptions where they belong**

» **Forming balanced sentences**

» **Avoiding confusing pronouns**

» **Deleting double negatives**

Chapter **17**

Avoiding Common Mistakes

I often see tourists in New York City, my hometown. As a local, I can spot potential problems — railroad stations during rush hour, for example — and avoid them. This chapter helps you become a local, not a tourist, in the world of grammar. Each question spotlights common grammar mistakes — placing descriptions in the wrong spot, unbalanced sentence structure, confusing pronouns, and double negatives.

Putting Descriptive Words in Their Proper Place

An inch to the left, an inch to the right . . . who cares? You should! Placing descriptive words in the wrong spot may change the meaning of a sentence. Chapter 4 explains how to identify descriptions. In this section, you practice inserting descriptions where they belong.

Describing nouns and verbs

Descriptions can be sorted into two big baskets. Some describe *nouns* — words that name people, places, or things. Others describe *verbs* — action or being words. The rules for placing both types of descriptions are simple. Here are some guidelines:

>> **Most single-word descriptions of nouns appear in front of the noun they're describing.**

The <u>young</u> child played with <u>stuffed</u> animals in her <u>tiny</u> house. (*young* describes *child, stuffed* describes *animals, tiny* describes *house*)

>> **Single-word descriptions of verbs may correctly appear in more than one spot in the sentence as long as the meaning is clear.**

<u>Often</u>, I make soup. (*Often* describes *make*)

I make soup <u>often</u>. (*often* still describes *make*)

I <u>often</u> make soup. (again, *often* describes *make*)

>> **Longer descriptions should appear near the noun or verb they describe.**

I need a car <u>with snow tires</u>. (*with snow tires* describes *car*)

The road <u>that was plowed last night</u> is icy today. (*that was plowed last night* describes *road*)

<u>When you have time</u>, stop by for a chat. (*When you have time* describes *stop*)

Identify the sentence(s) with correctly placed descriptions.

YOUR TURN Q.

I. Even before she passed the road test, Julie bought a plastic sleeve for her license that was given twice a month.

II. Even before she passed the road test that was given twice a month, Julie bought a plastic sleeve for her license.

A. II. The plastic sleeve may be bought anytime, but the test shows up only twice a month. Move the description *twice a month* closer to *test*, and the problem is solved.

I. Julie passed the eye examination given by a very near-sighted clerk with flying colors.

II. With flying colors, Julie passed the eye examination given by a very near-sighted clerk.

2

I. The written test inquired about a strategy for cars skidding on ice.

II. The written test for cars skidding on ice inquired about strategy.

3

I. Another question, which required an essay rather than a multiple-choice answer, inquired about defensive driving.

II. Another question inquired about defensive driving, which required an essay rather than a multiple-choice answer.

4

   I.   About a week after the written exam, the Department of Motor Vehicles sent a letter giving Julie an appointment for the road test without enough postage.

  II.   About a week after the written exam, the Department of Motor Vehicles sent a letter without enough postage and giving Julie an appointment for the road test.

5

   I.   Before the letter arrived, Julie asked her sister to drive her to the testing site.

  II.   Julie asked her sister to drive her to the testing site before the letter arrived.

6

   I.   Julie's examiner wrote messy notes on an official form.

  II.   Julie's examiner wrote notes on an official messy form.

7

   I.   The first page, which was single-spaced, contained details about Julie's turning technique.

  II.   The first page contained details about Julie's turning technique, which was single-spaced.

8

   I.   During the first minute of the road test, Julie scared a pedestrian.

  II.   Julie scared a pedestrian during the first minute of the road test.

9

   I.   The examiner relaxed in his aunt's house in Florida soon after Julie's road test.

  II.   The examiner relaxed soon after Julie's road test in his aunt's house in Florida.

10

   I.   By a wide margin, Julie failed the test.

  II.   Julie failed the test by a wide margin.

Four tricky descriptions

Four single-word descriptions require extra attention because the meaning of the sentence changes with their location. Fortunately, the rule is simple: *only, nearly, almost,* and *even* refer to what comes next in the sentence. Take a look at these examples:

Sherwood plays baseball <u>only</u> on Sundays. (He doesn't play on any other day of the week.)

<u>Only</u> Sherwood plays baseball on Sundays. (His friends don't play on Sundays.)

Sherwood plays <u>only</u> baseball on Sundays. (He won't play basketball or video games or anything else on Sundays.)

YOUR TURN

In each sentence, a description is underlined. In parentheses, you find information about the intended meaning of the sentence. If the description is in the proper place, write "correct." If not, rewrite the sentence.

Q. My Uncle Fred <u>only</u> wears green on St. Patrick's Day. (The rest of the year, he wears purple.) _____

A. **My Uncle Fred wears green only on St. Patrick's Day.** The word *only* is not a comment on *wears*. Instead, it refers to *St. Patrick's Day.*

11. Because she was in a good mood, the teacher <u>only</u> gave us one hour of homework, a report on gray whales. (The work can be completed in an hour.) _____
_____

12. Usually, she <u>almost</u> assigns five hours of work! (The usual amount of assigned work is a little less than five hours.) _____
_____

13. After I'd written <u>nearly</u> 200 words about gray whales, my phone rang. (I wrote 197 words and then the phone rang.) _____
_____

14. Roberto even did the assignment because he likes whales. (Roberto usually doesn't do homework.) _____
_____

15. When I finished my homework, I made a pot of coffee and <u>almost</u> drank the whole thing. (I left some in the pot.) _____
_____

16. She sounded cheerful, <u>almost</u> excited, when I told her about my assignment. (The tone of voice approaches excitement.) _____
_____

17. My mom works for a natural history museum, and she said she will <u>only</u> text me a photo of the whale exhibit if she has time. (If she has a free minute, she will text.)
_____
_____

18. Reading about whales is fun, and I've <u>nearly</u> read everything in the library about this topic. (The library has 10 books about whales, and I've read 9.) _____
_____

Dangling descriptions

Some sentences begin with descriptions that look like verbs. (In official grammar terminology, they're *verbal phrases*. Verbal phrases can show up elsewhere in the sentence; in this section, I'm just dealing with those that introduce sentences.) Usually, a comma separates these introductory descriptions from the main portion of the sentence. When you begin a sentence this way, the introductory description must refer to the *subject* — the person or thing you're talking about in the sentence. (Chapter 7 tells you more about subjects.) In these examples, the introductory description is italicized:

> *Dazzled by her friend's new diamond ring,* Lulu reached for her sunglasses. (The introductory description gives more information about *Lulu,* the subject.)

> *To block out all that light,* Lulu's glasses have been coated with a special plastic film. (The introductory description gives more information about the subject, *glasses.*)

Another type of introduction is a statement without a stated subject. The rule for this type of sentence is that the missing subject must match the subject that appears in the main portion of the sentence. Take a look at this sentence:

> *While wearing these glasses,* Lulu can see nothing at all.

If you expand this sentence by stating the subject, you get

> While Lulu is wearing these glasses, Lulu can see nothing at all.

A common mistake is a disconnection between the introduction and the subject, resulting in a sentence that doesn't make sense:

> While wearing these glasses, nothing is visible.

In this incorrect sentence, *nothing is wearing these glasses.* Grammarians call this error a *dangling modifier.*

Check these sentences for dangling modifiers. Identify the correct sentence(s).

YOUR TURN **Q.**

    I. After waiting for a green light, the crosswalk filled with people rushing to avoid Keisha and her speeding skateboard.

    II. After waiting for a green light, people rushed into the crosswalk to avoid Keisha and her speeding skateboard.

A. II. In the first sentence, the *crosswalk* is *waiting for a green light* because *crosswalk* is the subject of the sentence, and an introductory verbal phrase describes the subject. The second sentence has the people escaping from the sidewalk, which is the intended meaning.

19

I. To skateboard safely, kneepads help.

II. To skateboard safely, skaters need kneepads.

20

I. Sliding swiftly across the sidewalk, Keisha smashed into a tree.

II. Sliding swiftly across the sidewalk, a tree was smashed into by Keisha.

21

I. Although Keisha was bleeding, she wouldn't stop skateboarding.

II. Although bleeding, to stop skateboarding was out of the question.

22

I. While skateboarding, Keisha decided it would be a good idea to attach a small camera to her glasses.

II. While skateboarding, the decision to attach a small camera to her glasses was made.

23

I. Covered in sparkles, Keisha's glasses made a fashion statement.

II. Covered in sparkles, Keisha made a fashion statement with her glasses.

24

I. Discussed in the fashion press, many articles criticized Keisha's choice of eyewear.

II. Discussed in the fashion press, Keisha's choice of eyewear was criticized in many articles.

25

I. Removing some sparkles, Keisha cleared a spot for the camera.

II. Removing some sparkles, a spot for the camera was cleared.

Keeping Everything in Order: Parallel Sentences

Parallelism is the English teacher's term for order and balance in the sentence when meaning moves along smoothly, without any bumps or unnecessary detours. In this section, you practice making sentences parallel.

In a parallel sentence, everything performing the same function sentence has the same grammatical identity. In other words, they match. Most of the time, you can hear mismatches. Compare these two sentences:

Luis enjoys skiing, climbing, and camping.

His sister wants to sew or singing.

The first sentence is parallel. *Skiing, climbing,* and *camping* match. The second sentence isn't parallel. *To sew* and *singing* don't match. Parallel sentences sound balanced, but nonparallel sentences sound lopsided, as if you started out in one direction and then changed course.

In the sample sentences *and* and *or* link elements. They're *conjunctions.* (For more information, see Chapter 5.) Some conjunctions work in pairs: *not only/but also, either/or, neither/nor,* and *both/and.* These pairs must link parallel elements. What follows the first conjunction in the pair must match whatever follows the second. In these parallel sentences, the conjunctions are in italics, and the elements they join are underlined:

After the accident, Mei was determined *not only* <u>to walk as well as before</u> *but also* <u>to run a marathon</u>.

Jess will go *either* <u>to the concert</u> *or* <u>to the rehearsal</u>.

Neither <u>where he went to school</u> *nor* <u>what he studied</u> was discussed in his job interview.

Omar's hobbies include *both* <u>sewing</u> *and* <u>knitting</u>.

WARNING

The time period verbs express — their *tense* — is consistent in a parallel sentence. Don't change tenses unless the meaning requires it:

NOT PARALLEL: Stanley <u>arrived</u> after we <u>finished</u> and <u>offers</u> to help.

WHY IT'S NOT PARALLEL: *Arrived* and *finished* are in the past tense. *Offers* is in the present tense.

PARALLEL: Stanley <u>arrived</u> after we <u>finished</u> and <u>offered</u> to help.

ALSO PARALLEL: Stanley <u>arrives</u> after we <u>finish</u> and <u>offers</u> to help.

TIP

Parallelism is especially important in presentation slides and bullet points. Each item in the list must match grammatically. For more information, see Chapter 14.

Which sentences, if any, are parallel? You may find one, two, or none.

YOUR TURN

Q.

 I. Speeding down Thunder Mountain, spraying snow across his rival's face, and to get the best seat in the ski lodge were Robert's goals for the afternoon.

 II. To speed down Thunder Mountain, to spray snow across his rival's face, and to get the best seat in the ski lodge were Robert's goals for the afternoon.

A. II. Each sentence has three subjects. In choice I, the first two subjects are verb forms ending in *-ing* (*gerunds,* in official grammar terminology). The third is an *infinitive* (the *to* form of a verb). Mismatch! Choice II turns the subjects into infinitives *(to speed, to spray, to get).* When the subjects match, the sentence is parallel.

26

I. The ski pants that Robert favors are green, skintight, and stretchy.

II. The ski pants that Robert favors are green, skintight, and made of stretch fabric.

27

I. When he eases into those pants and zips up, Robert felt cool.

II. When he eased into those pants and zipped up, Robert felt cool.

28

I. In other ski outfits, Robert can breathe not only without difficulty but also forcefully.

II. In other ski outfits, Robert can breathe not only without difficulty but also with force.

29

I. Looking good is worth the trouble, and how he feels uncomfortable, according to Robert.

II. Looking good is worth the trouble and discomfort, according to Robert.

30

I. Also, sliding down the mountain and coasting to a full stop is easier in tight clothing.

II. Also, to slide down the mountain and to coast to a full stop is easier in tight clothing.

31

I. Robert objects to secondhand clothing and used equipment.

II. Robert objects to secondhand clothing and how some equipment is used.

32

I. "With a good parka or wearing a warm face mask, I'm ready for anything," he says.

II. "With a good parka or a warm face mask, I'm ready for anything," he says.

33

I. He adds, "The face mask is useful on the slopes and doing double duty in bank robberies."

II. He adds, "The face mask is useful on the slopes and does double duty in bank robberies."

34

I. The ski pants can also be recycled if they are rip-free and clean.

II. The ski pants can also be recycled if they are rip-free and without stains.

35

I. Robert cares not only about the environment but also about outdoor sports.

II. Robert not only cares about the environment but also outdoor sports.

Making Sure Your Pronouns Are Clear

Pronouns have caused many arguments recently. I deal with current pronoun issues in the introduction to this book. In this section, I focus on unclear pronouns. What's unclear? Well, suppose I write, "John spoke with his father about <u>his</u> car accident." Who had the accident? John? His father? Either could be true. The underlined pronoun isn't clear. Many solutions are possible: "Dad, we need to talk about your car accident," "I had a car accident, Dad," or "Concerned about his father's car accident, John sat down to talk with him."

To avoid confusing pronouns, keep these points in mind:

>> **Every pronoun needs one clear antecedent.** An *antecedent* is what the pronoun refers to. Problems occur when you have more than one possible antecedent in the sentence, as you see in the car accident example at the beginning of this section.

>> **The pronoun must match its antecedent.** When I say match, I mean that the antecedent and the pronoun could be interchanged without changing the meaning. In this sentence, they can't be interchanged: "Jane's an architect, and I want to study it too." The pronoun *it* refers to *architect,* but you can't write "I want to study *architect* too." Many corrections are possible, including this one: "Jane's an architect, and I'd like to learn more about her profession."

>> **Pronouns shouldn't refer to whole sentences or paragraphs.** A singular pronoun refers to one noun or one pronoun. A plural pronoun may stand in for more than one noun (for example, *they* may refer to *Nancy* and *Joe*). But you run into problems when you try to refer to an entire sentence or even more with *which, this,* or *that.* Take a look at this sentence: "Joe was a day late and a dollar short when he paid his rent, which annoyed his landlady." What bothered the landlady — the lateness or the dollar or both? The pronoun *which* doesn't work here. Try this version (or something like it) instead: "His landlady was annoyed because Joe's rent was a day late and a dollar short." Or this one: "Joe's landlady didn't mind receiving the rent a day late, but the fact that Joe was a dollar short annoyed her."

Often, the best way to clear up a pronoun problem is to rewrite the sentence with no pronoun at all.

TIP

Clear or unclear? Check out the underlined pronoun and decide. Note: As you answer this question and all the others in this section, be aware that the pronouns Ella and Rachel use are *she/her/hers.* The pronouns that Chad uses are *he/him/his.*

YOUR TURN

Q. Ella and Rachel photographed <u>her</u> tattoos.

A. **Unclear.** Did Ella and Rachel photograph Ella's tattoos? Perhaps they photographed Rachel's tattoos. Because you can't tell, the pronoun is unclear.

36 Chad and his sister Ella are campaigning for an Oscar nomination, but only <u>she</u> is expected to get one.

37 Chad sent a donation to Mr. Hobson, the president of the awards committee, in hopes of support for <u>his</u> nomination.

(38) If Chad wins an Oscar, he will place the statue next to his Emmy, Tony, and Grammy awards. <u>It</u> is his favorite honor.

(39) Ella has already won one Oscar for <u>her</u> role as a successful painter.

(40) Rachel, who tried out for the role before Ella got the part, thought <u>her</u> interpretation of the role was the best.

(41) Rachel worked hard to prepare for the part by attending art classes and drawing many pictures, <u>which</u> made her acting more realistic.

(42) Rachel's interest in art isn't new; she has wanted to be <u>one</u> ever since she was a child.

(43) "I see you as a poet, not a painter," said the director as he watched Rachel's performance, <u>which</u> disappointed her.

(44) In the film, the artist creates giant sculptures out of discarded baseball bats, but athletes don't appreciate <u>them.</u>

(45) During one rehearsal, Chad hit a sculpture with his elbow, <u>which</u> broke.

Dropping Double Negatives

In some languages, the more negatives you pile into a sentence, the more strongly you're saying no. In formal English, though, two negative words make a positive statement. For example, "Enrique did not want no vegetables" means that Enrique wanted some vegetables. Unless you're trying to say something positive, steer clear of these double negatives, presented here with examples:

> WRONG: Lucette cannot help but dance when she hears flamenco music. (*not* and *but* = negatives)
>
> RIGHT: Lucette cannot help dancing when she hears flamenco music.
>
> WRONG: Elizabeth can't hardly wait until her favorite singer releases a new album. (*can't* and *hardly* = negatives)
>
> RIGHT: Elizabeth can hardly wait until her favorite singer releases a new album.
>
> WRONG: Claudeen, a champion skier, hadn't but ten minutes until it was time to head down the mountain. *(not*, which appears in the contraction *hadn't*, and *but* = negatives)
>
> RIGHT: Claudeen, a champion skier, had only ten minutes until it was time to head down the mountain.

Identify the double negatives. Rewrite the sentence correctly.

 YOUR TURN

Q. I can't help but think that your questions about the final exam are extremely annoying.

A. I can't help thinking that your questions about the final exam are extremely annoying.

The expressions *can't help but* and *cannot help but* are double negatives. The two negatives (*not* and *but*) cancel each other and express a positive meaning. Thus, the original sentence means that you can stop thinking this way if you want to do so.

46 Tomas is humming so loudly that I can't hardly think.

_____

_____

47 Candice ain't got no problem with Tomas's noisy behavior.

_____

_____

48 The teacher looked at Tomas and declared, "I do not allow no singing here."

_____

_____

49 Tomas hadn't but five minutes to finish the math section of the test.

_____

_____

50 "I can't help but think that your rule is unfair to musicians," said Claudeen.

_____

Calling All Overachievers: Extra Practice with Common Mistakes

Below are ten sentences from a book about yoga. (Not a real book. I made it up!) Check each sentence for misplaced descriptions, unbalanced sentences, unclear pronouns, and double negatives. Mark the sentence "Correct" if everything is fine, and "incorrect" if you find any problems.

(1) Deciding which yoga class to take, the level of skill is important. (2) If you only know a little, enroll in Yoga for Beginners. (3) The work in that class can hardly be easier! (4) A former student told me that he took five classes with three different teachers and liked them very much.

(5) Here are instructions for one yoga pose, so you will know not only what we expect but also what muscles you'll use. (6) Stand up straight and with flexed muscles. (7) Bend one elbow and one knee, lifting it to your nose. (8) You should almost bend the other elbow to your ear, touching as high on your neck as possible. (9) Tucking your chin, both elbows should stay still. (10) You can't help but love this pose!

Answers

1. **II.** You can easily see what's wrong with choice I. You don't want a clerk *with flying colors.* Choice II places *with flying colors* at the beginning of the sentence, where it's close enough to the verb *passed* to tell you how *Julie passed,* the meaning you want.

2. **I.** In choice I, the two descriptions — *written* and *for cars skidding on ice* — are close to the words they describe. *Written* describes *test* and *for cars skidding on ice* describes *maneuvers.* Choice II places *for cars skidding on ice* after *test.* The test isn't for cars, so this choice is wrong.

3. **I.** Defensive-driving techniques don't include essays, but test questions do. The description *which required an essay rather than a multiple-choice answer* belongs after *question,* its location in choice I. Choice II incorrectly places the description after *driving.*

4. **II.** The *letter* is described by *without enough postage,* so that description must follow *letter,* as it does in choice II. Choice I places the description after *test* — which doesn't need postage!

5. **I.** Both sentences mention two actions: *asked* and *drive.* The time element, *before the letter arrived,* tells you when Julie *asked,* not when she wanted her sister to *drive.* The description should be closer to *asked* than to *drive,* as it is in choice I, because *asked* is the word it describes.

6. **I.** The description *messy* describes *notes,* not *official form,* so it belongs in front of *notes.*

7. **I.** The *page* is *single-spaced,* not Julie's three-point turn. Choice I, which places the information about spacing after *page,* is correct.

8. **I, II.** *During the first minute of the road test* describes the verb *scared.* Both choice I and choice II place the description near the verb, so both are correct.

9. **I.** The relaxing took place *in his aunt's house in Florida.* The road test took place on a road. Choice I places the description close to the word it describes. Choice II has the road test taking place inside a house — not the most likely meaning.

10. **I, II.** *By a wide margin* describes the verb *failed.* Both choices work because, in each, the description clearly refers to *failed.*

11. **Because she was in a good mood, the teacher gave us <u>only</u> one hour of homework, a report on gray whales.** The word *only* refers to the amount of time (*one hour*), not to the action *gave.*

12. **She usually assigns <u>almost</u> five hours of work!** *Almost* refers to the amount of time, *five hours,* not to the action, *assigns.*

13. **Correct.** The word *nearly* appears before the number of words, showing that the number of words written was a little less than 200.

14. **<u>Even</u> Roberto did the assignment because he likes whales.** This sentence comments on *Roberto,* so *even* belongs in front of his name.

15. **When I finished my homework, I made a pot of coffee and drank <u>almost</u> the whole thing.** *Almost* refers to how much of the coffee *I drank.* In the original sentence, *almost* is in front of *drank.* In that spot, *I* didn't drink anything. In front of *the whole thing,* I drank most of it.

16. **Correct.** She didn't sound *excited,* but close to it, so the word *almost* correctly appears in front of that word.

(17) **My mom works for a natural history museum, and she said she will text me a photo of the whale exhibit only if she has time.** *Only* refers to the condition (*if she has time*) that will allow Mom to text, so *only* belongs in front of that expression.

(18) **Reading about whales is fun, and I've read nearly everything in the library about this topic.** *Nearly* refers to how much *I* have read. Not *everything*, but *nearly everything*. The original places *nearly* in front of *read*. In that position, *I* read nothing at all.

(19) **II.** No one is skateboarding in choice I. Choice II has *skaters*, so it's correct.

(20) **I.** The description at the beginning of the sentence appears without a subject, so the subject of the main part of the sentence is the one *sliding swiftly*. That's *Keisha* (choice I), not *a tree* (choice II).

(21) **I.** Who's *bleeding?* In choice I, *Keisha* is, so that one's correct. In choice II, no one is bleeding. It's incorrect.

(22) **I.** A description without a subject at the beginning of a sentence picks up the subject from the main part of the sentence. Choice I makes sense because *Keisha* is *skateboarding.* Choice II is incorrect because *the decision* isn't *skateboarding.*

(23) **I.** Choice I correctly states that *Keisha's glasses* are *covered in sparkles.* In choice II, *Keisha* herself is *covered in sparkles.* That's possible, but not likely.

(24) **II.** Choice I incorrectly has *many articles* being *discussed.* Choice II correctly says that *Keisha's choice of eyewear* was *discussed.*

(25) **I.** *Keisha* was *removing some sparkles, a spot* wasn't, so choice I is correct.

(26) **I.** Choice I relies on three adjectives (*green, skintight,* and *stretchy*) to describe Robert's favorite pants. Choice II isn't parallel because the original sentence links two adjectives (*green* and *skintight*) with a verb form (*made of stretch fabric*).

(27) **II.** Choice I is illogical, not parallel, because two verbs (*eases, zips*) are in the present tense *and* one is in the past (*felt*). In choice II, all three verbs are in the past tense, so the sentence is parallel.

(28) **II.** In choice I, the conjunctions *not only/but also* link *without difficulty* (a prepositional phrase) and *forcefully* (a description). These two don't match, so the sentence isn't parallel. In choice II the conjunctions join two phrases (*without difficulty* and *with force*), creating a parallel sentence.

(29) **II.** Choice I joins a noun, *trouble* and a subject/verb combo (*how he feels uncomfortable*). Not parallel! Choice II links two nouns, *trouble* and *discomfort.* Choice II is parallel.

(30) **I, II.** Choice I connects two *ing* forms (*sliding* and *coasting*). Verdict: parallel. Choice II links two infinitives (*to slide* and *to coast*): also parallel.

(31) **I.** Choice I is parallel because it pairs two nouns (*clothing* and *equipment*). Choice II isn't parallel because it pairs a noun (*clothing*) and a statement with a subject and a verb (*how some equipment is used*).

(32) **II.** The *or* in Choice I links *with a good parka* and *wearing a warm face mask.* The second term includes a verb form (*wearing*), and the first doesn't, so it's not parallel. In choice II, *parka* and *face mask* are linked. Because they're both nouns, the sentence is parallel.

(33) **II.** The first choice isn't parallel because *is useful* and *doing* don't match. The second choice pairs *is* and *does*, two verbs, so the sentence is parallel.

34 **I.** *Rip-free* is an adjective, but *without stains* is a phrase, so choice II isn't parallel. Choice I has two adjectives (*rip-free* and *clean*), so it's parallel.

35 **I.** In choice I, a conjunction pair (*not only/but also*) joins two phrases (*about the environment* and *about outdoor sports*), so it's parallel. Choice II links a verb expression (*cares about the environment*) with a noun (*sports*).

36 **Clear.** Chad uses male pronouns, and his sister uses female pronouns, so *she* may refer only to one person, Chad's sister.

37 **Unclear.** Does *his* mean Chad's or Mr. Hobson's? The way the sentence reads, either answer is possible.

38 **Unclear.** Maybe the Tony is his favorite honor, or maybe the Grammy.

39 **Clear.** The pronoun *her* can refer only to Ella. Everything is clear.

40 **Unclear.** You can't tell what *her* means — *Rachel's* or *Ella's*, so the pronoun is unclear.

41 **Unclear.** What does *which* refer to, the art classes or the drawing? The pronoun should clearly refer to another pronoun or noun, and in this sentence, *which* doesn't.

42 **Unclear.** *One* what? *One art?* The most likely meaning is that *one* means *artist*, but that word isn't in the sentence.

43 **Unclear.** What does *which* refer to? The director's statement or the performance? *Which* doesn't clearly refer to either of these, so the pronoun is unclear.

44 **Unclear.** You have two groups of objects in the sentence: the *sculptures* and the *bats. Them* could refer to either, so the pronoun is unclear.

45 **Unclear.** What broke, the *sculpture* or the *elbow*? Because you can't tell, the pronoun is unclear.

46 **Tomas is humming so loudly that I can hardly think.** The double negative *can't hardly* should be *can hardly*.

47 **Candice has no problem with Tomas's noisy behavior.** *Ain't* isn't standard, and pairing it with *no* creates an additional problem, a double negative. Another possible correction: "Candice does not have a problem with Tomas's noisy behavior."

48 **The teacher looked at Tomas and declared, "I do not allow singing here."** If you place *not* and *no* together, you have a double negative. Either get rid of *no*, as I did, or delete *do not*: "I allow no singing."

49 **Tomas had but five minutes to finish the math section of the test.** The contraction *hadn't* contains *not*, a negative, and *but* is also negative. Change *hadn't* to *had* and the sentence is fine. You can also substitute *only* for *but*.

50 **"I can't help thinking that your rule is unfair to musicians," said Claudeen.** Inside *can't* is the negative word *not. But* is also negative. Change *but think* to *thinking* and the sentence is correct.

Answers to "Overachievers Questions"

1. **Incorrect.** The sentence begins with a description containing a verb (*Deciding which yoga class to take*). That description must apply to the subject of the sentence, which is *level*. *Level* isn't deciding what class to take! One possible correction: "When you are deciding which yoga class to take, the level of skill is important."

2. **Incorrect.** *Only* should be in front of *a little* because it refers to the amount of knowledge, not to the verb *know*.

3. **Correct.** *Can hardly* is a positive statement, which is the intended meaning of the sentence.

4. **Incorrect.** Did the student like the *classes* or the *teachers*? You can't tell because the pronoun *them* is unclear.

5. **Correct.** Take a close look at the conjunction pair, *not only/but also*. The elements that follow each half of the pair (*what we expect*, *what muscles you'll use*) should match, and they do. The sentence is parallel.

6. **Incorrect.** Here the conjunction *and* joins a single-word description (*straight*) and a phrase (*with flexed muscles*). That's a mismatch, so the sentence is incorrect. One possible correction: "Stand up straight and flex your muscles."

7. **Incorrect.** What should you lift to your nose, the elbow or the knee? The pronoun *it* is unclear.

8. **Incorrect.** *Almost* should appear in front of the idea it applies to, which is the position, *to your ear*.

9. **Incorrect.** Who's *tucking*? No one appears in the sentence, and *both elbows* can't tuck a chin. One possible correction: "Tucking your chin, keep your elbows still." The understood subject, *you*, is now *tucking*.

10. **Incorrect.** *Can't help but* is a double negative and not acceptable in Standard English. Change it to "you can't help loving."

Chapter **18**

Sharpening Your Verb Skills

I f you've mastered the basics of dealing with verbs (see Chapters 3 and 6), give yourself a gold star. Ready to go deeper? In this chapter, you dive into voice (active or passive), mood (yes, verbs have moods), and the proper tense for descriptive verb forms.

Voicing an Opinion: Active and Passive Verbs

In the world of grammar, verbs have a *voice* — either *active* or *passive*. A verb's voice depends on its relationship with its subject. (I explain how to locate the subject in Chapter 7.) In *active voice*, the subject performs the action or exists in the state of being expressed by the verb:

> Millie *cracked* a priceless vase." (*cracked* = active-voice verb)

With *passive voice*, the subject receives the action:

> The priceless vase *was cracked*. (*was cracked* = passive-voice verb)

Active voice is often better than passive. Why? Sometimes, active voice gives you more information. If your company insured the *priceless vase* mentioned in the sample sentences, you probably want to know who cracked it, and an active-voice sentence tells you. True, you could tack on *by Millie* after the passive-voice verb, but the resulting sentence sounds a bit stiff.

TIP

Passive can be useful, too. Sometimes, you don't know who performed an action, and sometimes, you don't care: "The winning lottery numbers *were drawn* last night." In that sentence, the focus is on the lottery, not on the person pulling numbered balls out of a container.

YOUR TURN

Q. Label the underlined verb forms as active voice (AV) or passive voice (PV).

Charles <u>arrived</u> three hours after curfew. He <u>was grounded</u> for three weeks.

A. **arrived (AV), was grounded (PV).** *Charles* is the subject. Because he performs the action in the first sentence (*Charles arrived*), that verb is in active voice. In the second sentence, someone else grounded him. The subject, *Charles*, receives the action. *Was grounded* is in passive voice.

1. The job opening <u>was posted</u> on a networking site.

2. About a thousand resumes <u>were emailed</u> within an hour.

3. When Pete first <u>heard</u> about the position the day after it <u>was announced</u>, he was already too late.

4. The job <u>had been given</u> to someone else.

5. Pete <u>set</u> an alert on his computer. Now, when resumes <u>are requested</u> for someone with a degree in philosophy, Pete <u>is informed</u> immediately.

6. Philosophers <u>have</u> a high unemployment rate, and Pete <u>must apply</u> for every position he <u>can find</u>.

7. "Only so many burgers <u>can be flipped</u> before boredom <u>sets</u> in," <u>explained</u> Pete.

8. Pete <u>has been given</u> free room and board by friends and relatives for the last year, but they <u>are losing</u> patience with him.

9. Lola <u>offered</u> free tattoo training, but Pete <u>refused</u>.

10. "I <u>think</u> for a living," he <u>declared</u>.

YOUR TURN

Now, try your hand at changing these passive-voice sentences to active voice. To keep you on your toes, I tucked in a couple where no change is possible.

Q. The score was kept by Ahmed throughout the season.

A. **Ahmed kept score throughout the season.** In the original, *score* receives the action of the verb, *was kept.* In the new version, *Ahmed* performs the action of scoring.

11. The ball was hit out of the park by the home team 562 times.

_____

12. Most balls were retrieved by fans and kept as cherished souvenirs.

_____

13. One baseball, though, wasn't found until more than a year after it was hit.

_____

14. It was placed by the team groundskeeper in a glass case near the locker room and labeled "the one that almost got away."

_____

15. According to Joe Smokey, the owner, fans are allowed to see the display only when the players aren't there.

_____

16. When outsiders were first invited to the locker room, a complaint was filed by the players' union.

_____

17. After the union's complaint was read by the owner, visits were strictly limited.

_____

18. The coach told the attendant to lock the locker room when players were there.

_____

19. Some players were not pleased by the new policy.

_____

20. Their friends and family were barred also!

_____

In the Mood: Selecting the Right Verb for All Sorts of Sentences

Verbs have three moods:

>> **Indicative** Nearly every sentence you write or say has a verb in the indicative mood. An indicative verb makes a statement or asks a question:

The dishes <u>are</u> dirty.

<u>Will</u> you <u>wash</u> them?

>> **Imperative** An imperative verb issues a command:

>> Load the dishwasher.

>> Stop whining.

Note: No subject appears in a sentence with an imperative verb. The subject is always *you* (understood but not stated).

>> **Subjunctive** The most common use of a subjunctive verb is to state something that isn't true, what English teachers call "condition contrary to fact":

>> If I were rich enough to hire a maid, I wouldn't ask for help. (I'm not rich.)

>> If the dishes had been washed, I wouldn't be complaining now. (The dishes are dirty.)

You don't need to know the grammatical terms. You just have to put verbs in the right mood. In this section, you practice identifying all three moods and using them correctly.

Indicating facts: Indicative mood

Just about everything I *say* about verbs in this book actually *applies* to indicative verbs, which, as the name implies, *indicate* facts. Indicative mood *is* the one you *use* automatically, stating action or being in any tense and for any person. *Do* you *want* to see some samples of indicative verbs? No problem. Every verb in this paragraph *is* in indicative mood. I *have placed* all the verbs in italics so you *can locate* them easily.

The form of an indicative verb changes according to the time period you're talking about — the *tense* — and, at times, according to the person doing the action. (Chapters 3 and 6 explain verb forms.)

If you're in the mood, circle the indicative verb that works best in each of the following sentences. The verb choices are in parentheses.

YOUR TURN

Q. Mr. Adams (holds/held) a performance review every June.

A. **holds.** Both choices are indicative, but the present tense works better. The clue is the expression *every June.*

21 Each employee (is/was) summoned annually to Adams's office for what he calls "a little chat."

22 All the workers (know/will know) that the "chat" is all on Adams's side.

23 Adams (likes/like) to discuss baseball, the economy, and the reasons no one (will/would) receive a raise.

24 "(Is/Was) business good these days?" he always says.

25 He always (mentions/will mention) that he may have to make personal sacrifices to save the company.

26 Sacrifices! He (means/meant) that he (earns/will earn) only a million instead of two million next year!

Issuing commands: Imperative mood

Commands, also known as the imperative mood, are easy. An imperative verb is the same whether you're talking to one person or 20, to a peasant or to a queen. The command form is simply the infinitive minus the *to*. In other words, the unchanged, plain form of the verb, which you see in italics in these examples:

> *Stop* complaining, Henry.
>
> *Pull* yourself together and *meet* your new in-laws.

Negative commands are slightly different. They take the infinitive-minus-*to* and add *do not*. In these examples, the imperative verbs are in italics:

> *Do* not *mention* our engagement.
>
> *Do* not *let them find* out we're getting married!

Are you wondering why *not* is not italicized? *Not* is not a verb.

Fill in the blanks with commands for Henry, who is meeting his future in-laws. The base verb you're working with appears in parentheses at the end of each sentence.

YOUR TURN

Q. _____ quietly on the couch, Henry, while I call Daddy. (*to sit*)

A. **Sit.** The command is formed by dropping *to* from the infinitive.

27 Henry, _____ my lead during the conversation. (*to follow*)

28 If Mom talks about Paris, _____ your head and _____ _____ interested. (*to nod, to look*)

29 Dad doesn't understand any language but English, so _____ French to him. (*to speak*, negative command)

30 _____ them to show you slides of last year's trip to Normandy. (*to ask*)

31 _____ asleep during the slide show! (*to fall, negative command*)

32 _____ some of Mom's potato salad, even if it's warm. (*to eat*)

33 _____ about food poisoning. (*to talk, negative command*)

34 _____ to the emergency room immediately after eating. (*to go*)

Telling Lies: Subjunctive mood

The subjunctive mood pops up only rarely, mostly in "condition-contrary-to-fact" sentences. *Condition-contrary-to-fact* means that you're talking about something that isn't true. In these examples, the subjunctive verb is in italics:

> If I *were* famous, I would wear sunglasses to hide my identity.
>
> *Had* I *known* the secret password, I would have used it.

Did you notice that the subjunctive changes some of the usual forms? When it isn't subjunctive, *was* pairs with *I*. Yet, as you see in the first example, *I* is paired with *were*. That's because I'm not famous! In the second example, *had* doesn't do its usual indicative job, which is to place events earlier in the past than other past-tense events. (See Chapter 6 for more details on this use of *had*.) Instead, in a subjunctive sentence the *had* shows that I didn't know the secret password.

WARNING

Condition-contrary-to-fact sentences always feature a *would* form of the verb. In Standard English, the *would* form never appears in the part of the sentence that's untrue. Don't say, "If I would have known . . ." when you didn't know. Say, "If I had known, I would have . . ."

YOUR TURN

Write the correct verb in the blank for each exercise in this section. The verb you're working with appears in parentheses after each sentence. Just to keep you honest, I tucked in a sentence that doesn't require subjunctive.

Q. If Ellen _____ for her road test, she wouldn't have dented the car. *(to prepare)*

A. **had prepared.** The *had* creates a subjunctive here because Ellen didn't prepare for her road test.

35 If the examiner _____ an appointment available in late afternoon, Ellen, who prefers to sleep until lunchtime, would have signed up for that slot immediately. *(to make)*

36 The test would have gone better if Ellen _____ a morning person. *(to be)*

37 "If it _____," explained the instructor, "you will take the test anyway." *(to snow)*

38 If Ellen _____ the weather report, she would have canceled. *(to hear)*

39 If Ellen _____ not on the road-test list, she would have stayed home when the first flake fell. *(to be)*

40 If an examiner _____ about Ellen's poor driving skills, he would have stayed home also. *(to know)*

Speaking Verbally

Some words look like verbs but act as descriptions or nouns. (*Verbs* are words that express action or state of being. See Chapter 3 for more information.) Grammarians call these words *verbals*. Like verbs, verbals have tenses. Their tense places the action or state of being on a timeline. In this section, you practice identifying verbals and selecting the correct tense for each.

Identifying verbals

Time to meet the verbal family. Here's the lowdown on *infinitives, participles,* and *gerunds* — the three types of verbals.

>> **Infinitives** are what you get when you tack *to* in front of the most basic form of the verb. Infinitives may act as a description or function as a noun.

- *To be* safe, Alice packed a roll of breath mints. *(to be = infinitive describing packed)*

- *To win* was Jamal's goal. *(to win = subject of the verb was)*

>> **Participles** are the *ing* or *ed* or *en* form of verbs, plus a few irregulars. Sometimes, participles act as part of the verb in a sentence, attaching themselves to *has, have, had* or *is, are, was,* or *were.* When they're not functioning as part of a verb, participles act as descriptions.

- *Broken,* the antique vase was worthless. *(Broken = participle describing vase)*

- The *dancing* statue is famous. Everyone *seeing* it takes a selfie. *(dancing = participle describing statue, seeing = participle describing everyone)*

>> **Gerunds** are the *ing* form of verbs, used as nouns.

- *Going* to the beach is fun. *(Going = gerund functioning as the subject of the verb is)*

- My dog loves *swimming.* *(swimming = gerund functioning as the object of the verb loves)*

TIP

Verbals can be alone or in phrases, with an object and descriptions. In the infinitive phrase *to learn algebra immediately,* for example, *algebra* is the object of the infinitive *to learn,* and *immediately* is a description.

YOUR TURN

Check out the underlined portions of each sentence and label them "I" for *infinitive,* "P" for *participle,* or "G" for *gerund.* If none of these labels fit, write "N" for *none.*

Q. Sam flew <u>to Phoenix</u> for a conference on "<u>Rebuilding</u> Your Company's Image."

A. N, G. *Phoenix* is not a verb, so *to Phoenix* is not a verbal. *Rebuilding* is a gerund. In case you were wondering, *rebuilding* is the object of the preposition *on. Rebuilding Your Company's Image* is the entire gerund phrase.

41 <u>Arriving</u> in Arizona, Sam was eager <u>to settle</u> in at his hotel.

42 The hotel room, newly <u>redecorated</u>, was on the same floor as an <u>overflowing</u> ice machine.

43. <u>To reach</u> his room, Sam had <u>to skate</u> across a miniature ice rink.

44. <u>Sliding</u> across a slippery floor <u>to his room</u> was not one of Sam's happiest moments.

45. Sam, <u>usually easygoing</u>, nevertheless decided <u>to complain</u>.

46. "I don't want <u>to practice</u> winter sports!" Sam stated <u>firmly</u>.

47. The manager, not <u>knowing</u> about the ice machine, found Sam's comment <u>confusing</u>.

48. <u>Reaching</u> 100 is not unusual during summer in this part of the country.

49. <u>Choosing</u> his words carefully, the manager replied, "Of course, sir. I will cancel your ski trip."

50. Sam <u>protested</u> because his lifelong dream was <u>to go</u> downhill on skis.

Telling time with verbals

Verbals, like everything associated with verbs, give time information. The plain form (without *have* or *having*) shows action happening at the same time as the action expressed by the main verb in the sentence:

> *Rooting* for her favorite team, Josie *forgot* about dinner. (*Rooting, forgot* = happening at the same time, in the past)

> *Rooting* for her favorite team, Josie *forgets* about dinner. (*Rooting, forgets* = happening at the same time, in the present)

> *Rooting* for her favorite team, Josie *will forget* about dinner. (*Rooting, will forget* = happening at the same time, in the future)

The perfect form (with *have* or *having*) places the action expressed by the verbal before the action of the main verb:

> *Having bought* a team jersey, Josie *wore* it to the game. (*Having bought* and *wore* = happening in the past, with *having bought* occurring before *wore*)

> *Having bought* a team jersey, Josie *wears* it to the game. (*Having bought* = happening in the past, *wears* = happening in the present)

> *Having bought* a team jersey, Josie *will wear* it to the game. (*Having bought* = past, *will wear* = future)

TIP

Choosing either the plain or perfect form can be tricky. First, figure out how important the timeline is. If the events are closely spaced and the order doesn't matter, go for the plain form. If the order matters, select the perfect form (with *have* or *having*) for the earlier action.

YOUR TURN

In the example and the practice exercises that follow, get out your time machine and read about a tooth whitener called "GreenTeeth." (It's not real. I made it up!) Circle the correct verbal form.

Q. (Perfecting/Having perfected) a new product, the chemists asked for some marketing research.

A. **Having perfected.** The two events occurred in the past, perfecting the product and asking for market research. The chemists' request is closer to the present moment. *Having perfected* places the act of *perfecting* earlier than the action expressed by the main verb in the sentence, *asked*.

51 (Looking/Having looked) at each interview subject's teeth, the researchers gasped.

52 One interview subject, (hearing/having heard) the interviewer's comment about "teeth as yellow as sunflowers," screamed.

53 (Refusing/Having refused) to open her mouth again, she frowned silently.

54 With market research on GreenTeeth (completed/having been completed), the team analyzed the results.

55 The tooth whitener (going/having gone) into production, no further market research was scheduled.

56 Additional interviews will be scheduled if the legal department succeeds in (getting/having gotten) participants to sign a "will not sue" pledge.

57 "(Sending/Having sent) GreenTeeth to the stores means that I am sure it works," promised the company president.

58 (Deceived/Having been deceived) by this man several times, reporters did not believe his promise.

59 (Interviewing/Having interviewed) dissatisfied customers, one reporter began to plan an announcement that GreenTeeth did not whiten teeth.

60 (Weeping/Having wept), the marketing team told the chemists to change GreenTeeth's formula.

Calling All Overachievers: Extra Practice with Verbs

Take a look at these sentences. Answer the question that matches the number of the sentence.

(1) As the director of Panux Travel, I am delighted <u>to have invited</u> you on a tour of the world's most mysterious castle. **(2)** I am confident that <u>my tour will be enjoyed by you</u>. **(3)** If I <u>were</u> not sure of that fact, I would not offer this tour. **(4)** <u>Visiting this castle alone,</u>

tourists often miss the most interesting parts. **(5)** Also, if you <u>are</u> alone when you visit, the entrance fee is higher. **(6)** During our tour, <u>stay</u> with the group! **(7)** <u>Having survived</u> a night alone in the castle, I know that ghosts are everywhere. **(8)** <u>To get lost</u> in the castle is common. **(9)** <u>Wearing</u> comfortable shoes. **(10)** Tickets <u>may be purchased</u> on my website.

1. Is the underlined portion of the sentence correct or incorrect?

2. Change the underlined portion of the sentence to active voice.

3. Is the underlined portion of the sentence correct or incorrect?

4. Is the underlined portion of the sentence correct or incorrect?

5. Should *are* be changed to *were*?

6. Is *stay* an imperative verb (a command) in this sentence?

7. Is the underlined portion of the sentence correct or incorrect?

8. Does *to get lost* act as a verb, a noun, or a description?

9. Change the underlined word to the imperative (command) form.

10. Is the underlined verb active or passive?

Answers to Verb Questions

(1) **was posted (PV).** The *job opening* didn't do the posting. It received the action of the verb, *was posted*, so it's passive.

(2) **were emailed (PV).** The *resumes* (subject) didn't do the emailing. Whoever sent them did. *Were emailed* is a passive-voice verb.

(3) **heard (AV), was announced (PV), was (AV).** The subject of *heard* is *Pete*, who performs the action. *Heard* is in active voice. *It* is the subject of *was announced*, but *it* didn't do any announcing. *It* receives the action and is a passive-voice verb.

(4) **had been given (PV).** The subject is *job*, which didn't perform the action of giving. The verb is in passive voice.

(5) **set (AV), are requested (PV), is informed (PV).** *Pete* is the subject of the verb *set*. Because Pete is performing the action, *set* is an active-voice verb. *Resumes* is the subject of the verb *is are requested*. The resumes don't perform the action, so the verb is passive. Next up is the subject-verb combo *Pete is informed*. Because the action happens to the subject, the verb *is informed* is passive.

(6) **have (AV), must apply (AV), can find (AV).** The first subject-verb pair is *Philosophers have.* *Philosophers* are the ones who *have*, so this is an active-voice verb. Next is *Pete must apply. Pete* is doing the applying, so the verb is in active voice. Finally, *he can find* creates another active-voice situation because *he* does the action expressed by *can find*.

(7) **can be flipped (PV), sets(AV), explained (AV).** Three subject-verb pairs appear here: *burgers can be flipped, boredom sets*, and *explained Pete*. The first is passive because the flipping happens to the *burgers*. The next pair contains an active-voice verb because the *boredom* does the setting. The last pair reverses the usual subject-verb order, but that doesn't matter. This is an active-voice verb because the subject, *Pete*, does the action, *explained*.

(8) **has been given (PV), are losing (AV).** The subject, *Pete*, isn't giving. Instead, he's receiving, so *has been given* is in passive voice. The second pair has an active-voice verb because *they* are doing the action (*are losing*).

(9) **offered (AV), refused (AV).** Two active-voice verbs here, because *Lola* did the offering and *Pete* did the refusing.

(10) **think (AV), declared (AV).** Because the subject, *I*, does the thinking, *think* is an active-voice verb. The subject of *declared, he*, also does the action, so *declared* is also an active-voice verb.

(11) **The home team hit the ball out of the park 562 times.** Instead of the passive verb *was hit*, this revised sentence has an active-voice verb, *hit*.

(12) **Fans retrieved and kept most balls as cherished souvenirs.** Instead of the passive verbs *were retrieved* and [*were*] *kept*, you have the active verbs *retrieved* and *kept*.

(13) **No change.** You don't know who found the baseball, and the identity of the finder isn't important. Nor do you know who hit the ball. The passive verbs *wasn't found* and *was hit* work fine here.

(14) **The team groundskeeper placed it in a glass case near the locker room and labeled it "the one that almost got away."** The groundskeeper did the work (*placed, labeled*), and this active-voice sentence gives him the credit.

15 Joe Smokey, the owner, allows fans to see the display only when the players aren't there. Instead of the passive *are allowed*, you have the active *Joe Smokey allows*.

16 When the owner first invited outsiders to the locker room, the players union filed a complaint. The original sentence doesn't tell you who invited outsiders, but *the owner* is a good guess. (You could also write *Joe first invited*.) If you left that part of the sentence unchanged, though, count yourself right. In the second part, *players union* is the subject of the active-voice verb *filed*.

17 After the owner read the union's complaint, he strictly limited visits. Passive verbs *(was read, were limited)* change to active *(read, limited)*. *Joe* could easily substitute for *the owner* if you wish.

18 No change. The verbs *told* and *were* are in active voice already.

19 The new policy did not please some players. The passive *were pleased* changes to the active *policy did not please*. Notice that the helping verb *did* helps create this negative statement. For more on helping verbs, turn to Chapter 3.

20 The policy barred their friends and family also! I wrote *the policy*, but if you substituted *Joe* or *the owner*, count yourself correct.

21 is. The sentence speaks of an ongoing situation, so present tense is best.

22 know. The workers have been through this "chat" many times, so the act of knowing isn't in the future but in the present.

23 likes, will. The present-tense form for talking about someone *(Adams, in this sentence)* is *likes*. The future-tense verb *will* explains that in the coming year, as always, employees will be shopping for bargains.

24 Is. The expression *these days* is a clue that you want a present-tense verb that talks about something or someone.

25 mentions. If an action *always* occurs, present tense is the best choice.

26 means, will earn. The boss is talking about the future (the clue is *next year*). The talking takes place in the present (so you want *means*), but the earning is in the future (hence, *will earn*).

27 follow. The command is formed by stripping the *to* from the infinitive.

28 nod, look. Drop the *to* and you're in charge, commanding poor Henry to act interested even if he's ready to call off the engagement rather than listen to one more story about French wine.

29 don't speak or do not speak. The negative command relies on *do* and *not*, as two words or as the contraction *don't*.

30 Ask. Poor Henry! He has to request boredom by dropping the *to* from the infinitive *to ask*.

31 Do not fall or Don't fall. Take *to* from the infinitive and add one *do* and *not* or the short form, *don't*, and you have a negative command.

32 Eat. Henry's in for a long evening, given the command *eat*, which is created by dropping *to* from the infinitive.

33 Do not talk or Don't talk. The negative command needs *do*, or it dies. You also have to add *not*, either separately or as part of *don't*.

34 Go. Create this command by dropping *to* from the infinitive *to go*.

(35) **had made.** The subjunctive *had made* is needed for this statement about available time slots because it's contrary to fact. No time slot was available in the afternoon.

(36) **were.** Ellen is not a morning person, so you need the subjunctive verb *were* to express condition-contrary-to-fact.

(37) **snows.** The instructor is talking about a possibility, not a condition that didn't occur. Therefore, you don't need subjunctive. The normal indicative form, *snows*, is what you want.

(38) **had heard.** Ellen didn't listen to the weather report, so subjunctive is needed.

(39) **were.** Ellen isn't a licensed driver, so you need subjunctive here.

(40) **had known.** The examiner didn't know, so you need the subjunctive here.

(41) **P, I.** The participle *arriving* gives information about *Sam*, the subject of the sentence. The verb in the sentence is *was*. *To settle* is an infinitive.

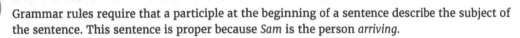

TIP

Grammar rules require that a participle at the beginning of a sentence describe the subject of the sentence. This sentence is proper because *Sam* is the person *arriving*.

(42) **P, P.** *Redecorated* (from the verb *redecorate*) is a participle describing *room*. *Overflowing* (from the verb *overflow*) is a participle describing *machine*.

(43) **I, I.** These infinitives perform different jobs in the sentence. *To reach* describes the verb *had*; *to skate* is the object of the verb *had*.

(44) **G, N.** *Sliding* is the subject of the verb *was*. *To his room* is a prepositional phrase, not a verb. (For more information on prepositional phrases, turn to Chapter 5.)

(45) **N, I.** *Easygoing* isn't a verbal because the verb "easygo" doesn't exist. *To complain* is an infinitive acting as the object of the verb *decided*.

(46) **I, N.** *To practice* is an infinitive acting as the object of the verb *want*. *Firmly* is an adverb, not a verbal. (For more information on adverbs, read Chapter 4.)

(47) **P, P.** Both *knowing* and *confusing* are participles. The first describes *manager*, and the second describes *comment*.

(48) **G.** *Reaching* is a gerund acting as the subject of the verb *is*.

(49) **P.** *Choosing* is something the manager is doing, but it's not the verb in the sentence. It's a description, what grammarians call an *introductory participle* because it sits at the beginning of the sentence.

(50) **N, I.** *Protested* isn't a verbal; it's a verb. *To go* is an infinitive acting as a subject complement. (For more information on complements, see Chapter 7.)

(51) **Looking.** Here the two actions take place at the same time. The researchers check out the subjects' teeth and *gasp*. The perfect form (with *having*) is only for actions at different times.

(52) **hearing.** Once again, two actions take place at the same time. Go for the form without *having*.

(53) **Refusing.** *Refusing* and *frowned* happen at the same time, so the plain form is best.

(54) **having been completed.** The plain form *completed* would place two actions (the completing and the analyzing) at the same time. Yet common sense tells you that the analyzing follows the completion of the research. The form with *having been* places the completion before the analysis.

(55) **having gone.** The decision to stop market research is based on the fact that it's too late; the tooth whitener is already being manufactured. Because the timeline matters here and one action clearly happens earlier, the form with *having* is needed.

(56) **getting.** Two actions — succeeding and getting — happen at the same time, so the plain form (*getting*), not the perfect form (*having gotten*) is appropriate.

(57) **Sending.** The president's statement places two things, sending and being sure, at the same time. Therefore, *sending*, not *having sent*, is best.

(58) **Having been deceived.** The point of the sentence is that one action (deceiving the reporters) comes before another (*did not believe*). You need *having been deceived* to make the timeline work.

(59) **Having interviewed.** The first action involves interviews. Then the planning starts. Because one action comes before the other, *having interviewed* fits well.

(60) **Weeping.** The marketers were *weeping* as they *told*, so you don't need a helping verb, and the plain form, *weeping*, is correct.

Answers to "Overachievers Questions"

(1) **Incorrect.** The feeling expressed by *am delighted* and the act of inviting take place at the same time, so you want the plain infinitive, *to invite*.

(2) **that you will enjoy.** Now the subject, *you*, performs the action, *will enjoy*, making it an active-voice verb.

(3) **Correct.** This is a condition-contrary-to-fact statement because the speaker (*I*) is sure. The subjective verb *were* is correct here.

(4) **Correct.** Two actions, *visiting* and *miss*, take place at the same time, so the plain form of this participle is what you need here.

(5) **No.** *Visiting* alone is a real possibility, so you should not use a subjunctive verb here.

(6) **Yes.** The subject of *stay* is *you*, although that word is understood, not stated.

(7) **Correct.** The past (*Having survived*) and the present (*know*) are placed in order by the perfect-tense form, *having survived*.

(8) **Noun.** *To get lost* is the subject of the verb *is*.

(9) **Wear comfortable shoes.** The command form is the infinitive (*to wear*) minus the word *to*.

(10) **Passive.** *Tickets* aren't purchasing. Customers are! Because *tickets* receive the act of purchasing, the verb is passive.

Chapter **19**

Mastering Picky Pronouns and Avoiding Confusing Comparisons

I n this chapter, you take a deep dive into two error magnets: pronouns and comparisons. Chapter 2 covers pronoun basics. Here, you work on combining pronouns with nouns ending in *ing*, as well as the choice between *who* and *whom*. Chapter 4 explains simple comparisons. In this chapter, you tune up your comparison skills, so every comparison you make is complete and logical.

Matching Pronouns to "ing" Nouns

Many nouns end with the letters *ing* — *thing*, *pudding*, and *king*, to name just three. Some nouns ending in *ing* are made from a verb (*swimming, smiling, dining,* and similar words). Grammarians call these nouns *gerunds*. You don't need to remember that term. You do need to be careful when you place a pronoun in front of an *ing* noun made from a verb. If the focus is on the action, the pronoun should be possessive: *my, his, her, its, their, our*, and so forth. Take a look at this example:

Carrie hates <u>his</u> auditioning for the new reality show, *Nut Search.*

The sentence doesn't tell you about Carrie's feelings for *him*. The sentence tells you that Carrie hates the involvement in a reality show. The possessive form shifts the reader's attention to *auditioning.*

If a noun appears before an *ing* noun (a gerund), and the focus is on the action, the noun should be possessive, too:

Carrie hates <u>Olaf's</u> auditioning for the new reality show, *Nut Search.*

TIP

Pronouns attached to an *ing* noun, like all pronouns, should match the word they refer to in number (singular or plural) and gender (masculine, feminine, nongendered). For a complete discussion of pronouns, turn to Chapter 2. For help with possessive nouns, see Chapter 9.

YOUR TURN

Circle the correct word from the parentheses. To keep you alert, I've inserted a few sentences that don't call for possessives.

Q. (He/Him/His) writing a novel on his phone is a bad idea.

A. **His.** The bad idea here is the *writing*, not *he* or *him.* The possessive pronoun shifts the attention to the task, which is the point of the sentence.

1. Peter Lincoln of the *Times* needs help with (*him/his*) editing and plans to hire two assistants.

2. Lincoln looks forward to (*they/them/their*) correcting his grammar.

3. Lincoln objected to the employment (*agency/agency's*) sending him too many candidates.

4. When I went for an interview, I saw (*him/his*) reading the latest bestseller.

5. (*I/Me/My*) saying that the book was trash bothered Lincoln.

6. "I object to (*you/your*) judging my reading," he muttered.

7. However, Lincoln did look favorably upon (*I/me/my*) editing.

8. He also hated (*I/me/ my*) pronouncing his last name incorrectly.

9. (*He/Him/His*) ignoring the second *L* in his name is a mistake, I believe.

10. In the end, he gave (*I, me, my*) the job.

To "Who" or To "Whom"? That Is the Question

Lately, some grammarians have given up on *whom* and *whomever*. In their view, only a few people use *whom* and *whomever*, and even fewer use these words properly. They argue that *who* and *whoever* are all anyone needs. In some circles, though, the difference between *who/whoever* and *whom/whomever* still matters. If you're writing or speaking to someone in those circles, you should understand the proper usage of these pronouns.

Because they tend to appear in complicated sentences, it's a good idea to untangle the meaning and figure out *who* is doing what to *whom*. Here's the deal: If you need a subject (someone doing the action or someone in the state of being described in the sentence), *who* or *whoever* are correct. If you need an object (a receiver of the action), go with *whom* or *whomever*. (Chapter 7 explains how to find subjects and objects.)

TIP

Are you wondering whether you need the shorter pronoun or the one with *ever* tacked on? *Whoever* and *whomever* don't refer to anyone specific. They refer to a person, but the person's identity is unknown or unimportant. *Who* and *whom* often refer to someone mentioned in the sentence. They may also refer to an unknown person whose identity matters.

YOUR TURN

Take a ride on the *who/whom* train and select the proper pronoun from the parentheses in the following sentences.

Q. (Who/Whom) can decode the secret message? Codebusters!

A. **Who.** The verb *can decode* needs a subject, someone to do that action. *Who* is for subjects, and *whom* is for objects.

11 Does Pete know (who/whom) should receive the secret message after Maria has decoded it?

12 Maria will discuss the message with (whoever/whomever) the buyer sends.

13 (Who/Whom) is the buyer?

14 His buyer is someone (who/whom) believes the message reveals where a treasure is buried.

15 Matt, (who/whom) wrote the code, is also selling copies of the message.

16 He rejected an offer from an astronaut, (who/ whom) offered Matt a $50 bill.

17 Do you know (who/whom) the astronaut consulted?

18 No one seems to know (who/whom) paid the most money.

19 Matt, (who/whom) I never believe, has the most sincere face you can imagine.

20 Peyton, (who/whom) Matt trusts, has a reputation for sincerity.

21. I once heard Peyton explain that (whoever/whomever) has an honest face can get away with anything.

22. "If you are one of those people (who/whom) can fake sincerity," he said, "you can accomplish a lot."

Writing Logical Comparisons

Comparison (and competition) seem to be hard-wired into the human mind. Who's got more "likes" on social media — Jean or John? Which player has the highest batting average? Is today's stock price higher than yesterday's? Comparisons are everywhere. Unfortunately, poorly written comparisons are everywhere, too. In this section, you practice creating correct comparisons.

Completing half-finished comparisons

A comparison may discuss two things or people in relation to each other. The comparison may also identify the extreme in a group and explain how it's extreme. Here are two examples:

> She throws more pies than I do. (comparing *she* and *I* in terms of pie-throwing)

> Of all the clowns, he throws the most pies. (identifying the extreme in a group of clowns in terms of pie-throwing)

A comparison may also examine something in relation to a standard:

> Her shoelaces were so tightly knotted that she had to cut them open. (comparing *her shoelaces* to those that can be untied)

A comparison may be any of these things as long as it is complete. If someone says, "The salmon is not *as* fresh" or "The sea bass is *more* delicious," you are left with questions. *As fresh* as what? *More delicious* than what? You have no way of knowing. These comparisons are incomplete and, therefore, incorrect.

Of course, in context, these sentences may be perfectly all right. If I say, "I considered the salmon. In the end, I chose the flounder. The salmon is not as fresh," the logic is clear.

TIP

Some words in a comparison may be implied without loss of meaning. Take a look at this sentence:

> The salmon is less expensive than the flounder.

You understand the logical ending:

> The salmon is less expensive than the flounder is.

The key point is that the reader must have enough information to understand the comparison.

Identify the correctly written comparison in each pair.

Q.
   I. "There are more fish in the sea," commented the nature photographer.

   II. "There are more fish in the sea than you can imagine," commented the nature photographer.

A. II. The key here is to define the term *more*. *More than* what? Choice I doesn't answer that question, so it's incomplete. Choice II adds *than you know* to complete the comparison.

23

   I. The photographer, who is wealthier than a tech titan, spends a lot of money on waterproof cameras.

   II. The photographer, who is wealthier, spends a lot of money on waterproof cameras.

24

   I. The film editor plays more video games than the photographer.

   II. The film editor plays more video games.

25

   I. Mermaids are the most interesting character in the editor's favorite game.

   II. Mermaids are the most interesting character because of the tail.

26

   I. On the other hand, mermaids have fewer powers.

   II. On the other hand, mermaids have fewer powers than other characters in the game.

27

   I. Not many players realize that the mermaid tail fins are so sensitive that special tail protection is a must.

   II. Not many people realize that mermaid tail fins are so sensitive.

Being smarter than yourself: Illogical comparisons

If I say that Babe Ruth was a better baseball player than any Yankee, I'm making an error that's almost as bad as a wild throw into the stands. Why? Because the Babe was a Yankee. According to the logic of my original statement, the Babe would have to be better than himself. I don't think so! The solution is simple. Insert *other* or *else* or a similar expression into the sentence. Then, the Babe becomes "a better slugger than any other Yankee."

Don't insert *other* or *else* if the comparison is between someone in the group and someone outside the group. I can correctly say, for example, that "the current Yankee shortstop is faster than all the Mets" — in terms of grammar, at least. You can time them as they run to first base to see if that statement is true in real life.

Time for some comparison shopping. Check out the following sentence pairs. Which one (if any) is logical?

YOUR TURN

Q.

    I. The average pigeon is smarter than any animal in New York City.

    II. The average pigeon is smarter than any other animal in New York City.

A.   **II.** Pigeons are *animals*, and pigeons flap all over New York. (I've even seen them on subway cars, where they wait politely for the next stop before hopping onto the platform.) Without the word *other* (as in choice I), pigeons are smarter than themselves. Nope! Option II, which includes *other*, is logical.

    I. Except for the fact that they don't pay the fare, subway pigeons are no worse than any human rider.

    II. Except for the fact that they don't pay the fare, subway pigeons are no worse than any rider.

    I. A pigeon waiting for the subway door to open is no stranger than anything else you see on an average day in New York.

    II. A pigeon waiting for the subway door to open is no stranger than anything you see on an average day in New York.

    I. I once saw a woman on a New York street shampooing her hair in the rain, an experience that was weirder than anything I've seen in New York City.

    II. On a New York street, I once saw a woman shampooing her hair in the rain, an experience that was weirder than anything else I've seen in New York City.

    I. Singing with a thick New York accent, she appeared saner than city residents.

    II. Singing with a thick New York accent, she appeared saner than other city residents.

    I. A tourist from England, peeking through the window of a sightseeing bus, was more surprised than New Yorkers on the street.

    II. A tourist from England, peeking through the window of a sightseeing bus, was more surprised than other New Yorkers on the street.

33

   I. Is this story less believable than what you read in this book?

   II. Is this story less believable than the rest of what you read in this book?

34

   I. You may be surprised to know that it is more firmly fact-based than the material in this chapter.

   II. You may be surprised to know that it is more firmly fact-based than the other material in this chapter.

35

   I. Tourists to New York probably go home with stranger stories than visitors to other big cities.

   II. Tourists to New York probably go home with stranger stories than visitors to big cities.

Calling All Overachievers: Extra Pronoun and Comparison Questions

Check the underlined words in these sentences. If everything is fine, write "correct." If you see a mistake, write "incorrect."

Dinah was a parakeet (1) <u>who</u> we found when she was just a baby. (2) <u>Our</u> giving her a home was (3) <u>better than anything we ever did</u>. Dinah slept in her cage every night, but she flew out (4) <u>faster</u> when we got up in the morning. She usually perched on a curtain rod and watched (5) <u>us</u> making breakfast. Anyone (6) <u>who</u> spoke in a loud voice knew that Dinah would squawk in reply. She stayed in the kitchen (7) <u>more than in the rooms of the house</u>. She also paid attention to (8) <u>my</u> turning on the television in the early evening when her favorite show was on. Dinah was (9) <u>more intelligent than any bird I ever knew</u>. Once, she was voted (10) <u>best pet</u>!

Answers to Pronoun and Comparison Questions

1. **his.** *Lincoln* doesn't need help with a person; he needs help with a task *(editing)*. Whose editing is it? *His.*

2. **their.** Lincoln doesn't look forward to people but to an action *(correcting)*. Whose *correcting*? *Their correcting.*

3. **agency's.** Lincoln didn't object to the agency. He objected to *their sending* too many candidates. The possessive pronoun shifts the focus to the action, where it should be.

4. **him.** I snuck this one in to see if you were awake. *I saw him.* What was he doing? *Reading*, but the *reading* is a description tacked onto the main idea, which is that I saw *him*.

5. **My.** What bothered Lincoln? The *saying.* To possessive pronoun *my* keeps the focus on that word.

6. **your.** The objection probably isn't to a person, *you*, but to the *judging*. The possessive pronoun *your* keeps the reader's attention on the action.

7. **my.** The sentence isn't reporting Lincoln's opinion of a person. It's reporting his opinion of how the person performs the task of editing. *My* places the focus on *editing.*

8. **my.** Isn't it amazing that this person got hired? Here Lincoln has a problem with the *pronouncing* of his last name. The possessive pronoun *my* spotlights that action.

9. **His.** The person isn't a mistake, but in the opinion of this writer, *ignoring* the second *L* is. The possessive form focuses on the action.

10. **me.** Here, you need an object pronoun to indirectly receive the action of the verb *gave.* That pronoun is *me.* (For more information on indirect objects, see Chapter 7.)

11. **who.** Focus on the part of the sentence containing the *who/whom* issue: *who/whom should receive the message.* The verb *should receive* needs a subject, so *who* is the proper choice.

12. **whomever.** The *buyer* is sending someone, so the pronoun you plug in receives the action of *sending.* Receivers are always object pronouns, so *whomever* is correct.

13. **Who.** The verb *is* needs a subject, and *who* is a subject pronoun.

14. **who.** The verb *believes* needs a subject. *Who* is a subject pronoun.

15. **who.** The verb *wrote* needs a subject. *Who* is a subject pronoun.

16. **who.** The verb *offered* needs a subject. *Who* is a subject pronoun.

17. **whom.** This sentence is easier to figure out if you isolate the part of the sentence containing the who/whom choice: *who/whom the expert consulted.* Now, rearrange those words into the normal subject–verb order: *the expert consulted whom. Whom* is the object of the verb *consulted.*

18. **who.** The verb *paid* needs a subject. *Who* is a subject pronoun.

19. **whom.** Focus on the portion of the sentence that contains the pronoun *(who/whom I never believe)*. Rearrange the words into the normal order for a statement: subject, verb, object *(I never believe who/whom)*. Because you need an object, *whom* is the correct pronoun. (For more on subjects and objects, turn to Chapter 7.)

20 **whom.** Concentrate on the part of the sentence between the commas. Rearrange the words into the normal subject-verb order: *Matt trusts who/whom.* Now do you see that it has to be *whom? Matt* is the subject, and *whom* is acted upon, not an actor.

21 **whoever.** The verb *has* needs a subject, so *whoever* is the correct choice.

22 **who.** The verb *can fake* pairs with the subject pronoun *who* in this sentence.

23 **I.** The problem with the choice II is that you can't tell what or who is being compared to the photographer. The missing element of the comparison must be supplied, as it is in choice I (*tech titan*).

24 **I.** Choice II begins the comparison nicely (*more video games than*) and then flubs the ending (*than* what? *than* who?). Option I supplies an ending — *than the photographer* — so it's complete.

25 **I.** The first comparison defines the group — the characters *in the editor's favorite game.* Choice II talks about the tail, but that information isn't part of the comparison.

26 **II.** Choice I is incomplete: *fewer powers* than what? Choice II finishes the comparison by adding *than other characters in the game.*

27 **I.** In common speech, *so* is often used as a substitute for *very.* In proper English, however, *so* begins a comparison. Choice II contains an incomplete comparison. *So sensitive* that what? Choice I supplies the needed information: *that special tail protection is a must.*

28 **I.** Choice I adds *human,* therefore correctly comparing *pigeons* to another group, *humans.* Verdict: logical. Choice II fails because it presents pigeons as no worse than themselves, an impossible situation.

29 **I.** In choice I, the *else* serves an important purpose: It shows the reader that the pigeon waiting for the subway is being compared to *other* events in New York City. Without the *else,* as in choice II, the sentence is irrational because then the sentence means that seeing pigeons in New York is no odder than what you see in New York.

30 **II.** The *else* in choice II creates a logical comparison between this event (which actually happened!) and other strange things I've seen in New York City. Because choice I lacks *else,* it's illogical.

31 **II.** If she's got a New York accent, you can assume she's a city resident. Without the word *other,* as in choice I, you're saying that she's saner than herself. Not possible! Choice II repairs the logic by inserting *other.*

32 **I.** The tourist isn't a city resident, so the tourist may be compared to *New Yorkers on the street* without the word *other.* Choice I is fine. Choice II becomes illogical because of the word *other.* A tourist isn't a New Yorker, so that word is unnecessary.

33 **II.** The story is in the book, and it can't be compared to itself, as choice I does. The phrase *the rest of,* which appears in choice II, differentiates the story but preserves the logic.

34 **II.** The story is in this chapter, so you need *other* or a similar word to create a logical comparison, which choice II does.

35 **I.** New York is a big city, but the second sentence implies otherwise. The word *other* in the first sentence solves the problem.

Answers to Overachievers Questions about Pronouns and Comparison

1. **Incorrect.** In this sentence, *we* is the subject of the verb *found*. *Whom* acts as the object of the verb *found*.

2. **Correct.** The focus in this sentence is on the action, *giving*. The possessive pronoun *our* pulls the reader's attention to *giving*.

3. **Incorrect.** Giving Dinah a home was something the narrator did, so how can that action be better than *anything we ever did*? To correct this illogical comparison, add *else* before *anything*.

4. **Incorrect.** *Faster* than what? The comparison is incomplete.

5. **Correct.** Dinah's focus is on the people, not on the action. Therefore, *us* makes sense.

6. **Correct.** *Who* is the subject of the verb *spoke*.

7. **Incorrect.** The *kitchen* is in the house, so the comparison should be "more than in any other room in the house."

8. **Correct.** The focus is on the action, *turning on*. The possessive pronoun *my* draws the reader's attention to that word.

9. **Incorrect.** Dinah is a bird, so the comparison should be "more intelligent than any other bird."

10. **Incorrect.** Who voted? The narrator's family, the community, everyone in the world? The comparison is incomplete.

Chapter **20**

Putting the Right Letters in the Right Place: Spelling

A young friend asked me why she had to learn spelling. "The computer tells me when a word is spelled wrong. Then, it fixes it! The computer knows everything." I hate to disappoint her, but no, the computer doesn't know everything. Sometimes, the computer (actually, the computer's word-processing program) "fixes" a word that isn't wrong or suggests a "correction" that makes the problem worse. Plus, sometimes you write on paper, without a computer. In these situations, you need good spelling skills.

The bad news is that English spelling usually isn't logical. The good news is that a few simple rules will help you put the right letter in the right place. In this chapter, you practice applying those rules. You also look at commonly misspelled words. Master those, and your spelling troubles will fade away.

Obeying the Rules

You often have to memorize words or look up the correct spelling. However, English does follow some patterns. Not many, but some! In this section, I explain a few rules that help you write correctly.

I before E

Here's a rhyme to remember:

> *I* before *E*
>
> except after *C*
>
> unless sounded like *A*
>
> as in *neighbor* and *weigh*

The rhyme explains a spelling rule:

>> **The letter *i* comes before the letter *e* most of the time.**

>> **After the letter *c*, put the letter *e* before the letter *i*.**

>> **If the letters *e* and *i* combine to sound like the letter *a*, the *e* comes before the *i*.**

WARNING

Some words don't follow this rule, such as *ancient*, *science*, and *efficient*. If you're not sure how to spell a word, check the dictionary.

YOUR TURN

Q. Is the word spelled correctly? If not, what is the proper spelling?

Word	Correct? Proper Spelling?
Neice	

A. **niece.** The letter *i* generally precedes the letter *e*.

Question	Word	Correct? Proper Spelling?
1	receive	
2	chief	
3	deciet	
4	weight	

Question	Word	Correct? Proper Spelling?
5	acheive	
6	shield	
7	breif	
8	their	
9	thief	
10	nieghbor	

Double letters

When you're spelling, pay attention to vowels — *a, e, i, o, u*, and sometimes *y*). If the sound of the letter matches its name, the vowel is *long*. In the word *pay*, for example, the vowel *a* is long. In the word *pat*, the vowel *a* is short. All the letters that aren't vowels are consonants. You have to check consonants and vowels when you're adding *ed* or *ing*. The last letter often doubles under these conditions:

>> The word is short.

>> The vowel sound is short.

>> The word ends with a consonant.

Watch this rule in action with the word *dot*. It's short, it has a short vowel sound, and it ends with a consonant (*t*). Therefore, when you add *ed* or *ing*, you double the *t*: *dotted, dotting*. If these three conditions aren't present, don't double the last letter.

Sometimes, you double the final consonant in longer words, too, when you add *ed* or *ing*. Read these words. Pay attention to the sound of the original words in the first column:

Original	With ed or ing
begin	beginning
occur	occurred
commit	committing
control	controlled

When you say the original words aloud, you hear that the accent — the stress — is on the last part of the word. You say

be-GIN, not BE-gin

In this situation, check the last vowel sound. If it's short, usually you need to double the final consonant when you attach *ed* or *ing*.

YOUR TURN

Q. Is the word spelled correctly? If not, what is the proper spelling?

Word	Correct? Proper Spelling?
Containned	

A. **contained**. The word is pronounced con-TAIN, with the stress on the second syllable. The vowel sound in that syllable is long, so the consonant *n* isn't doubled when you add *-ed*.

Question	Word	Correct? Proper Spelling?
11	topping	
12	admited	
13	moldded	
14	baged	
15	claimmed	
16	followed	
17	spinning	
18	putting	
19	runing	
20	beged	

TIP

Double letters cause trouble in other situations, too. See "Mastering Spelling Demons," later in this chapter, for more information.

Sounding out words with a silent letter e

Many English words end with the letter *e*, but the *e* is silent. Although you can't hear it, you can hear the effect of a silent *e*. With a silent *e*, the word *hat* becomes *hate*, and *hop* turns into *hope*. If you say those words aloud, you notice that the silent *e* is a signal that the vowel before it is long. A long vowel is pronounced like the name of the letter. *Hate* and *hope* have long vowels (long *a* in *hate*, long *o* in *hope*.) The words that don't end with a silent *e* have short vowels (short *a* in *hat*, short *o* in *hop*). If you pay attention to this rule, you won't text sick friends that you "hop" they feel better.

YOUR TURN

Q. Circle the word that fits the definition.

sit, site: to take a seat

A. **sit.** A *site* (long *i*) is a place.

(21) cut, cute: to use scissors

(22) dud, dude: friendly term for a guy

(23) pin, pine: a tree

(24) cub, cube: a solid with six equal sides

(25) star, stare: to look at intensely

(26) ton, tone: 2000 pounds

(27) nap, nape: a short rest

(28) dun, dune: a pile of sand

(29) far, fare: fee to ride a train

(30) ban, bane: to make something illegal

Dropping the silent E

What happens with you add letters to a word ending with a silent *e*? The spelling rule for this situation has two parts:

>> Keep the silent *e* if the first added letter is a consonant (any letter except *a, e, i, o,* or *u*):

- hate → hate**ful**
- pale → pale**ness**
- manage → manage**ment**

>> Drop the silent *e* if the first added letter is a vowel (*a, e, i, o,* or *u*):

- arrive → arriv**ing**
- pure → pur**ity**
- nerve → nerv**ous**

You probably won't be surprised to hear that the silent *e* rule has exceptions. All English spelling rules have exceptions! Here's one:

dye (to change the color of cloth) — dyeing

As always, if you're not sure how to spell a word, check the dictionary.

YOUR TURN

Q. Is the underlined word spelled correctly? If not, what is the proper spelling?

Word	Correct? Proper Spelling?
Peter is <u>timeing</u> me, but his watch is not always accurate.	

A. **timing**. The word *time* has a silent *e*, and the added letters (*ing*) begin with a vowel. Therefore, you drop the silent *e*.

Question	Word	Correct? Proper Spelling?
31	If a tiger is <u>biteing</u>, you may die.	
32	Mary is <u>giveing</u> a concert this evening.	
33	<u>Haveing</u> a cold is miserable.	
34	Andrew was <u>driving</u> when he hit that tree.	
35	The <u>pavment</u> is icy. Don't slip!	
36	Play <u>nicely</u> with the other children!	
37	This tool is <u>useful</u> because it can do many things.	
38	Page 12 comes after page 15. The <u>pageing</u> is wrong!	
39	Otto is f<u>ameous</u> because his last post went viral.	
40	The <u>ruling</u> body of that country is greatly respected.	

Mastering Spelling Demons

"Spelling demons" are not supernatural monsters. They're words that often trick writers. With a little care, though, you will always spell these words correctly.

How does the word end?

Read this paragraph. Look closely at the underlined words:

> Sandy said she couldn't go to school because she had to see a <u>doctor</u>. Really, she was not ready for the <u>grammar</u> test. Sandy's mom, a <u>professor</u>, wrote a note to the <u>teacher</u>: "Please excuse my <u>daughter</u> from this exam."

Every underlined word ends in *ar, er,* or *or*. These ending letters are different, but when you say the words aloud, the endings sound the same. (Isn't English great? Three ways to spell the same sound! Three spelling problems!) When you write these words, be careful. Here's a table to help you remember.

AR Endings	ER Endings	OR Endings
grammar	lawyer	doctor
scholar	plumber	tutor
dollar	builder	actor
collar	better	mentor
polar	counter	bachelor
burglar	writer	author
circular	kinder	director
molar	anger	editor
similar	climber	creator
spectacular	gangster	favor

TIP

The word *kinder* is a comparison: "Mary is *kinder* than Tom." When you're making a comparison, the word usually ends with *er*.

Another type of spelling demon is a word that ends with either *ant* or *ent*. These three-letter groups sound the same, so they're easy to confuse. Check this table:

ANT Ending	ENT Ending
important	different
pleasant	dependent
constant	argument
elegant	requirement
assistant	accent
instant	adolescent
irrelevant	client
immigrant	department
protestant	employment
tenant	monument

Another pair of word endings — *ible* and *able* — also confuses people. Read the words in this table:

IBLE Words	ABLE Words
visible	dependable
possible	washable
incredible	affordable
horrible	acceptable
sensible	understandable
responsible	reasonable

TIP

No rule guides you automatically to the right choice between *ible* and *able*. However, *able* generally attaches to complete words. If you cross out *able* in every word in the second column, you see a real word (*depend, wash,* and so on). If you cross out *ible,* you do not find a real word.

If you read these lists aloud once a week, gradually, you will remember how to spell the words. Of course, these lists could be much longer because many English words end the same way. If you do not know how to spell an ending, the dictionary helps.

YOUR TURN

Write "Correct" if the underlined word is spelled properly. If it isn't, correct the spelling.

Q. Your worries are <u>understandable</u>, but I still think that my plan is <u>possable</u>.

A. correct, possible.

41 My <u>assistent</u> will take note of your suggestions for a more <u>sensible</u> solution.

42 Jamal, who is an <u>author</u>, wants a <u>spectaculer</u> party to celebrate his new book.

43 It's <u>importent</u> to treat <u>writers</u> well!

44 <u>Creaters</u> aren't always <u>dependible</u> when it comes to deadlines.

45 I am not concerned about lateness, but poor <u>grammer</u> is not <u>acceptable</u>.

One or two?

Are you *dissapointed* or *disappointed* or *disapointed* in your spelling skills? Deciding when to double a letter is annoying. Most often, you have to memorize the spelling. Note: One rule will help you figure out whether you need to double a letter when you add *ing* or *ed* to a word. See "Double Letters," earlier in this chapter, for more information.

Here are some demons that may give you double trouble. I underline the spots where many people make a spelling error (doubling when one letter is needed or placing one letter where two is correct):

enroll	disgust	wedding	usually
embarrass	baggage	really	sudden
apartment	occur	commitment	excellent
opposite	unnatural	casually	lose (not be able to find)
appear	special	immediately	loose (not tight)

TIP

Two phrases are sometimes mistakenly written as one word when two words are correct: *a lot* (many) and *all right* (fine, agreed).

Which vowel?

Short vowels — *a, e, i, o, u* when they don't sound like their names — can confuse spellers. Why? Short vowels often sound like each other. Also, sometimes their sound blends into the word, so you may not realize that they're present. Here are some spelling demons that cause vowel problems. The trouble spots are underlined:

separate	Definite	cause	among
persuade	recognize	despair	jewelry
obey	nursery	division	officer
extraordinary	February	category	disguise

YOUR TURN

If the word is spelled properly, write "Correct." If it isn't, correct it.

Q. Febery

A. February.

46 jewlery

47 pursuade

48 obey

49 commitment

50 embarasment

Calling All Overachievers: Extra Practice with Spelling

Check each underlined word in this advertisement for a boat tour. Mark the word "correct" if it is spelled properly. If it isn't, write the correct spelling.

(1) <u>Loose</u> your tension and enjoy an hour of fun and education on our boat tour. As you watch the shoreline, many (2) <u>fameous</u> sights will (3) <u>appear</u>. Wear (4) <u>washible</u> clothing, because sometimes a wave swamps the boat. You shouldn't be worried, though, because our (5) <u>safty</u> record is excellent. The boat is (6) <u>controlled</u> by an expert pilot and meets every state and local (7) <u>requirment</u>. Every customer will (8) <u>recieve</u> a (9) <u>bagged</u> lunch. Plan on (10) <u>arriving</u> early, as the streets around our dock have heavy traffic.

Practice Questions and Answers

(1) **correct.** Following the letter *c*, the letter *e* comes before the letter *i*.

(2) **correct.** Generally, the letter *i* comes before the letter *e*.

(3) **deceit.** Following the letter *c*, the letter *e* comes before the letter *i*.

(4) **correct.** When you say this word, you hear a sound that matches the name of the letter *a*. In that situation, the letter *e* comes before the letter *i*.

(5) **achieve.** Generally, the letter *i* comes before the letter *e*.

(6) **correct.** Generally, the letter *i* comes before the letter *e*.

(7) **brief.** Generally, the letter *i* comes before the letter *e*.

(8) **correct.** When the letters *e* and *i* sound like the name of the letter *a*, the letter *e* comes before the letter *i*.

(9) **correct.** Generally, the letter *i* comes before the letter *e*.

(10) **neighbor.** When the letters *e* and *i* sound like the name of the letter *a*, the letter *e* comes before the letter *i*.

(11) **correct.** The word *top* has a short *o*, so the final consonant, *p*, is doubled when you add *ing*.

(12) **admitted.** In the word *admit*, the stress is on the second syllable (*ad-MIT*). The vowel in the second syllable is a short *i*, so you double the final consonant, *t*, when you add *ed*.

(13) **molded.** The word *mold* is short, but the vowel, *o*, is long. Therefore, you don't double the final consonant, *d*, when you add *ed*.

(14) **bagged.** The word *bag* is short, and so is the vowel, *a*. Therefore, you double the final consonant, *g*, when you add *ed*.

(15) **claimed.** *Claim* has a long *a*. Don't double the final consonant after a long vowel sound.

(16) **correct.** The accent is on the first syllable of the word *follow* (*FOL-low*). You don't double the final consonant, *w*, is doubled when you add *ed*.

(17) **correct.** The word *spin* has a short *i*, so the final consonant, *n*, is doubled when you add *ing*.

(18) **correct.** The word *put* has a short *u*, so the final consonant, *t*, is doubled when you add *ing*.

(19) **running.** The word *run* has a short *u*, so the final consonant, *n*, is doubled when you add *ing*.

(20) **begged.** The word *beg* has a short *e*, so the final consonant, *g*, is doubled when you add *ed*.

(21) **cut.** The word with the silent *e*, *cute* means "pretty, appealing."

(22) **dude.** The word without the silent *e* means "a flop, a failure."

(23) **pine.** The word without the silent *e* means "a metal tack."

(24) **cube.** The word without the silent *e* means "a baby bear."

(25) **stare.** The word without the silent *e* means "a shining heavenly object, an actor with a leading role."

(26) **ton.** The word with the silent *e* means "a sound."

(27) **nap.** The word with the silent *e* means "back of the neck."

(28) **dune.** The word without the silent *e* means "to nag about a loan repayment."

(29) **fare.** The word without the silent *e* means "not near."

(30) **ban.** The word with the silent *e* means "hardship or suffering."

(31) **biting.** When a tiger uses its jaws, the word is *bite*, which has a silent *e*. When you add a group of letters beginning with a vowel, in this case, *ing*, you drop the silent *e*.

(32) **giving.** *Give* has a silent *e*. When you add *ing*, which begins with the vowel *i*, drop the silent *e*.

(33) **having.** *Have* has a silent *e*. When you add *ing*, which begins with the vowel *i*, drop the silent *e*.

(34) **correct.** *Drive* has a silent *e*, which you drop when you add a group of letters beginning with a vowel, in this case *ing*.

(35) **pavement.** *Pave* has a silent *e*. When you add a group of letters beginning with a consonant, you don't drop the *e*.

(36) **correct.** When you add *ly* to *nice*, you keep the silent *e* because *ly* begins with a consonant, *l*.

(37) **correct.** When you add *ful* to *use*, you keep the silent *e* because *ful* begins with a consonant, *f*.

(38) **paging.** When you add *ing* to *page*, you drop the silent *e* because *ing* begins with a vowel, *i*.

(39) **famous.** When you add *ous* to *fame*, you drop the silent *e* because *ous* begins with a vowel, *o*.

(40) **correct.** When you add *ing* to *rule*, you drop the silent *e* because *ing* begins with a vowel, *i*.

(41) **assistant, correct.**

(42) **correct, spectacular.**

(43) **important, correct.**

(44) **creators, dependable.**

(45) **grammar, correct.**

(46) **jewelry.**

(47) **persuade.**

(48) **correct.**

(49) **correct.**

(50) **embarrassment.**

Answers to "Overachievers Questions"

1. **Lose.** *Lose* and *loose* differ by only one letter, but the meanings are far apart. *Lose* means "to misplace." *Loose* is "free, not tied down."

2. **famous.** When you add letters beginning with a vowel (*o*, in this case) to a word ending with a silent *e*, drop the *e*.

3. **correct.** A double *p* should appear in *appear*.

4. **washable.** Don't confuse words ending with *ible* with those ending with *able*.

5. **safety.** When you add letters beginning with a consonant to a word ending with a silent *e*, don't drop the *e*.

6. **correct.** This word is correctly spelled with a double *l*.

7. **requirement.** *Require* ends with a silent *e*. When you add to it, and the first letter is a consonant (any letter but *a, e, i, o,* and *u*), don't drop the silent *e*.

8. **receive.** After the letter *c*, *e* comes before *i*.

9. **correct.** *Bag* is a short word, with a short vowel, ending in a consonant. Therefore, you double the *g* when you add *ed*.

10. **correct.** *Arrive* ends with a silent . When you add *ing* to it, don't drop the silent *e* because *ing* begins with a vowel, *i*.

Index

About the Author

Geraldine Woods has taught every level of English from 5th grade through adult writing classes. She's the author of more than 50 books, including *Basic English Grammar For Dummies*, 2nd Edition, *All-in-One English Grammar For Dummies*, and *1001 Grammar Practice Questions For Dummies*, 2nd edition (all published by Wiley). She also wrote *25 Great Sentences and How They Got That Way* and *Sentence. A Period-to-Period Guide to Building Better Readers and Writers*, both published by WW Norton. She blogs at www.grammarianinthecity.com about current trends in language and ridiculous signs she encounters on her walks around New York City. Her current favorite sign reads, "Pay inside before entering."

Author's Acknowledgements

I owe thanks to my elementary school teachers — nuns who taught me how to diagram every conceivable sentence and, despite that fact, also taught me to love language and literature. I appreciate the efforts of Rick Kughen, an excellent and attentive project editor; Lindsay Lefevere and Hanna Sytsma, Wiley's acquisitions editors; Catherine Conley, the technical reviewer; and Lisa Queen, my supportive agent.

Dedication

In memory of Harriet, true friend.

Publisher's Acknowledgments

Executive Editor: Lindsay Berg
Development Editor: Rick Kughen
Copy Editor: Rick Kughen
Technical Editor: Catherine Conley

Production Editor: Saikarthick Kumarasamy
Cover Image: © Sezeryadigar/Getty images